Communicating for Life

RenewedMinds

RenewedMinds, an imprint of
Baker Academic, publishes quality
textbooks and academic resources to
guide readers in reflecting critically
on contemporary issues of faith and
learning. While focused on the
needs of a Christian higher education curriculum, RenewedMinds
resources will engage and benefit
all thoughtful readers.

The Council for Christian Colleges & Universities is an association of over ninety-five member colleges and universities, each of which has a curriculum rooted in the arts and sciences and is committed to the integration of biblical faith, scholarship, and service. More than thirty Christian denominations, committed to a variety of theological traditions and perspectives, are represented by these member institutions. The views expressed in these volumes are primarily those of the author(s) and are not intended to serve as a position statement of the Council membership.

For more information, please contact www.cccu.org, council@cccu.org, or The Council for Christian Colleges & Universities, 321 Eighth Street N.E., Washington, DC 20002-6518.

Communicating for Life

Christian
Stewardship
in Community
and Media

QUENTIN J. SCHULTZE

Foreword by Martin E. Marty

A RenewedMinds Book

Baker Academic
Grand Rapids, Michigan

Published by Baker Academic
a division of Baker Publishing Group
P.O. Box 6287, Grand Rapids, MI 49516-6287
www.bakeracademic.com

Printed in the United States of America

Library of Congress Cataloging-in-Publication Data
Schultze, Quentin J. (Quentin James), 1952–
    Communicating for life : Christian stewardship in community and media /
    Quentin J. Schultze ; foreword by Martin E. Marty.
        p.   cm.
    Includes bibliographical references and index.
    ISBN 10: 0-8010-2237-1 (pbk.)
    ISBN 978-0-8010-2237-1 (pbk.)
    1. Communication—Religious aspects—Christianity. I. Title.
BV4319.S39 2000
261.5′2—dc21   00-042910

To
Karen Longman,
friend, colleague, and sister in shalom

This book benefited enormously from the advice, support, and critique of an advisory group formed by the Council for Christian Colleges and Universities (CCCU):

Elvera Berry, Roberts Wesleyan University
Clifford Christians, University of Illinois, Urbana-Champaign
Mark Fackler, Calvin College
Karen Longman, Greenville College (formerly with the CCCU)
Martin Medhurst, Texas A & M University
Kathaleen Reid-Martinez, Regent University
Greg Spencer, Westmont College
Helen Sterk, Calvin College
Nicholas Wolterstorff, Yale University

Contents

Foreword

WHO WOULD EVER HAVE THOUGHT to combine the words *communicating* and *stewardship?* I would not have, and I have not seen such a combination before. But Quentin Schultze would, and did, and the product of his juxtaposition of the two concepts is in your hands. And you are in for some refreshing surprises.

The question now is not "Who would connect the concepts?" but rather, now that we have an author in our sights and his book in our hands, "Why did he connect them?"

Thousands of young people take college and university courses in communications and graduate bearing degrees in that field. The government needs Federal Communications Commissions. There are regulatory agencies, investment companies, and all sorts of outlets for communications. Therapists and counselors concentrate on the difficulty people have communicating, for example, in marriage.

So far, so good. Communicating is "in." But how does it relate to stewardship? We have to know that Quentin Schultze did not include that word in the subtitle of his book to boost sales. If that was his reasoning, don't trust him as a communicator, because he's not a very good observer and listener.

Observers and listeners know that stewardship is a theme most of us like to duck. Many ministers resent the fact that they have to devote the month of November, certain Sundays, and a few minutes each week to stewardship. Laypeople may work hard to complete stewardship campaigns, but they may also groan a bit in the process and feel relieved when the task comes to an end. The word *stewardship* has become tainted.

Part of Schultze's task, therefore, is to set the theme of stewardship into a larger context than the one many Christians hear about during stewardship month. While such a theme often involves talk of money, or with a bit of alliterative stretching, time, talent, and treasure (and while we could benefit from good books on those subjects), Schultze presents a larger frame, or chooses a different frame for his discussion. He connects stewardship with how we speak and listen, how we interact in word and gesture, what we have to say and hear, whether one-on-one, in community, or in mass communications within our culture.

My minister-son once told me and his congregation that during the Olympics he heard a televised interview with an equestrienne champion. The reporter asked, "How does your horse know when it has to leap the hedges and hurdles, and why do some horses turn away or stumble?" The woman answered something like this: "That's very simple. You tear your heart out of your body and throw it over the hedge. The horse knows what is going on and how desperate you are to catch up to your heart. So it leaps."

A crude analogy, perhaps, but in stewardship, you tear out your heart and plunge it ahead in a Godward direction. Once it has been placed ahead of you, you will work to catch up with it. For where your treasure is, there your heart is also; and, as well, where your heart is, there your treasure is also.

When the heart has been committed, there is still work to do, and Schultze offers guidance. We have been given God's heart in our world, and God pursues it here, desperately—desperately enough to enter the world God created through Jesus Christ, who mirrors the fatherly heart of God. And in that world we now have to be—no, we *get* to be—cocreators. Schultze is well read in the literature and keeps from jumping out of his Calvinist skin, or at least his Calvinist context. That is, cocreation here does not mean usurping the role of the sovereign God. Rather, it means we are graced with the gift of cocreation.

And much of that cocreation has to do with language, words, intentions, concerns. Some years ago I shared a platform with a great theologian, Joseph Sittler. By then he was blind, but he could *really* see, and hear. Someone asked him to put his vision of church reform into as few words as possible. He said, simply, "Watch your language!"

Watch your language, Schultze tells us in elaborate and intricate ways, if you love or would love your neighbor. Or if you would help criticize and then improve cultural signals, mass media, and other agencies of communication. Watch your language and you will learn to confront what is dehumanizing and demeaning in others.

For years I have read Quentin Schultze on Christian communication and the mass media, so I was a bit surprised that he did not get around to his specialty until chapters 8 and 9. I would have profited from almost anything he had to say on that subject, but seeing it framed in the context of stewardship and cocreation gave me a chance to read and hear something quite fresh and challenging. I hope his book will convert others to this approach to communicating and then inform them as they go about living up to their new resolves.

Martin E. Marty
Fairfax M. Cone Distinguished Service Professor Emeritus
The University of Chicago

Acknowledgments

MANY PEOPLE GAVE TIME, advice, and encouragement to me as I worked on this book over a three-year period. Chief among them is the advisory group appointed by the Council for Christian Colleges and Universities (CCCU): Elvera Berry, Clifford Christians, Mark Fackler, Martin Medhurst, Kathaleen Reid-Martinez, Greg Spencer, and Helen Sterk. Their ideas and suggestions made this a much better manuscript. Nicholas Wolterstorff chaired the group and helped keep this project on track from the beginning.

My students at Calvin College served like colleagues to make this manuscript readable, interesting, and compelling. I owe special debts of gratitude to Brad Van Arragon, Derek Benthem, Stacey Wieland, Brian ("Train") Vos, Brenda Cooke, and Sara Jane Toering. Thanks as well to my interim class of January 1999: Tim Bogertman, Jeff Byma, Rachel deKoning, Carolyn deVries, Matt Dyksterhouse, Autumn Edwards, Mark Haan, Kyle Hack, Jessica Hillstrom, Melissa Kamara, Heath Krueger, Benjamin McCloskey, John Miller, Sarah Porter, Rob Prince, Adam Stout, and Chris Veltman. Together we experienced shalom on earth.

Moreover, various colleagues at the CCCU and other institutions reviewed versions of the manuscript for style and substance. They included Ron Johnson and his students (Steph, Jared, Melanie, and Sean); Tim Detwiler and his communication theory class at Cornerstone University; Kyong Kim, Charlie Marler, Veronica Ross, Scott Turcott, Bruce Montgomery, and Brian Fuller; and Doug Walker and his ethics students.

My colleagues at Calvin College deserve special mention for their unrivaled support and encouragement. Randy Bytwerk, Bob Hubbard, Bill Romanowski, David Holquist, and Neal Plantinga merit special mention. My entire department, Communication Arts and Sciences, is an irreplaceable source of ideas and stimulating discussion. There is probably no better undergraduate communications faculty at any liberal arts college in North America.

My family provides daily nurture and insightful critique of my work. My daughter, Bethany, served as my typist and file clerk for an entire summer. My son, Stephen, challenged me to be intellectually transparent. And my wife, Barbara, helped shape the tone of the manuscript. Her warm spirit and personal enthusiasm for my work are constant sources of joy. Her love is grace.

I dedicate this book to Karen Longman, who indefatigably championed the cause of this and many other manuscripts for the CCCU. She humbly exudes wisdom, joy, and peace. I thank God for her friendship, which has enriched my life and given me peeks at shalom.

To God be all glory, now and forever.

Introduction

CONCENTRATION CAMP SURVIVOR Simon Wiesenthal recalls what happened to him in Poland during World War II. Camp officials sent him to work at a makeshift hospital for German soldiers. When Wiesenthal arrived, a nurse led him to a twenty-one-year-old Nazi soldier named Karl, who was covered with bandages and barely able to communicate.[1]

Karl, a member of Hitler's notorious SS, confessed a horrendous crime to Wiesenthal. Karl had killed a family that was trying to flee from a building the Nazis had filled with Jews and set ablaze. Karl explained how the faces of the terrified family members still haunted him. "I know that what I have told you is terrible," Karl said. "In the long nights while I have been waiting for death, time and time again I have longed to talk about it to a Jew and beg forgiveness from him. Only I didn't know whether there were any Jews left."[2] Then Karl said that he wanted to die knowing that at least one Jew had forgiven him. Wiesenthal responded by silently leaving the room.

Years later, Wiesenthal asked various leaders to write short essays about what they might have done in that situation.[3] Several writers suggested that only someone who had lived through the Holocaust could offer a meaningful perspective on Wiesenthal's dilemma. A person who had not experienced Wiesenthal's pain had no right to comment on whether Wiesenthal should have forgiven Karl. Perhaps others who had suffered in the death camps could decide whether or not Wiesenthal should have treated Karl as his "neighbor."

We have all faced important personal predicaments that hinged on communication. Maybe someone apologized to us after years of mutual hatred, dissolving deep feelings of alienation. We might recall a relationship that turned on our words—or on our silence. Perhaps a teacher told us that we have a special talent, inspiring us to pursue excellence. Or maybe an unexpectedly intimate conversation with a close friend led us to drop our defenses and to share some of our deepest fears and hopes. The Christian tradition often focuses on the moment a person declares the gospel as truth and Jesus Christ as Lord.

These kinds of life-changing events illuminate the close connection between our relationships with each other and our communication with God. Sometimes our communication transcends the limitations of daily life and reveals "the rousing good fellowship" in heaven, says theologian Eugene H. Peterson. "Assemble in your imagination all the friends that you enjoy being with most," he writes, "the companions that evoke the deepest joy, your most stimulating relationships, the most delightful of shared experiences, the people with whom you feel completely alive—*that* is a hint of heaven."[4] If Peterson is correct, our communication on earth can give us a taste of eternal life and an intimate friendship with God.

For many people, communication sometimes is a road to sublime relationships and personal healing. Even skeptical people pray in times of crisis. British scholar C. S. Lewis once said that pain is God's "megaphone to rouse a deaf world."[5] Personal difficulties can turn our attention to higher matters. We are "much more likely to find passionate prayer in a foxhole than in a church," says Peterson.[6] Perhaps our words can be powerful paths to wisdom, love, holiness, and even God.

Unfortunately, communication scholars sometimes squeeze this divine mystery out of human communication. Often they reduce communication to a drab, mechanical process of sending and receiving messages. Researchers tend to secularize communication as if it has nothing to do with religion.[7] Communication is far more interesting, creative, and spiritual than most scholars and students recognize.

The study of communication should take us beyond the ordinary in life to ultimate matters of life and death. Karl reached out for forgiveness. Wiesenthal sought justice. Both men struggled to communicate deeply in a broken world.

In this book I offer a perspective on communication that is anchored in a Christian worldview, but I do not pretend to offer *the* Christian perspective on communication. I expect that even friends in the faith will take issue with some of my ideas; in fact, I encourage lively discourse about this book. Also, I admit that my ideas are not completely original. I have borrowed heavily from the Old and New Testaments, and I have adapted ideas from St. Paul and St. Augustine, from contemporary communication scholars, and from a range of academic fields. Because, as Augustine said, all truth is God's truth, I discerningly borrowed from any sources that offered wisdom about communication.[8]

In addition to offering my own view of communication, I reveal and evaluate some other scholars' religious assumptions. Many of the most respected scholars hold quasi-religious beliefs about human communication. They often cling to assumptions with profound philosophical implications when they ask questions about communication: What is the origin of human communication? Why do we communicate? Will effective communication produce a better world? How can we encourage people to communicate openly and honestly? When it comes to these kinds of philosophical questions, many communication scholars live by their own implicit faith.

In chapters 1 and 2, I suggest that God creates human beings as caretakers of creation, as symbol-using stewards who can create life-giving cultures, or ways of life. I believe that God intends for all people to use the gift of communication to love God and neighbor, not just to exchange messages. When we communicate responsibly, we establish communities of justice and peace—what Scripture calls *shalom*. As recipients of God's grace (unmerited favor), we can spread God's love in all areas of life.

In chapter 3, I consider the way that many models of communication dehumanize the process. By scientifically reducing human communication to a mechanical process of sending and receiving messages, scholars sometimes rob it of its creativity and spiritual mystery. Moreover, these *transmission* views of communication tend to foster manipulation and control instead of love and service. I argue for a *cultural* view of communication that emphasizes the human ability to cocreate culture. If we are not careful, our *theories* of communication will crowd shalom out of our *real* interaction with each other.

In chapters 4 and 5, I address the disturbing fact that human communication is fundamentally flawed. We all communicate imperfectly. Worse yet, human arrogance, portrayed in the scriptural account of the fall, corrupts our motives and alienates us from each other, from God, and from ourselves (see Genesis 3). Sometimes we even naively believe that we can become great communicators and easily eliminate conflict in life. Instead, we descend regularly into confusion, misunderstanding, and deception. As Wiesenthal and Karl discovered, shalom is clouded by human sin. We all use words and images to confuse and confound others, to deceive, belittle, and destroy our neighbors. If communication is a path to human hope, it is also a road to destruction. Each person's communication invariably becomes a legacy that influences how future generations will communicate.

As I suggest in chapters 6 and 7, the ability to communicate gives all people the potential to powerfully influence community. In spite of the fall, God still enables us to cocreate shalom. Using Christ's own incarnational example of selfless love, I suggest that humankind should use the power of communication to serve others rather than to exploit them. In short, God calls us to communicate on behalf of weak and exploited people.

In chapters 8 and 9, I examine the role of mass media in contemporary society. Unfortunately, the media are often driven by the love of Mammon, or earthly riches. I suggest that the media are implicitly religious storytellers that sometimes (like prophets) challenge secular mainstream culture, but more often (like priests) affirm it. The media even demonize particular groups in society by appealing to people's existing prejudices and arrogance.

In chapters 10 and 11, I address the importance of ethical communication. I suggest that communication is willful action as opposed to passive behavior. God holds us responsible for how we communicate, for what we communicate, and for how our communication affects others. I believe that God requires us all to be virtuous communicators who live authentic lives and who engage detractors civilly. Because we live in the deep ethical confusion wrought by the fall, we need to foster communities of virtue that provide "soul food" for nurturing responsible action.

Finally, in chapter 12, I invite all communicators to become disciples of Jesus Christ. Jesus once walked the earth, calling common people to become faithful communicators. Today he calls us to offer our gifts in service to others and to the glory of the Creator. As Augustine wrote, we "should be an alleluia from head to foot."[9] Ultimately all human communication is a form of worship, a love ballad.

After surviving the Holocaust, Wiesenthal began writing and speaking about the horrors of totalitarianism. He dedicated his life to telling stories that illuminate the human condition for all people. Whether or not he made the right decision with Karl, Wiesenthal dedicated his life to fostering peace and justice in the world.

I hope this book will inspire you to celebrate God's gift of communication by dedicating your life to promoting shalom in work and play. Thanks for reading these pages. I expect to learn much from my critics as well as my supporters. To all, shalom!

ONE

Symbolic Stewardship

The Meaning and Purpose of Human Communication

Wetlands ecologist Calvin DeWitt stopped his car one night along a busy section of interstate highway in northern Indiana in order to read aloud Psalm 19: "The heavens declare the glory of God" (v. 1). DeWitt recalls that he "looked up into the night sky and couldn't see any stars because of all the lights and pollution. The noise of traffic was deafening. Semitrailers slammed by, literally sucking at my car. The psalm made no sense at all there. I thought, 'Here is a community that has deprived itself of nature's testimony.'"[1]

Determined not to let a similar thing happen in his own community, DeWitt ran for office and spoke passionately with residents about the importance of ecological planning. At town meetings he listened to the residents' concerns and hopes. He encouraged the community to publish a study of its natural resources so residents would know their own habitat. DeWitt helped the town develop an ecological plan to protect and enhance the local environment. "Cal is so amazing," said one resident, "how he could have a room full of hostile people, and he could calm the crowd. He would let them talk, would really try to understand them. Then he would start explaining his side. He would just calm things down. He always listens to people."[2]

DeWitt's effectiveness depended on his ability to communicate well. He first listened because he respected his neighbors' opinions. He then communicated awe and wonder, built trust, sought the truth, and encouraged consensus. In the process, DeWitt cocreated community.[3] Using his God-given rhetorical gifts, DeWitt helped his neighbors to live harmoniously with the physical world and with each other. He became known as a caretaker of creation, a servant of his community, and an agent of grace.

DeWitt's communication demonstrates that our talking and listening can be rooted in death or in life. He could have promoted ecological irresponsibility by pushing for projects that would have polluted the water and destroyed the natural beauty of the area. Instead he called for environmental stewardship. In every situation, our words help or hurt people, nurture or destroy community. "Are we cynical," asks one Christian scholar, "measuring the talk of others according to the waste of limited resources, or are we charitable, looking with grace upon the efforts of others?"[4] Our communication is a two-edged sword.

In this chapter, I charge into the spiritual thicket of human communication. I ask why people communicate—and why they should communicate. These questions stretch back to our human origins, they complicate our lives today, and they reach forward to the ideal community that God intends for us to savor. Our language is more than a tool for communicating; it is the "home in which human beings live."[5]

First, I examine how God's gift of communication enables us to cocreate cultures, or ways of life. Our cultures include webs of relationships in everything from business to entertainment. For example, DeWitt communicated with neighbors to foster the ecological aspect of culture. He persuasively offered his town a vision of harmony between people and nature.

Second, I suggest that God created us all to be stewards of creation who use the gift of communication to care for the world. Every person on earth is meant to be a caretaker of God's creation, but God holds us accountable for the kind of culture we cocreate. Our Creator expects us to cocreate culture that reflects our role as servants of God and of our neighbors. Every human being is made in the image of God and is our neighbor. DeWitt realized that his ability to persuade and educate his geographic neighbors was God's gift to him to use for serving others. Like DeWitt, we need to recognize that we are symbol-using stewards of God's world.

Third, I turn to how communication enables us to cocreate life-giving community. When we see little or no place for God, our communication will foster broken communities of fear, hatred, and oppression. But when God is the center of our communication, we are more likely to cocreate peaceful and justice-loving communities of shalom. When we are connected to God, our language is the "marrow" of community life.[6]

Finally, I suggest that our Creator wants us to become God-listening communicators. Ultimately, the quality of our community life and interpersonal relationships depends on how well we listen to God's discourse. When DeWitt stopped his car along the highway to recite Psalm 19, he communicated obediently. Moreover, obedience may have been the most important aspect of his rhetorical skill for cocreating with neighbors the ecological future of their community. Our ability to communicate for shalom is a kind of sacred covenant with God. We have to listen to God in order to faithfully establish communities of shalom. Otherwise we tend to create a self-destructive culture of death.

Cocreating Culture

Chinese writer Zhang Jieying has become a thorn in the side of China's traditionalists and a beacon of freedom for many young readers. In her book *Absolute Privacy*, Ms. Zhang interviews citizens about intimate topics such as broken marriages, premarital sex, and childlessness—all subjects that are taboo for public discussion in China. As her words slice through traditional social norms, Zhang has become both a hero and a rebel. Her journalistic colleagues shun and criticize her, while lovelorn readers celebrate her courage to address formerly unmentionable subjects.[7] For good or for bad, she has helped to usher new ways of life into China.

God gives us the gift of communication so that we can actively cocreate our *culture*, our whole way of life.[8] When we communicate, we expand God's original creation by making and sharing our ways of life. Like craftspersons and traders at international ports, we exchange culture through communication of all kinds. Of course, we do not invent all of our culture ourselves. We inherit most of it from previous generations. Then we shape it and share it with others.

The word *communication* comes from the Latin *communis*, which means to share, to make common, or even to have "possession of a common faith."[9] When we communicate, we create, maintain, and change shared ways of life. Communication enables us to cultivate education, engineering, business, the media, and every other aspect of human culture. Together we design and construct buildings, fall in love, establish households, and perform music. Perhaps this ability is part of what Scripture refers to as the *imago Dei* (image of God) in us (Gen. 1:26–27).

Every time we communicate, we creatively exercise God's gifts by contributing good or bad pieces of culture to the world. We mimic the Creator, fashioning in our *own* image the kinds of culture that *we* desire. Our communication becomes "a faithful index of the state of our souls."[10] Zhang's columns invariably reflect her own vision of what Chinese culture should be like. That is why some readers celebrate her new cultural vision for China while traditionalists condemn or ignore her.

In the broadest sense, culture is everything that exists on earth because of human effort. God created the world but then turned it over to human beings to cultivate it. From this perspective, culture includes our *values* (what we believe), our *practices* (what we do), and our *artifacts* (the physical things that we make).

At the heart of all of this humanly created culture is a system of meaning—what people think and believe. Adolescents' dating practices, for example, convey a particular meaning, namely, what it means to date someone. At one Midwestern Christian college the system of meaning defines dating as a prelude to marriage. If you date the same person more than once or twice, the rest of the campus considers you virtually engaged (values), and no one else expresses an interest in dating you. The meaning within the system of dating on that campus also shapes where people go on dates (practices) and what types of clothing they wear on dates (artifacts). Even who pays for the date (another practice) can reveal much about the meaning of gender roles and expectations (values).[11] Everything we do with other human beings—all of our social practices—is grounded in cultural ideals, attitudes, and assumptions.

But what people believe about the world around them may not reflect the way the world actually operates. In other words, a particular cultural system can be out of sync with social realities. Nevertheless, our systems of meaning are always grounded in society—the social structures and economics of everyday life. No matter what college students believe about dating, they will somehow have to pay for the dates, select from among available places to go, observe campus regulations about off-campus activities, and probably even follow some socially prescribed dating rituals. Similarly, a television network might profess to distribute family-oriented programs, but somehow it has to pay for the programs, generate a large enough audience to attract adequate advertising revenue, and even obey various governmental regulations for program content. Zhang depends on China's laws, economy, technology, and transportation system in order to finance, print, and distribute her work. We cannot just create our own personal beliefs and values if we intend to get along with others in society.

In a narrower sense, then, *culture* is only a people's system of meaning, whereas *society* comprises the rules, regulations, and social structures with which we live. Culture is especially what we carry around in our heads and hearts, the everyday meaning of our lives. Society, on the other hand, consists only of the external political and economic structures that set limits on what we can do. Clearly human beings create both culture (in this narrow sense) and society through the process of communication. Communication enables us to cocreate with others both our systems *of* meaning (culture) and systems *for conveying* meaning (society).[12]

For the sake of this book, I will use the term *culture* broadly to refer to both culture and society—to all human values, practices, and artifacts, and to the context within which these values, practices, and artifacts operate. Without the ability to communicate, human beings would be unable to cocreate any area of culture, from music to architecture to education.

We are marvelously made creatures who imitate God's own creative ability to cultivate creation. Before we get too carried away about our own communication ability, however, we should contrast it with God's ability. Scripture says that God "spoke" this world out of nothing *(ex nihilo)* (see Genesis 1). Unlike God, we do not create words or images out of nothing. Instead, we conceive new words by combining existing sounds or existing words. We can cocreate a language to talk spiritually about the environment—as DeWitt and many others have done,[13] but we cannot create a new language out of nothing. Zhang may have invented a few new words in her column, but she depended overwhelmingly on the existing language to communicate with her readers.

All of our communication seems fragile, limited, and utterly dependent on the shared goodwill of others. Author Richard Foster expresses wonderment that his "squiggles on paper" actually "work in the hearts and minds" of readers.[14] But as a communicator he has the benefit of his culture's existing words and common meanings. We can communicate only because we already live in a shared culture. By making us cultural creatures, God empowers us to communicate through shared ways of life.

Every culture is cocreated through four types of relationships. First, God is our primary cocreator in communication. When we cocreate culture, we collaborate with God—or God cocreates through us! We commune with God through prayer, through listening to Scripture, through enjoying the created world, and through experiencing Christian community and tradition.[15] In other words, God can speak through all aspects of creation and culture.

Second, we cocreate culture by communicating with our neighbors. Biblically speaking, every person with whom we interact becomes our neighbor. We are a part of economic, political, and religious communities. Schools, for example, provide a means for us to educate our children as neighbors and citizens. Participating in a community means that we agree to cocreate culture with others.

Christian traditions typically offer a rich history of culture and communication that form a common life for a group of neighbors. The books, songs, liturgies, and creeds of a church provide a tradition of how and what to communicate. A tradition is a communal memory that keeps speaking to people as long as they listen together to its voice through books, recordings, holiday celebrations, and other media. We love God partly by loving each other in traditional communities of neighbors (see Matt. 22:37–39).

Third, we cocreate culture by having a dialogue with creation. God initiates some of this dialogue. Martin Luther said, "God writes the gospel not in the Bible alone, but on trees, flowers, clouds and stars."[16] One novelist suggests that the "earth itself is His handiwork, and my treading on it is communicated through a network so complex that even our mightiest computers can't begin to estimate its effect."[17] When DeWitt parked his car along the highway and looked up to the heavens, he heard and saw that people had muffled the glory of God's creation. The physical world spoke to him, and he responded creatively by awakening the ecological voice of his own community. Physical scientists dialogue with each other and with creation. Hoping to understand creation, they creatively apply the language of science to it, naming new elements and devising theories about how the physical world works.

Communication theory is partly a dialogue with God's creation. Just as a chemist charts the elements, a communication scholar tries to categorize forms of human interaction and to explain or predict what happens when people communicate. Scholars cocreate theories of communication partly by observing how people use God's gifts. All communication scholars interact with the creation as well as with each other.

Fourth, we cocreate culture by communicating with ourselves. This is a great mystery. Somehow we introspectively dialogue with our own thoughts, ideas, and feelings. In the process, we think about what others have said to us, or about what we believe God is saying to us, directly or through his creation. Strangely enough, our cultures are partly created when we dialogue with ourselves. For example, we might think to ourselves about what to say to someone before we say it. Also, we might listen thoughtfully to a politician before deciding whether to vote for that person. All of our "external" communication with others takes place in the context of our communication with ourselves.

All four kinds of relationships—with God, with our neighbors, with the created world, and with ourselves—influence culture. God's gift of communication enables us to fashion incredibly complex combinations of all four types of interaction. Every day we cocreate ways of life shaped by these four relationships. In the process, we act wisely or foolishly as stewards of God's creation.

Defining Reality under God

Pastor Bill Hybels of Willow Creek Community Church recalls the time that he met with a man who was devoted to shutting down producers of adult entertainment. "You'd be amazed at what people can justify," the man told Hybels. "Film directors call what's going on in the beds 'acting.' The government . . . calls it 'art.' Producers and distributors call it 'free enterprise.' Video stores call it 'entertainment.'" Meanwhile, consumers call it "'a good night of fun.'"[18]

Human communication is a powerful means of defining reality. What some people call "pornography" or "smut," the industry calls "adult entertainment." German philosopher Ernst Cassirer writes, "Whatever has been fixed by a name, henceforth is not only real, but is Reality."[19] Cassirer overstates our creative power, but he rightly suggests that our symbols shape how we view the world. Our communication defines how we see others and ourselves.

I believe that God created us to be stewards of symbolic reality. Our task as *symbolic stewards* of creation is to echo God's reality, not merely our own. "What is truth?" asked Pilate, who would not stay around for the answer (John 18:38). Without God we merely define our own, often-selfish version of the truth.

The key to our ability to define reality is our use of symbols. As we cocreate culture, we attach definitions or interpretations to our ways of life. Just as Adam named the creatures in the Garden of Eden, we define ideas and objects by using vast vocabularies of verbal and nonverbal symbols that subtly represent (or misrepresent) the reality of God's world. For instance, scientists have identified and named roughly 1.6 million species of living things, and some scholars believe that there may be another five to forty million, primarily in rain forests, awaiting identification.[20] These classifications represent scientists' attempt to define the physical world accurately. The way scientists organize their understanding of the world will ultimately define many people's view of the creation.

How should we define what is commonly known as "pornography"? Is it entertainment or sin—or both? Supreme Court Justice Potter Stewart once said that he couldn't define pornography, but he knew it when he saw it.[21] Perhaps he could identify pornography, but then why could he not define it? And what would we do about the fact that another judge might come to a different conclusion when confronted with the same products? Symbols do seem ambiguous sometimes. G. K. Chesterton called human language a "bewildering" and "arbitrary system of grunts and squeals."[22] Still, no matter how arbitrary symbols can be, they are the primary means by which we define reality.

Our use of symbols is a powerful tool for making distinctions in culture. Our naming differentiates between what "is" and what "is not," between what is "right" and what is "wrong." Water is not fire, just as capitalism is not communism. Our shared symbols depend on this human capacity for the *negative*.[23] If we could not distinguish between what "is" and what "is not," our attempts at communication would fail. Imagine if we could not distinguish between a green traffic light and a red one, between "go" and "don't go!"

Our capacity for distinguishing between yes and no reflects our human nature. Eugene Peterson says that the negative is "our access to freedom. Only humans can say no. Animals can't say no. Animals do what instinct dictates. The judicious, well-placed no frees us from many a blind alley, many a rough detour, frees us from debilitating distractions and seductive sacrilege. The art of saying no sets us free to follow Jesus."[24]

At one level, defining reality does not seem all that important. We decide the rules of sports, the names of our children, and words for what we call "snow" and "sun." A large golf club is a Big Bertha (named after a cannon). Crispy toast becomes Melba toast (named after opera star Nellie Melba). Our idea of a "doozy" is based on the name of Frederick Duesenberg, the onetime king of custom-made cars. A Zamboni ice-grooming machine is named after the now-legendary Southern California family. We create these kinds of everyday symbols without much concern for ultimate reality.

At a deeper level, however, our symbols define our self-identity as well as other people's identities. Advertising presents its versions of beauty, popularity, and happiness. In the 1920s, public relations legend Edward Bernays redefined cigarette smoking for women in the United States. He secretly convinced health experts and movie stars and other celebrities to endorse the idea of female smoking. Soon female Hollywood personalities were smoking in public and extolling the virtues of cigarettes for helping people to lose weight. Bernays's catchy slogan, "Reach for a Lucky [cigarette] instead of a sweet," helped legitimize smoking for millions of women. Bernays associated smoking with a slim, attractive figure, and soon smoking was viewed not as an evil practice for females but as part of sophisticated culture.[25]

Definitions of certain groups' identities are used to justify atrocities and to subjugate people. During the 1930s and 1940s, Adolf Hitler enacted the "final solution," the systematic extermination of the Jews, in preparation for the day when his master race would control the world. The calamity of six million murders occurred on the shoulders of a language of oppression: Jews were called "parasites," "bacilli," and "vermin." Similarly, in the United States, immigrants called Native Americans "savages" and "barbarians."

Racist slurs and sexist language help people to redefine reality so that it will be in tune with their prejudices.[26] This kind of name-calling creates false versions of reality.

Our communication can constructively or destructively define reality. Reporters can promote social justice or advance stereotypes. Teachers can inspire or provoke students. Filmmakers can illuminate forgiveness or incite revenge. In every aspect of culture we see a mixture of responsible stewardship and irresponsible destruction.

God calls us as caretakers of creation to anchor our symbolic reality in God's truth. The Old Testament idea of naming suggests God's authority over all human communication. *Naming* was a banking term that meant "in the account of." When someone named an item, she or he decided who owned it. As Adam named the animals, he took inventory for the owner: God. He named God's creatures on behalf of God, not merely for his own pleasure.[27] Throughout the Old and New Testaments, people who have authority over others get to name their subjects. Nebuchadnezzar's chief official gave Daniel and his friends new names (Dan. 1:7). Jesus changed Simon's name to Peter (Matt. 16:18). Godly namers were people who had both the authority and the wisdom to define reality, whereas ungodly namers used symbols to create their own, selfish version of reality. In this biblical sense, naming always requires "a thorough, sympathetic knowing."[28] Our responsibility today is the same: to define symbolic reality under God's authority and in tune with God's truth, especially the gospel. In this sense, we are called to be "symbolic stewards" of God's creation.

Fortunately, God created us so that we can be aware of our unique role as symbolic stewards of creation. We engage in communication about communication—what scholars call *metacommunication*. Rhetorician Kenneth Burke points out that dogs do not bark about barking.[29] Animals cannot "talk" about themselves. They live in a kind of conceptual silence that makes it impossible for them to understand the reality of their own communication. God formed humans, on the other hand, with the ability to communicate about communication, as this book attests.

God's gift of communication equips us to represent the Creator on earth. We see, hear, and speak under God's authority. God even commanded us to "rule" over the earth (Gen. 1:28). Our vocation is to cocreate culture that honors God and serves our neighbor.[30] We should not use our symbolic creativity to exploit the creation selfishly, to define reality apart from God's Word. As Bill Hybels's friend discovered, we all too easily delude ourselves and others. In a Christian worldview, the core of truth is the gospel. God's truth is not "abstract ideas or mystical experiences, but a story of our redemption from a Fallen world."[31] When the gospel forms our communication, we become a community of truth. We then live knowing the name of God.[32] We become cultural carriers of shalom in God's world.

Tasting Shalom

When we communicate faithfully, we experience a taste of heaven on earth. Writer Philip Yancey speculates that heaven will "offer faithful Christians whatever they have sacrificed on earth for Jesus' sake." Yancey's mountain-climbing friend who chooses to live in a Chicago slum will "have Yosemite Valley all to himself." Meanwhile, a missionary doctor "in the parched land of the Sudan will have her own private rain forest to explore." Maybe, says Yancey, this is why the New Testament "commends poverty while portraying heaven in such sumptuous terms."[33]

Yancey's speculations about heaven remind us that we all wish for a better life. We yearn for joy. In myriad ways, we try to appease our appetite for a taste of heaven on earth. Some people watch romance movies. Others read Scripture. We all desire shalom, God's peace and justice. We feel that creation is not complete until we experience the wholeness of community in shalom.[34]

Shalom is an ancient Hebrew word that suggests the presence of God in our everyday relationships. The Jews strongly sensed God's presence in the cloud by day and the fire by night. I borrow partly from Jewish tradition the idea that God profoundly desires for all people to live together in harmony with the Creator, with each other, with themselves, and with nature. Our Creator does not want us to live in broken relationships, hurting each other with words and images that destroy our joy and delight and spread hatred and despair. God desires instead that we experience the joy of shalom with our neighbors.

A community of shalom is a responsible community in which sinful people obey and are reconciled in joyful peace with God and each other, a community in which justice and peace are embraced. As philosopher Nicholas Wolterstorff puts it, shalom is a way of living that reflects "both God's cause in the world and our human calling."[35] In such a community, everyone enjoys harmonious relationships filled with delight.[36] Shalom, or peace, is first articulated in the poetic and prophetic literature: "The wolf will live with the lamb, the leopard will lie down with the goat, the calf and the lion and the yearling together; and a little child will lead them" (Isa. 11:6). Shalom is where the "mountain of the LORD's temple" is "raised above the hills" so that "all nations will stream to it" (Isa. 2:2). Shalom is a taste of heaven on earth.

In the New Testament, shalom is expressed in *koinonia* and *agape*. *Koinonia* emphasizes fellowship and participation. *Agape* signifies selfless love of others and ourselves. Paul says that even if one can speak in tongues and prophesy, one is nothing without love. Real love is patient, kind, humble, and selfless. Love is the greatest thing we can do for another person (see 1 Corinthians 13). In a community of peace and justice, we use communication both to have fellowship with others and to love them.

Jesus Christ is the strongest expression in the New Testament of the peace of shalom. Luke says that Christ's birth caused the angels to sing: "Glory to God in the highest, and on earth peace" (Luke 2:14). Christ is both the message (the Word) and the messenger of shalom (the Word of God). Jesus is the one whom Simeon worshiped: "Sovereign Lord, as you have promised, you now dismiss your servant in peace" (Luke 2:29). Jesus preached the "good news of peace" to Israel (Acts 10:36). Every time Jesus "healed, forgave or called someone, He demonstrated *shalom*."[37] Followers of Christ cannot "stand around, hands folded, waiting for Shalom to arrive." Rather, we are all to be God's shalom spreaders, or "peace-workers."[38]

Shalom may represent ultimately the peace and harmony that God experiences in the Trinity—the Creator, the Redeemer, and the Comforter. Because we are made in the image of a Triune God, we can share some of the deep relational harmony of the Trinity. In other words, shalom on earth might reflect God's own eternal shalom; it is our foretaste of the community of heaven. In heaven we will experience the joy and delight, the richness and beauty of shalom even more fully and deeply than we can on earth. Shalom is a deep "longing for being together, for being 'in and with each other,' for the ways of setting each other free, of mutual openness, of sacrificing and receiving . . . successful unity of life."[39] We taste shalom when we deliver a worthwhile speech, report the truth compassionately, listen empathically to a friend's tales of woe, and help recover someone's ability to write after she has suffered a stroke. Whenever we communicate peacefully in accord with God, we taste heaven.

Imagine a major airport terminal. God created gravity, wind, and the basic materials that people use to build planes. God even created the pilots. But someone has to manage the flow of planes into and out of the airport, or flights will be delayed and cancelled. Air traffic controllers are charged with the responsibility of using two-way radios located in the control tower and on each plane to guide the traffic. Under their leadership, the airport should operate smoothly, enabling people to visit relatives, conduct business, and travel for pleasure. Air traffic controllers are the heart of the airport, using symbols literally to shape the destiny of millions of travelers annually.[40] Dedicated air traffic controllers enjoy directing aircraft gracefully through the skies and along the runways. Even under stress, they empathize with pilots and care for passengers' safety. When they think and

27

communicate well, the entire airport can be a harmonious place for people traveling for work and play.

Just as air traffic controllers are responsible to officials for airline traffic at airports, humans are responsible to God for communication on earth. We all regulate our communication, shaping the quality of our daily interactions. In shalom, we act responsibly for the good of the community and in accord with God's Word. We see our communication in the larger context of God's desires for creation. We become symbolic stewards who listen to God's plans for peace and justice, especially when the stakes are high and we feel the pressure. When we communicate obediently, we taste heaven on earth, and we help others to do so as well.

Listening for God in the Shadowlands

Our own quest for shalom begins when we listen obediently. The Latin root *(audire)* for the word *obedience* means "to listen." Our obedience always requires "a discerning ear, an ear that listens for the reality of the situation, a listening that allows the hearer to respond to that reality, whatever it may be."[41] Theologian Eugene Peterson writes, "Christian spirituality does not begin with us talking about our experience; it begins with listening to God call us, heal us, forgive us."[42] Having heard God's Word, we can begin our own walk toward shalom. Calvin DeWitt heard the call to obedience while reading God's Word on a noisy highway in northern Indiana. Bill Hybels's friend heard the call while listening to rhetoric about the virtue of pornography. Both of them then used the gift of communication to cocreate shalom.

Shalom depends on our listening to a God who "still speaks."[43] As philosopher Nicholas Wolterstorff argues in *Divine Discourse,* there is plenty of reason to believe that God has a voice among faithful people who listen.[44] According to Scripture, God's Word is "like fire . . . and like a hammer that breaks a rock in pieces" (Jer. 23:29). But do we listen? Or is the cultural noise too loud? We need to listen if we hope to hear God's shouts and to savor the Lord's whispers.[45]

No matter how God speaks, all of our daily communication occurs in what C. S. Lewis called the "shadowlands."[46] We taste shalom but never dine only on its peace and justice. Someone always spoils the pudding. In Psalm 83 the psalmist prays for the judgment of his people for not carrying out their duties. They were following false gods and irresponsibly defending wicked people at the cost of oppressing the weak and needy.[47] Forgetting their status as caretakers of God's creation, they had become their own arrogant gods by failing to hear and heed God's Word. Shalom was a distant memory lost in the shadows of their minds and the noise of their culture.

Christian communicators listen ultimately to Jesus Christ. We thereby become agents of shalom even in the shadowlands. We listen *to* God, and we listen *for* God. We hear the call to become symbolic stewards of the creation. Breaking out of daily darkness for glimpses of eternal heaven, we see the cross of Christ and listen to the Word of God. In short, we hear and enact the Good News with our neighbors in community.[48]

Conclusion

The best communication theory sometimes resembles theology and sounds like a search for shalom. Rhetorician Kenneth Burke, for example, has developed one of the most compelling theories of communication. In fact, his rich work has become a "bible" for many communication scholars. Burke saw the symbolic power that humans use to shape culture. He perceived the urge that people have to associate with others in community. Burke's writings speak of the nature and purpose of life, not just of the process of communication.[49] He defined human beings poetically:

Man is
the symbol-using (symbol-making, symbol-misusing) animal
inventor of the negative (or moralized by the negative)
separated from his natural condition by instruments of his own making
goaded by the spirit of hierarchy (or moved by the sense of order)
and rotten with perfection.[50]

In one sense, Burke had it right. We are symbol-using creatures. We do have the capacity to define between "is" and "is not," including what is morally right and wrong. Moreover, our symbolic "instruments" such as language and media can separate us from nature—even from our own natures. As Scripture says, we are fearfully and wonderfully made, if not "rotten with perfection."

But in another sense, Burke was misguided by his own reality-defining language. When Burke was advanced in years and had mourned the deaths of friends and family members, he added another human ability to his definition: "acquiring foreknowledge of death."[51] Burke's worldview perhaps cynically captured both the inherent goodness of human communication and its terrible imperfections. He glimpsed human communication as it exists in the shadowlands between heaven and hell. But he seemed never to accept Jesus Christ as the center of all reality-defining wisdom.

Burke rightly recognized that the study of human communication is invariably a religious exercise. All of us who study communication implicitly assume religious definitions of reality. Burke's idea that humans are "rotten with perfection" surely flowed from his sense that people are created above other creatures. Burke's late-life addition to his definition—"acquiring foreknowledge of death"—may be the most profound of his insights and surely the most sobering. Perhaps Burke saw the imagery of Psalm 23, the "valley of the shadow of death" (v. 4). But he apparently never recognized our sacred covenant with God that requires all of us to communicate obediently. Nevertheless, perhaps because of its religious language, Burke's work has provided one of the most compelling and widely followed paradigms of human communication in the discipline. Although Burke may never have offered any ultimate hope for the human condition, he tasted shalom.

When Calvin DeWitt looked into the night sky, he expected to see the glory of God's handiwork. Observing only city lights and pollution, he resolved to save his own community from environmental blight. God's gift of communication enables us all to cocreate the kind of culture that celebrates shalom. Symbols are human equipment for responsibly cultivating God's creation. Our quest for faithful communication begins when we taste shalom and listen to God.

TWO

Inexplicable Grace

The Mystery of Human Communication

Two days before Christmas, a drunk driver killed a Kentucky couple's eighteen-year-old son, their only child. Consumed with hatred, the grieving couple fought for justice. They doggedly pursued the killer through the courts, seeing to it that he would be required to fully pay for the crime. When he eventually pleaded guilty and was freed on probation, they made sure that he spent the required night in jail every other weekend. For years they monitored all of the accused young man's court appearances. After all, their son was dead. They deserved revenge. As the distraught mother said of the killer, "All I can think of is that he should die, and how he should die."[1]

Over time, the couple's preoccupation with revenge softened. Discovering details about the driver's background, they realized that he was human, not a monster. They heard that he had grown up without the kind of love and support that they had lavished on their own son. As the couple identified with him, they began to emphathize with their son's killer, to feel some of his pain, confusion, and regret. Eventually the couple invited him to their home to share meals. In word and deed, they began to love him. As a remarkable testimony to grace, they accepted like a son the man who had killed their only son. Freed of a vengeful spirit, they nurtured their "adopted" child, loving him as they once had loved the son whom he had killed.[2]

This true story is a modern parable about grace in communication. It points to an inexplicable reality beyond the everyday lives of the people involved. We cannot fully explain in human terms what happened between the grieving parents and the lost young man. The plot has an unexpected, even unbelievable, ending. Why did this grieving couple begin forgiving the driver? How did the couple convince him that they were sincere? Why did he trust their efforts to help him? And why did they choose to forgive when many others would not have? In short, how did all the fear and vengeance turn into the love and joy of shalom?

In this chapter, I first examine the mystery of grace in human communication. Grace is all of the "good" that God blends into communication, often invisibly. Grace is forgiveness, understanding, empathy, and love—every one a taste of shalom. Strangely enough, we cannot force people to understand, to forgive, to love; we cannot force grace. We can only invite it into our lives. Sometimes no matter how hard we try, our communication falls apart. At other times our communication mysteriously ushers us into grace. The Kentucky couple could not easily forgive—but they did.

The second section of this chapter reveals how communication enables us to identify with one another. Living in shalom, we share the stories of our lives and come to know and love our neighbors as distinct persons. The Kentucky couple discovered that by identifying with their only son's killer they were eventually able to love him. They all tasted shalom because of God's gift of identification. Jesus Christ identified with a suffering humanity. So can we identify with others in order to cocreate peace and harmony on earth.

The third section illuminates the implications of identification for our understanding of human nature. As we identify with others, we discover our common humanity. At its best, this deep, universal empathy enables us to commune with others as if they are our neighbors.

Finally, I describe some of the incredible richness in human communication. Humankind has an amazingly multimedia character. Every one of our senses contributes to our communion with others. Moreover, almost everything we do as humans can become a means of communication. Each person's communication gifts have the potential to contribute to shalom and to testify to God's grace, which pervades our symbolic activities. Every glimpse of grace in our lives is a love letter of shalom from God.

From Entropy to Shalom

William Rodriguez learned the *mystery of grace* in communication when gang members in Los Angeles shot and killed his son. Rodriguez was a twelve-time North American champion in kickboxing and a black belt in karate, but as a Christian he had decided not to seek revenge through physical violence. When he realized that one of the three men convicted for killing his sixteen-year-old son had really just been riding in the backseat of the killers' car, Rodriguez asked the judge for mercy on the man. The man's "family was very grateful," recalls Rodriguez. "I just believed it was the right thing to do. That's my faith."[3]

Rodriguez had no idea where his words of grace would lead him, but he felt called to orchestrate peace treaties among warring gangs. The kickboxer sensed that he could show gangs how to communicate rather than fight. Although he lacked any training as a mediator, Rodriguez eventually planned a meeting with the gangs for the purpose of creating an area-wide truce. He recalls, "I went to that meeting where there was close to a thousand heads, and I didn't know what I was going to say."[4] He had no agenda other than peace, and Rodriguez suddenly realized that he could talk about the power of forgiveness. So he told the gang members about "the ability to live for the future and not be in bondage to your past."[5] Knowing that Rodriguez had lived that message, gang members identified with him. Soon Rodriguez was hosting meetings every Sunday. He became a powerful channel of grace among the gangs of Los Angeles.

God's grace mysteriously enables us to share shalom with others. The parables of Rodriguez and of the Kentucky couple reveal that life-affirming communication often is not the result only of our own effort, but is an inexplicable gift. As mere humans, we cannot fully determine the impact of our communication. Even when we try our hardest, our communication sometimes fails. At other times, we seem to reap unmerited rewards from even poorly crafted communication.

Professors know that this is true in their teaching. Sometimes an instructor labors intensely over a great lecture, then it bombs in the classroom. What went wrong? At other times an unprepared teacher only chats off-the-cuff with a class and receives rave reviews from pleased students. Why did the impromptu chat work better than the well-organized lecture? Some professors always leave room for spontaneity in their classroom lectures because they do not want to stifle the possibility that something wonderful will happen in the unpredictable interaction with students. No matter how carefully we communicate, results are mixed and unpredictable.

When our communication turns sour, grace seems to disappear. Relationships lacking grace can frustrate us and tear us down. Without grace, a self-conscious public speaker hyperventilates. An alcoholic lies to herself and to loved ones about her addiction. A dictator orders the execution of innocent victims. A young child quietly endures incest because Daddy said not to tell anyone. A college student breaks a strict confidence by gossiping about a roommate's date. Our communication sometimes reflects human fear, distrust, and disharmony. Where is grace in these kinds of situations? Are we just blind to it? Did we fail to invite it into our lives?

Apart from grace, all of our communication tends toward *symbolic entropy*. It simply falls apart. If Rodriguez had not spoken of forgiveness to gang leaders, the symbolic chaos of the streets would have produced even more name-calling, turf wars, and killings. We contribute to symbolic entropy when we hide our real feelings or express them inappropriately. But most of our communication simply dissipates in the daily noise of life. It just goes nowhere. We lose interest in a conversation. We start daydreaming. Entropy takes over. Grace seems to disappear.

The fact is that *all* human communication depends on God's grace. First, our Creator has established the physical laws of sound and sight that we need to communicate. Second, God goes a step further, creating situations in which we can spread shalom even with our imperfect talents. Third, our Creator grants each of us the gifts necessary to communicate. In all of these ways, grace arrests entropy and makes productive communication possible.

The Greek term *kairos* captures the idea of communication that is just right for a particular situation. *Kairos* operates when a preacher speaks the perfect words to comfort grieving people at a funeral service. Newlyweds experience it when they gaze at each other over candlelight during their first private dinner together as husband and wife. *Kairos* is at work when a physics teacher chooses just the right metaphor to capture for students the wonder of God's creation. We witness *kairos* when the vulnerable political leader responds patiently to a reporter's presumptuous criticism. God's grace is a kind of *kairos* that enables us to overcome momentarily the normal entropy of human interaction.[6]

In the Christian tradition, Pentecost represents special grace in human communication. Our Creator sent the Holy Spirit to earth, giving early Christians the miraculous ability to communicate effectively across linguistic and cultural barriers. A sound like the blowing wind filled the house in which the early apostles were sitting. Tongues of fire rested on them, and they spoke in other languages. Soon a crowd gathered, and the apostles' prophetic speech was mysteriously translated into the languages of listeners (see Acts 2:1–13). The Holy Spirit, God's unique gift to the church, enables believers to be not only technically good communicators of the Word but also rightly motivated and extra-humanly successful communicators. The Spirit is anti-entropy and pro-shalom and can insure our effectiveness when we least expect it. The Spirit enabled William Rodriguez to know what to say to the gangs and helped him to say it humbly and effectively.

I emphasize the importance of grace not to encourage people to be sloppy or lazy communicators but to reveal that God's ongoing care is necessary to redeem problematic communication. Grace comforts us and liberates us from the idea that the world's communication problems are all on our shoulders. We all struggle with imperfect symbols, erroneous definitions, broken communities, and confusing technologies. Filmmakers love to hear from people who are moved by their productions because from the inside the making of a movie seems too slipshod and imperfect. In fact, some movie actors will not even view themselves on the screen, because they see all of the flaws in their performance. But in the end the cinematic story can work even with imperfect people. God's grace in human communication mysteriously steers us away from entropy and toward shalom. All of our successful communication is like a love letter from God. William Rodriguez's kind words to the judge on behalf of one of the men accused of killing Rodriguez's son were surely a love letter to both the accused and his family and friends.

Identification

Harvard psychiatrist Robert Coles tells of his encounter with a fifteen-year-old young man who had stopped attending school and started smoking large amounts of marijuana, who sat alone in his room for hours on end listening to rock music. When Coles met with him, the young man shook his head and refused to talk. Coles had several possible professional diagnoses for the troubled patient—depression, maybe psychosis—but he was not sure what would open him up. Coles finally offered words of *identification:* "I've been there; I remember being there—remember when I felt I couldn't say a word to anyone." Tears welled up in the young man's eyes. Coles's words of identification had powerfully opened the door to communication.[7] The young man realized that Coles was not just a doctor but also a person. More than that, the young man and Coles could identify with each other. Both tasted the grace of shalom in identification.

We daily experience grace in our ability to identify—to sympathize and empathize—with our neighbors. Identification can help us to overcome divisions and differences, just as it overcame the impasse between Coles and his patient. It can motivate us to offer love and justice to others. Identification equips us to learn to speak others' languages, to interpret their gestures, and to understand their images. We can, like the apostle Paul, "become all things to all people" (1 Cor. 9:22 NRSV) in order to reach out to them. We can step out of our own selfish thoughts and into others' lives. People often have the opportunity to identify with another culture by learning about and enacting its literature and folktales and performing its music.

They might experience the stories of African-Americans in slavery, European Mennonites in times of persecution, and Jews in the Holocaust. God intends for us to identify with each other, just as the Father, Son, and Holy Spirit identify with each other as distinct persons in the same Godhead.

Every time we identify with someone else we practice what God perfected in Jesus Christ.[8] God took the form of a human being in order to identify fully with humankind. Christ touched the lepers and spoke with the prostitutes and the tax collectors. He communed with all types of people in all social classes, regardless of their standing in the religious community. As God's image bearers, we share some of that ability to identify with others every time we communicate. The couple from Kentucky identified with the man who killed their son. They were able to trust him, love him, and forgive him, just as Christ forgave us.

Missionaries know how crucial identification is for cross-cultural communication. As a missionary to China in the nineteenth century, Hudson Taylor wove his black hair into a braid and let his fingernails grow long because these were local marks of mature spirituality. He could not communicate fully with Chinese people simply by following his English Christian ways. He first had to listen to them and learn about them; then they listened to him as well.[9]

Only when entering into a people's conversations and stories can an evangelist begin to connect with them. Scholar John Shea tells the story of Damien, an evangelist to lepers who learned that ministry begins with identification. For some time Damien had been unsuccessful as a witness to lepers. But one evening when he "put his foot into the hot water after a futile day's evangelizing," he felt nothing. He had leprosy. "That Sunday he got into the pulpit and did not begin with the customary 'You lepers' but with '*We* lepers.'" From then on, Damien's ministry was "electric, fruitful beyond his wildest dreams."[10] Damien's identification with lepers had ushered him into their culture and their conversation. He lost his physical health, but he gained a powerful means of communication.

God's grace enables us to let go of our immediate assumptions and preconceptions so that we can identify with others. We no longer merely observe others; we begin to participate with them. When we communicate, we don't just exchange messages; we leave ourselves temporarily in order to enter into someone else's experience. Jewish philosopher Martin Buber says that we enter "the sphere of the between."[11] He developed a philosophy of communication grounded in the intimate character of the most basic oral human interaction. Dialogue—especially speaking and listening in person—can open up relationships to a sacred intimacy. A true dialogue is not just an instrument for exchanging information; it is also a means by which a person can enter deeply into the presence of another person and God.[12] Identification is the difference between merely imagining what it would be like to be Chinese and empathizing with Chinese people—even becoming like them, if not one with them.

During the Renaissance, Benedictine monks so identified with deaf people that they created a new definition of deafness that still shapes public perceptions in the twenty-first century. The monks lived in monasteries and took a vow of silence. Having developed their own nonverbal forms of interaction, they knew that significant daily human communication was possible without speech.[13] To them, Aristotle's belief that "those born deaf all become senseless and incapable of reason" made little sense.[14] Moreover, the Christian church's prejudices seemed absurd. How could the church routinely bar deaf people from receiving Holy Communion simply because they could not "confess aloud" their faith? Spanish Benedictine monk Pedro Ponce de Leon, the first teacher of the deaf, so identified with deaf people that he developed a sign language and wrote a book on the topic of how to teach "mute deaf."[15] Ponce de Leon's ideas were eventually exported to France and later to North America, perhaps changing deaf education forever.[16] Because of God's grace in the monks' strong identification, millions of people who have hearing and speech impairments are no longer treated as if they were subhuman.

God created us with the amazing ability to identify with each other so that we might cocreate communities of shalom. Identification can lift us out of the whirlpool of isolation and plunge us into fresh streams of flowing shalom.

Discovering Our Common Humanity

Photojournalist Susan Meiselas tries to capture images that enable viewers to identify with victims of injustice. One time, during Nicaragua's civil war, she drove up the "Hill of Lead" outside of Managua. The hill was known as a place where death squads executed citizens they thought to be rebels. She looked out the window and saw the remains of a human body scattered and decaying in the bloody grass, and vultures circling for the feast. Meiselas took a picture. In the background of the photo were a gorgeous Nicaraguan forest and a lake—in jarring contrast to the bodily remains of a victim of a horrendous act of violence. "I think the hardest thing for me as a photographer," wrote Meiselas, "is moving the viewer past the shock and horror of the image to identify with the dead as people. . . . It's not just that you're a reporter documenting something. You start to feel that it could have been you; it could have been your family."[17]

Identification can lift us out of our parochial culture so that we can recognize and share with others our *common humanity*. By temporarily losing ourselves we can find deeper communion with others. People who have spent many hours trying to feel and understand the alienation and confusion of others might be best able to speak to their neighbors. Identification can help us experience human wellsprings of both pain and joy. Literature can show us that the line between evil people and righteous people is not very fine. Russian writer Alexandr Solzhenitsyn poignantly remarked, "If only there were evil people somewhere, insidiously committing evil deeds, and it were necessary only to separate them from the rest of us and destroy them. But the line dividing good and evil cuts through the heart of every human being. And who is willing to destroy a piece of his own heart?"[18] Communication empowers us to share with others even the darkest reaches of our common humanness—and thereby to see ourselves as we all really are.

Without the ability to identify with our shared humanness, we would not be able to love our neighbors who have been our enemies (see Matt. 5:44). When William Rodriguez asked the judge for mercy on one of the men convicted of killing his son in Los Angeles, he transformed anger and hatred into love for an enemy. Although he recognized the need for justice, Rodriguez also identified with the accused man's vulnerability. Perhaps Rodriguez even imagined himself or his son in the same position. Similarly, when the Kentucky couple began to identify with the man who had killed their son, they recognized his humanity and started to love him. Identification can remind us that if it weren't for grace we could have been the perpetrator.

Theologian Lewis Smedes believes that the art of forgiving always begins with rediscovering the humanity of a person who has hurt us. Before we rediscover that humanity, we merely "filter the image of our villain through the gauge of our wounded memories." But as we begin to identify with our enemies, we see them through a "cleaner lens, less smudged by hate." Eventually we perceive the reality of a "real person, a botched self, no doubt a hodgepodge of meanness and decency, lies and truth, good and evil." Then grace melts our hatred as we see "a human being created to be a child of God."[19] We may never fully love people who have wronged us, but by the grace in identification we are freed from hatefulness and a vengeful spirit. After all, we could have been in their shoes.

As we identify with each other's foibles, we recognize that we are all imperfect people who need others' patience and understanding. A psychiatrist described a husband who was about to leave his wife because she did not screw the top back on the soda bottles. Relationships can "flounder on pebbles, insubstantial insults and injuries," said the psychiatrist. He concluded that seemingly minor issues can even destroy a marriage because neither person wants to surrender. Maybe "surrender itself is not as bad as it's been put up to be," he suggested. "It is extremely useful in relationships to learn flexibility of perspective." He explained that couples must be able "to see the other person's way, so that perhaps there is something very charming about leaving the cap off soda bottles."[20] Identification gives us the grace to accept each other's differences and weaknesses. Each bit of identification reveals our shared humanity.

Our ability to identify provides a glimpse of the complete "oneness" that people experience in heaven, a taste of eternal fellowship. Christ says, "I pray also for those who will believe in me through their message, that all of them may be one, Father, just as you are in me and I am in you. May they also be in us so that the world may believe that you have sent me. I have given them the glory that you gave me, that they may be one as we are one" (John 17:20–22). Scripture captures a fully reciprocal understanding among persons that we can only approximate in this life, but that believers will attain fully in the life to come, when we will know as we are known (1 Cor. 13:12). According to Christian tradition, all of our identification on earth points to complete identification with the community of saints in heaven.

Sheldon Vanauken tells about the deep identification he shared with his wife. The couple was so close in the "co-inherence of lovers" that they usually "knew by a glance or a tone of voice what the other was thinking and feeling." Once a visitor saw Vanauken's wife "glance fleetingly at the candles on the mantelpiece." A moment later Vanauken got up to light them, never knowing that his wife had just considered the same action. "It almost scared me," the friend later admitted. "It was too perfect."[21] This kind of identification is a foretaste on earth of the intimate communion of heaven.

Identification, then, is not only a communication technique but also a means by which we can witness God's grace in our shared humanity. We cannot fully love people in the abstract—only as particular persons with whom we have identified. Identification lets us go beyond mere knowledge *about* others to a specific knowledge *of* them. In Scripture, "knowing" is deep love between persons, or between a person and God (see Ps. 139:23).

Our universal humanity can also lead us away from the grace of shalom. We can be chameleons, becoming like those around us. Some missionaries identify with the native culture so thoroughly that they give up their own cultural background and their own faith in order to join the community.[22] Actors, too, can sometimes identify so strongly with their characters that they virtually become them. Certain theories of acting actually promote this kind of personal metamorphosis.[23] Some people identify strongly with rock music stars or television and film celebrities. Adolescents use movies, in particular, to help them make sense of sexuality and confusing interpersonal relationships.[24] Soap opera viewers identify vicariously with the fictional world of the shows; some even send cards and gifts when characters get married.

Humankind's Multimedia Character

In Belgrade, Yugoslavia, during the late 1990s, pro-democracy demonstrators wanted to send a public message to the ruling socialist government: "Give us our freedom." The government had refused to recognize the results of democratic elections and had then banned protest marches. So the demonstrators operated within the letter of the law by taking their protests on the road—literally. Thousands of Belgraders converged on the city center in their vehicles, blocking traffic in every direction for hours and creating a cacophony with horns and whistles. Hundreds of drivers suffered simultaneous "breakdowns," opened their vehicles' hoods, clutched their heads in mock incredulity, and joined the protest. One driver complained that someone had stolen his engine. Using humor and imagination, the demonstrators shared their message of freedom with the entire nation.[25]

Human communication is a remarkably rich and multifaceted gift from God that spans many forms of verbal and nonverbal media. We communicate through sight, sound, touch, taste, and smell. The church has communicated through incense, stained glass, statuary, paintings, books, scrolls, chants, candles, songs, sermons, confessions and professions, and even silence. All forms of communication are open as vehicles for shalom, to our joy and delight. Theologian Richard Mouw says that Jesus' approach to teaching is a kind of "sanctified tackiness." Jesus' parables "borrowed mundane images from ordinary life to talk about very profound matters. He referred to buried treasures, loans, coins, sheep, seeds, oil lamps, and daily wages in a vineyard."[26] God seems to have a sense of humor that delivers grace in the most unexpected ways. All forms of communication can be conduits of grace.

Often we do not recognize the special value of nonverbal communication. It is a sobering fact that virtually everything we do can communicate something to someone else. Filmmakers say that over half of what we experience when we view a movie is the musical score. Even architecture and living space can speak to us. The physical setting is often an important part of our worship experience. One graduate student wrote in her final exam about her desire for a meaningful worship space: "I think that much of modern society has lost a sense of divine, holy space." We sometimes worship now in gymnasiums and their impermanent spaces. A sanctuary, the student said, should radiate "the holiness of God . . . to my senses and to my spirits."[27] Although not everyone would accept her traditionalism, she rightly suggests that worship, like all human communication, should be powerfully rich and vibrant.

At one time or another, people of faith have used every means of communication to build communities of shalom. In Western society, Christians were often at the forefront of developing new media. Martin Luther used Gutenberg's press in the sixteenth century to print the vernacular Bible; Scripture had previously been available only in Latin and other ancient languages. Eventually millions of copies of the printed Scriptures were distributed from house to house and from town to town. Many later Bible printers selected attractive type fonts and adorned the holy text with lines, drawings, and even gilded pages. The same thing was done with some hymnals. Today's church banners and liturgical vestments are part of a long history of rich expressions of communal faith. The church has tried creatively to harness all forms of symbolism for worship and outreach.

Although much of our meaning is transmitted nonverbally, use of the human word, or linguistic communication, is probably the most important human form of communication. Language starkly differentiates us from other creatures. Rhetorician Kenneth Burke begins his analysis of human communication with the assumption that humans are "bodies that learn language."[28] Scripture says that God *spoke* the world into existence. Adam *named* the creatures (Gen. 2:19–20). In Christ the "Word became flesh" (John 1:1–14). Christians for millennia have *professed* faith publicly (Rom. 10:9). Believers have not only recorded and saved the Holy Scriptures but have also created catechetical teachings based on them. In most traditions, worship is very linguistic. Hymns and other Christian songs are anchored in the language of the faith. People who are unable to speak with their voices can communicate words with sign language, writing, special computer technology, and other means.

In every area of life, the human word drives culture and spreads grace. The classical rhetorician Isocrates said, "None of the things which are done with intelligence take place without the help of speech."[29] Clearly language is a crucial part of study and education. The visual artist uses words to think about her work, to explain it to others, and to study the work of others. Language permeates all human cultures. Without some form of language, there could be no deep human identification and no real shalom. Language is our strongest bridge to rich relationships with God, our neighbors, the creation, and ourselves.

Our linguistic ability enables us to tell stories, or narratives, that connect us to the past, present, and future. Says a former corporate CEO, "Every family, every college, every corporation, every institution needs tribal storytellers. The penalty for failing to listen is to lose one's history, one's historical context, one's binding values."[30] Stories help us to rediscover the past, learn from the present, and forecast the future. Walter Fisher, one of the leading scholars of narrative communication, says that "symbols are created and communicated ultimately as stories . . . to establish ways of living in common, in communities in which there is sanction for the story that constitutes one's life."[31] Christ used parables to make spiritual ideas relevant. The entire Bible narrative addresses the past, present, and future of God's relationship with humankind. Our understanding of the world, of ourselves, of God, of virtually everything is wrapped in rich biblical narratives. In fact, the gospel is Christianity's *metanarrative* that helps believers interpret all other stories.

Chenjerai Hove, an award-winning Zimbabwean writer, tells how the oral tradition of village storytellers shapes Shona culture from generation to generation. All villagers know that when the sun goes down it is time for a festival of music, story, and dance. The children ask to hear the story about when Hare and Hornbill went to look for a woman in another village. After cajoling the storyteller, the children receive the tale they knew they would get to hear once again. Later that night, a woman performs the story with the children, "harmoniously repeating the chorused refrain of their participation." They join the woman in swaying their bodies to the music that accompanies the story. Many more tales are told that evening, for these narratives provide the community's moral teachings as well as its entertainment. The tales show the children and remind the adults "how to respect the weak as well as the strong, and how to work hard for oneself and for the community." Although modern radio and television now compete with indigenous oral storytelling, these simple moral narratives have been the "pillar of indigenous communication in Zimbabwean society."[32] Stories can give life to a culture and sustain a common identity.

When William Rodriguez called for forgiveness in his meeting with the Los Angeles street gangs, he employed some of the most cogent means of linguistic persuasion. He identified with gang members and their families who had lost children to gang violence. He told the narrative of his own life, especially how God had given him the courage to forgive the man who had killed his son. He distinguished between the two choices that the gang members had—to return to street violence or to seek peace. His rhetorical ability helped turn the gangs toward shalom.

God made us all to be creative symbolizers who can transform almost anything into a form of communication. Words, images, music, and all of the other means of human communication are part of the tapestry of meaning in our lives. When the Serbians took to the streets with their cars and trucks, they created a powerful festival of freedom that spoke to themselves, to the government, and to the world. The horns, whistles, jokes, and posters became part of their urban celebration for democratic reform. The rich variety of human media allows us to commune at work and play, to share the gospel, and to celebrate life in shalom. Our multimedia ability to communicate can spread grace through all aspects of our lives and culture.

Conclusion

Philosopher John Dewey once said that of all things "communication is the most wonderful."[33] God's gift of communication exudes grace. The Kentucky couple found grace as they identified with their son's killer. William Rodriguez discovered grace in the mercy he expressed to the bystander. Psychiatrist Coles suddenly felt God's grace when his young patient wept in identification. Through God's rich gift, we can help each other to seek justice, love mercy, and walk humbly with our Creator (Micah 6:8). Because of grace we can spread the peace of shalom through every kind of symbolic activity.

THREE

Cockfights and Demographics

Two Views of Communication

As every school child in the United States learns, Christopher Columbus was disappointed when he discovered America. His maps had rightly told him that he was sailing west from Spain, but they greatly underestimated the distance from Europe to Asia. And America did not exist on the maps; Columbus had thought he was headed for India.

So when Columbus arrived in America, he began naming his discoveries as if he were in Asia. He called the people "Indians." The Caribbean islands were now the "West Indies." The Spaniards were so pleased with Columbus's new finds in "Asia" that they gave him major resources for a second trip: seventeen ships filled with fifteen hundred workmen and artisans. He was ready to begin creating some culture in the new Spanish lands. But as Columbus continued to probe new areas, he grew increasingly baffled and frustrated. Where was the fabulous East?

Eventually Europeans figured out that the world was much larger than they had previously assumed. Each generation of new maps added more land and water to their picture of geographic reality. Later explorers determined that the West Indies were not in Asia after all. Improvements in timekeeping, cartography, and astronomy helped them to create a more realistic representation of the globe.

The study of communication is like map making. Scholars try to express their observations about communication using theories or models that are intended to match reality. Like fifteenth-century European maps of the world, theories of communication are simplistic and imperfect representations of a complex, unpredictable process that we cannot fully comprehend. God made us so wonderfully complicated that we cannot fully understand ourselves, let alone understand others.

The history of communication studies offers many worthwhile models, but I agree with James W. Carey that there are two major types of theories—*transmission theories* and *cultural theories.*[1] In this chapter, I summarize and critique these two dominant types of communication theories.

First, I offer a few observations about the subjective nature of communication theory. Often scholars adopt a particular theory because it fits with their assumptions or motives, not because it is the most comprehensive or appropriate theory.

Second, I describe transmission theories of communication, which emerge primarily from the social and natural sciences and which define communication in mechanistic and monologic terms. Transmission theories of communication gained prominence after World War II, but their roots extend at least into the nineteenth century, when mass communication became an important part of public life. Proponents of transmission theories usually quantify communication in a search for the rules that will make communication effective.

Third, I briefly examine some of the weaknesses of the transmission view of communication. These models tend to disregard God, to assume that people are relatively passive communicators, to diminish the importance of human motives, and to promote exploitive relationships among people.

Fourth, I look at cultural theories of communication, which emerge primarily from the humanities and which view the communication process as highly interpretative, interactive, and creative. The roots of the cultural view of communication extend at least back to the Greek philosopher Aristotle. Although I side with this more creative cultural perspective, I recognize that it, too, has some major problems that potentially challenge a Christian worldview.

Fifth, I briefly examine the benefits and weaknesses of cultural theories of communication. These theories tend to capture the creative nature of human communication. They reflect existing culture and recognize that communities depend on communication. But they also tend to slip into cultural relativism.

Finally, I offer some thoughts about Christian theorizing. As we shall see, each of these types of communication theory assumes a particular view of human nature and a particular approach to the practice of communication.

I believe that the cultural view better captures the God-given complexity of human communication, but I also admit that even cultural approaches to understanding human communication are highly subjective and are not always applicable to real situations. Even today communication theorists are like Columbus, charging across the sea with an imperfect map of a big, complex world of symbols.

Why We Need Communication Theories

Just as all people use communication to cocreate culture, scholars use words and illustrations to create representations of the process of communication. And just like nonscholars, theorists may be motivated by many different things, including their religious faith, their drive for professional status, simple curiosity, and author royalties on textbook sales (ouch!). There are many schools of thought about communication: Marxist and feminist theories, a few Christian theories, and theories that focus on particular forms of communication such as small-group theory, mass-communication theory, and rhetorical theory. Overall, communication theory is a kind of hodgepodge of bits and pieces, mixed motives, and some remarkably helpful ideas.

Motives aside, communication theories serve two primary purposes. First, they are descriptive maps *of* human communication. In other words, theories help us to understand communication just as Columbus's maps enabled him to understand (or misunderstand) geography.

Second, theories are prescriptive maps *for* communication. They suggest how we should communicate.[2] When theories are accurate, they can help us communicate. When theories are inaccurate, on the other hand, they can get us into trouble. Most of Columbus's maps helped him successfully navigate his ships. When his maps were inaccurate, however, he was lost. If we use wrong or inaccurate maps of communication, we will find that we do not understand the communication process.

The Transmission View of Communication

By the mid-1920s, many people in the United States were concerned about the impact of motion pictures on the nation's youth. Religious leaders, journalists, and community leaders criticized the film industry for producing movies that depicted sex, violence, and crime. As a result, the Payne Fund, a private philanthropic foundation, financed a series of thirteen studies of the impact of movies on children. Over a three-year period, the well-known researchers examined film content, audience size and composition, and the effects of children's exposure to movie themes and messages. The results were published in the 1930s in ten book-length volumes. The Payne Fund studies were the first major attempt to uncover scientifically the cause-effect relationships between media and behavior.[3]

The Payne Fund researchers creatively developed a *transmission view of communication* to aid them in understanding how media work in children's lives. They assumed what nearly all producers of social-scientific studies of communication assume: that individuals' values, beliefs, and practices are determined by external stimuli, or messages.

The Payne Fund studies and similar research shaped the way later scholars would think about what communication is and how it works. Researchers developed social-scientific methods that are still widely used by communication scholars. Payne Fund researchers, for example, categorized and quantified the content of films and audience habits. They tabulated the number of children who watched movies and how often they did so. They used follow-up questionnaires to test children after they were shown movies in a laboratory setting. They tried to measure what the children recalled about the movies and how much the films changed the children's attitudes toward ethnic and racial groups and about social issues. In some lab studies, the researchers attached electrodes and mechanical devices to young viewers to see how the movies changed their galvanic skin responses and breathing patterns. The researchers also created a standardized "morality scale" for "measuring the mores" of young viewers. The scale enabled them to determine whether there was a correlation between viewers' moral values and their demographics, such as social class. Finally, using elaborate questionnaires, researchers tried to determine the relationship between students' movie-going and their school behavior, including course attendance, general conduct, and peer reputation.

The results of the Payne Fund studies and similar social-scientific communication research were both predictable and surprising. Predictably, they discovered that movies do have some impact on some children in some circumstances. Moreover, the impact was not always good. For example, some children strongly identified with movie characters and imitated their behaviors. The surprising result was that the more subjective, autobiographical parts of the studies, those that were based on lengthy interviews with children, may have "revealed a greater richness and insight into the effects of the films than the 'scientific' studies."[4] In other words, the more subjective and least "scientific," or quantitative, sections of the study seemed to bear the best fruit for researchers. Ironically, though, the subjective parts of the Payne Fund studies probably had the least long-term impact. Many researchers at the time believed that the study of communication could and should be a purely objective enterprise.

Early media-effects studies established the direction for a new field of research that was dedicated to mapping human communication scientifically within a stimulus-response model. Collecting and analyzing measurable data about senders, receivers, and messages, the new social-scientific researchers seemed to be studying the highly subjective process of human communication very objectively. After World War II, much of the newly emerging discipline of communication studies anchored itself in the assumptions and methods developed in the Payne Fund studies. Mechanistic sender-receiver models became part of the systems designed to map how mass communication affects people. These models were also used to study interpersonal, group, and organizational communication. As in the natural sciences, the goal of communication studies was to predict what would occur in particular communication situations: to foresee, for example, what would happen when children watched violent movies.

The social context of the rise of this type of scientific communication research is particularly telling. First, from World War I to the 1930s and 1940s, Americans were increasingly concerned about totalitarianism, especially the impact of communist and fascist propaganda on free nations. Would it be possible, they wondered, for a totalitarian nation to undermine Western democracy by using mass communication? The war had brought propaganda to the attention of fearful citizens, making it a subject for public discussion. Various popular writers published exposés of war propaganda and biographies of its chief practitioners.[5] Using engineering-like models and statistical analysis, communication researchers hoped to protect free society by revealing the real impact of totalitarian propaganda.

Second, Americans expressed growing confidence that science could enable people to discover truth and improve society. Engineers and chemists were making enormous gains in applying scientific findings to everyday life. Could mass-media research also furnish society with scientific information? After all, other "subjective" fields such as sociology and psychology were claiming success in constructing scientific approaches to the study of human behavior.[6] The stage seemed to be set for the development of a purely scientific discipline of communication.

Third, the emerging field of mass communication research met the needs of mass marketers, especially advertisers and broadcasters; both business and the academy sought to know how mass media affected consumers, and advertisers and broadcasters were increasingly willing to finance communication research.[7] After World War II, the advertising and broadcast industries in particular developed elaborate models for testing and predicting the impact of advertisements on consumers. Business experts began to study what came to be known as "consumer behavior."

Fourth, the rapid growth of mass media led to deepened public concern about the impact of popular culture on individuals. In fact, the term *popular culture* took on an increasingly negative connotation. Some scholars and other critics of the media differentiated between lowly popular art, on the one hand, and more authentic "folk" and "high" culture, on the other. They considered popular culture to be inherently standardized, manipulative, stereotypical, and superficial. The critics spoke not only against media messages but also against the systems that produced and distributed popular fare.[8]

These four aspects of the historical context—the postwar fear of totalitarianism, the growing faith in applied science, the needs of mass marketers, and the rise of critical attitudes toward popular culture—fostered the new, social-scientific approach to the study of human communication. As the Payne Fund studies illustrate, researchers were developing a fairly simple cause-effect theory of the way communication works. This "hypodermic needle" or "bullet" theory[9] posited that mass-mediated messages directly affect how individuals behave. It viewed mass communication using a mechanistic, sender-receiver model and assumed that audiences are relatively passive and easily affected by print and broadcast messages. The sender-receiver model looks amazingly like the stimulus-response theory of behavioral psychology: What people do and believe is a product of incoming stimuli. In short, the study of communication became a social science with the goal of objectively measuring and predicting the impact of messages on passive people.[10]

Although many studies have shown that communication is not so powerful, the basic idea of communication as "senders influencing receivers" has never disappeared. The cause-effect concept is simply too attractive, and apparently too quasi-scientific, to abandon. No matter how many studies have proven otherwise, many scholars still believe in a scientific metaphor of human communication founded on the idea that messages make the person, that "we are what we receive."

According to the transmission perspective, the purpose of communication research is to predict what factors will determine the effect of a given message on particular persons in specific situations. Researchers try to manipulate measurable factors to determine how the changes will affect receivers. The transmission view is most prevalent in mass-media research, but it is also the basis for the sender-receiver models that use terms such as *encoding, decoding, static, noise,* and *feedback.* These terms for communication are grounded in the idea that communication is the transmission of signals or messages over distance for the purpose of control—something the media seem to do pretty well.[11] As two communication researchers put it, "'Control' is basic to science, starting with the control arising from rigor in statements of problems, of concepts, and of conceptual schemes and hypotheses. Science means controlled observations and/or experimental methods that may be replicated by others."[12]

This simple cause-effect view of communication is deeply embedded in Western culture and long predates the formal study of mass communication. Scholar James W. Carey has suggested that the transmission view of communication originated in American Protestants' missionary rhetoric. He concluded that the Protestants saw mass communication as a means to "establish and extend the kingdom of God, to create conditions under which godly understanding might be realized, to produce a heavenly though still terrestrial city."[13] In other words, developing a science of communication was an evangelistic enterprise. Carey fails to recognize that Protestants, long before American colonization, had led the way in developing new mass media, perhaps beginning with the Gutenberg Bible during the Reformation. Clearly Protestants were using the transmission "map" of communication in the publication of books and Bible tracts in early eighteenth-century United States.[14] But European Protestants had already created a rhetoric of mass communication that linked God's providence to new communication technologies.

In any case, Protestants invented the modern communication theory that eventually became the backbone of the mass-persuasion industries of advertising and public relations. A theory that was developed for the purpose of evangelizing people became a magic formula for revealing how to persuade people to purchase soap, adopt new fashions, vote for a political candidate, and select a particular movie to view. In fact, the social-scientific approach to the study of communication is now directed nearly entirely toward the secular purposes of marketing and propaganda. Advertisements have become the secular evangelist of our time.

This may help explain why the transmission view is so prevalent in popular books and self-help literature. All of the faddish material about "dressing for success," "persuading anyone to do anything," and "winning every argument" is based largely on the simplistic bullet theory. Every year bookstores are flooded with new titles that seem to promise the reader great success in manipulating people with verbal and nonverbal symbols. The self-help industry seems to offer magical insights that will give the average person mysterious powers.

The Limits of Scientific Maps of Communication

From a Christian perspective, the transmission view of communication suffers serious drawbacks. First, transmission models eliminate God from the process of communication. They offer no room for supernatural presence or intervention in human culture. They tend to be closed models that assume all of the dynamics of communication take place within a definable system of senders, receivers, and other measurable factors. If we believe that God still speaks and that people still listen to God, a closed system inadequately describes what can happen in human communication. We will never be able to account for everything that happens when we communicate: We will always encounter serendipitous events that defy scientific explanation.

Ironically, when Protestants began devising systems for mass evangelism, they often focused on the impact of human technique instead of on the power of God. Especially during the Great Awakening of the mid-eighteenth century, mass evangelists such as George Whitefield refined dramatic techniques and rhetorical strategies that would "guarantee" conversions.[15] They viewed "soul winning" as a human-oriented enterprise. In the process, Protestant evangelists inadvertently advanced a secularized view of communication.

Second, transmission theories wrongly tend to assume that humans are passive receivers of communication. Human communciation is not a laboratory where researchers can manipulate and control all physical reactions. Because human beings creatively interpret symbols, no one can forecast with certainty what will happen in a conversation. Even formulaic mass-media messages elicit very different responses from various individuals and groups. In the early days of research into the effects of mass media, social scientists were stunned at how little impact media seemed to have on people.[16]

Researchers eventually tried to create models that were more complex than the hypodermic-needle theory of communication. They identified more and more factors that might help predict how receivers would be affected by a message. But they failed to address the deeply creative nature of communication. As I suggested in chapter 1, people *cocreate* communication; we constantly *interact* with others, including the mass media. This is why, for instance, viewers will often interpret the same television news story in very different ways. Humans are hardly passive consumers of communication.

Third, transmission theories usually diminish the importance of human motives in communication. Harold Lasswell's famous research question for the study of mass communication, "Who says what, in which channel, to whom, and with what effect?"[17] is a classic example of the failure to take human motives into account. Each of Lasswell's questions is reasonable and important. But what happened to the most important question: "Why?" Why do we communicate? Motive is a crucial aspect of human communication, but because it seems so subjective and immeasurable, it is excluded from most transmission theories.

Fourth, transmission models of communication tend to promote exploitative relationships among people. As I suggested earlier, models *of* communication are also models *for* communication. When we understand communication as a means of manipulation and control, we create cultures that promote symbolic exploitation and encourage monologic communication like advertising and propaganda in which senders' only goal is to manipulate receivers.

The concept of transmission focuses too strongly on the idea of selfishly controlling the receiver. Theologian John Bachman argues that "transmission does not provide for the exchange which is essential to genuine communication, and violates God's creative provision for human freedom."[18] Transmission models of communication can rob us of our dignity, grace, and mutuality.

The more we technologize our theories of human communication, the less human they become. The transmission view of communication does sometimes reflect the way people interact, but it cannot fully address the scope, variety, and dialogic complexity of most real-life human communication. It also misses much of the joy of improvised and serendipitous interaction. Transmission models based ultimately on manipulation and control leave little room for human and divine creativity.

Why, then, are transmission models of communication so widely reproduced in textbooks and self-help literature? Surely their simplicity is appealing. Maybe they reflect the general belief that quantification is powerful because it is scientific. Perhaps transmission models offer hope that human beings can improve their relationships and careers by controlling others. Transmission theories distort our calling to be caretakers of creation. They probably appeal to our urge to dominate our neighbors rather than serve them.

Mechanistic maps of communication can suffocate shalom by encouraging us to think about communication merely as a tool for influencing others for our own gain. In these theories, humans are generally reduced to pragmatic social engineers dedicated merely to increasing market share, manipulating coworkers, or impressing friends. We may find ourselves counting souls for Christ just like we follow baseball scores and stock market reports. But community is more than demographics and income statements. And communication is not just a matter of senders, receivers, and responses to stimuli. In their search to measure communication objectively by quantifying what people do, supporters of the transmission view simplify and distort a cocreative, dialogic process.

The Cultural View of Communication

When anthropologist Clifford Geertz decided to study the role of cockfights in the culture of Bali, he took an unusual approach. Geertz suspended his Western beliefs and scientific worldview and took on the Balinese way of life. As he communed with the culture, he uncovered an elaborate ritual.

Balinese cockfights begin late in the afternoon and run through sunset. Before each of the ten matches, men enter the ring with their birds and seek an opponent. Once two of them have been paired up, all of the men clear the ring and the opponents affix razor-sharp, pointed steel spurs to their cocks' feet. Finally, the handlers place the two cocks in the ring for the fight. Usually the cocks fly almost immediately at one another in "a wing-beating, head-thrusting, leg-kicking explosion of animal fury so pure, so absolute, and in its own way so beautiful, as to be almost abstract, a Platonic concept of hate."[19] All the while the audience crowds around the ring and watches silently, cheering on their favorite bird with hand motions, shifting shoulders, and turning heads.

Cockfights, Geertz concluded, are a Balinese art form. The fights symbolize "everyday life." They are an "image, fiction, a model, a metaphor," and above all a "means of expression." The fights are more than mere entertainment: They "enact" the "status relationships" of Balinese society. They bring alive for the participants and spectators all of the social differences among people—differences of jealousy, brutality, and charm. On the surface, Balinese society seems sedate and placid, but below the surface are all kinds of feelings and tensions among people. In effect, says Geertz, the cockfights are the Balinese people's reading of their own lives, the "story they tell themselves about themselves."[20] The Balinese cockfight may not seem like communication unless we compare it to a play, a movie, a professional sporting event, or a birthday party. Geertz joined the participants in order to find out what the fights "mean" to Balinese people and what they symbolize for Balinese culture.

According to Geertz's cultural approach, the study and practice of communication is more of an art than a science, more of a dialogue than a monologue, more of a ritual than a transmission of meaning. The cultural approach is more likely to involve anthropological fieldwork than scientific lab work or audience surveys. It assumes that communication is subjective and interpretive (open to interpretation). Moreover, in this view, communication is ritualistic or formulaic but not strictly mechanical and predictable. In other words, human communication is highly creative within the everyday patterns of interaction that humans invent. Cockfights, for instance, include set rules, but every fight is new, unique, and charged with spontaneous interaction among participants. Instead of using mechanistic terms such as *send* and *decode,* proponents of the cultural approach describe communication with words such as *interpretation, meaning,* and *context.* They speak of *sharing, participation, association, fellowship,* and even "the possession of a common faith."[21]

According to the *cultural view,* the study of communication is the art of subjectively interpreting the meaning and significance of people's shared cultural activities. Communication is a participatory ritual in and through which we create, maintain, and change culture. Rituals include the daily routine of reading the newspaper and eating meals together, and the weekly patterns of gathering for worship, viewing television, attending courses, taking exams, dating, and participating in cockfights. We do not merely exchange messages; we cocreate and share cultural rituals that define reality. Religious rituals such as Bible studies and worship shape our identities as Christians. Our faith becomes real to us as we sing Christmas carols and enjoy Easter celebrations, say mealtime prayers and share Sunday-afternoon dinner. Likewise, purchasing the right brand of jeans is part of a ritual of consumption that constructs as well as reflects personal identity. Even when they do not emphasize ritual, cultural models of communication do focus on the ways that people cocreate shared meanings.

Whereas proponents of the transmission view use tools such as demographics to dissect the communication process into measurable components, supporters of the cultural view aim to capture the *experience* of communication as fully and realistically as possible. While transmission scholars of communication seek to look at the process objectively from the outside as detached observers, cultural scholars seek to view the process subjectively from the inside as participant-observers.[22]

Benefits and Dangers of the Cultural View

There are many types of cultural approaches to communication, and while they share both weaknesses and strengths when analyzed from a Christian perspective, overall they are more compatible with the Christian faith than are transmission models.[23]

First, the cultural view generally captures more of the subjective, cocreative nature of communication. Because the cultural view recognizes the subjective nature of the meanings of symbols, cultural approaches are likely to be more open to scientifically inexplicable but meaningful communication, including the ways that God "speaks" grace into people's lives. The Balinese cockfight is a dynamic, exciting ritual charged with symbolic meaning created by participants. A film audience cocreates with the filmmaker an interpretation of the movie as the audience views the film. Even our faith is a creative dialogue with God and with each other.[24]

Second, cultural theories of communication generally evidence respect for existing cultures more fully than do transmission models. Cultural theories focus more on interpreting culture than on changing it. Because they more generously accept different cultures and affirm cultural pluralism, cultural theories of communication are more likely to question the right of some groups of people to influence or dominate other groups. For instance, some proponents of the cultural view question the right of mass media to shape local, regional, and especially traditional cultures that existed long before the media or modern cultures arrived in their communities.[25] In short, cultural approaches to communication generally emphasize understanding existing culture more than influencing it.

Third, the cultural view captures the interdependence of communication and community. A cultural map of communication focuses on shared meaning and collective symbolic action.

From a Christian perspective, communication enables us to keep the faith by sharing it with each other creatively in community. Down through the centuries believers have enjoyed and celebrated art that expresses their faith in concrete, often visual forms, helping them to remember what they believe. Paintings, sculptures, church buildings, vestments, and music help believers to affirm the faith among themselves and to carry that faith to the wider community. Similarly, hymnbooks, liturgies, creeds and confessions, and Christian literature keep alive particular Christian traditions. Technologies such as the printing press have helped the church to spread its community across space and have empowered the church to maintain its culture through time, from generation to generation. As Anabaptists know, one of the greatest witnesses of the church to the outside world is a strong, vibrant community life.

Finally, cultural theories of communication can easily slide into relativism. If communities create all of their own meaning, there is no objective truth. Cultural approaches tend to focus only on how particular cultures create and maintain their own meaning and rituals, not on what is ultimately true. Proponents of the cultural view often assume that cultural preference is merely a matter of personal taste and group mores. Geertz hoped only to understand the Balinese cockfight, not to evaluate it using standards of peace or justice. Christians should not agree uncritically with this kind of cultural relativism; however, we can admit that human beings do create versions of reality. The human fall from grace distorts our understanding of reality. Scripture makes clear that we can neither grasp all truth nor create perfectly truthful communities of belief.[26] Cultural theories can accurately capture how our misdirected symbols create distorted maps of reality—and thus distorted maps of communication.

In spite of the danger of relativism, cultural understandings of communication capture more of the image of God in humans than do transmission approaches. As God's creatures, we do not just send and receive messages. We also create meaningful cultural rituals, from cockfights to Easter pageants.[27] We are often spontaneous, imaginative, and unpredictable communicators. Moreover, our communication is relational and subjective. As one businessperson says about leadership, it is "more tribal than scientific, more weaving of relationships than an amassing of information."[28]

Conclusion

The transmission and cultural views of communication use different research methodologies and are premised on different understandings of human nature and culture. Proponents of the transmission view employ quantitative methods such as surveys and experiments, assume human passivity, and conceive of culture as fairly static and formal. In short, the transmission view tends to see culture as a kind of *organization*.

Proponents of the cultural view, on the other hand, prefer qualitative methods such as participant observation, emphasize human creativity, and assume that culture is highly dynamic and organic, even if it is very ritualistic. If proponents of the transmission view embrace the certainty of demographics and predictions, adherents to the cultural view focus on the interpretation of rituals. For them, culture is more of a dynamic *organism* than a static organization.

In the real world of communication studies, scholars combine and dilute the transmission and the cultural view of communication. Ancient rhetoric contributed substantially to the cultural view of communication even though rhetoric emphasizes persuasion. Many of the transmission models used in interpersonal, small-group, and organizational communication are modified with various interpretive and subjective elements. Communication theorists mix and match their maps of reality in the hope of creating a single theory that helps them either to understand or control all communication—or to do both.

There are no perfect theories. Sooner or later, all of them fail to explain particular instances of communication. While I favor cultural approaches, I admit that they, too, fail to adequately address complex cultural situations and God's inexplicable intervention.

Because these views *of* communication are also views *for* communication, we should pay attention to our own understanding of communication. Our notions about communication are sometimes the maps that we use to guide ourselves through life. When Columbus landed in the New World, his maps told him he was in Asia, so he began naming North America as an Indian land for Spain. For some time, cartographers believed that Columbus had found the way to the East. God graciously gives us the capacity to cocreate models of communication so that we might better understand God, others, creation, and ourselves, but any map of communication can lead us astray if we fail to test it, modify it, and hold it up to the light of God's Word.

Finally, we should always remember that God's grace transcends all of our theories of communication. God is able to enter into culture, to dialogue with individual believers, and even to direct history. We will never be able to explain or control all human communication. We now can only taste the ultimate power of God's Word.

FOUR

Symbolic Ambiguity

Limitations of Human Communication

Psychologist Martha Manning describes what it was like to grow up in a culture that stresses the importance of women being slim and attractive. She recalls looking into a mirror at eleven years of age and disliking her own reflection. "Over the next few years I came to equate growing up with getting fat," she says. "And I learned to hate my body." Manning battled her weight for years until finally she concluded that nothing she could do short of starving herself would give her a figure like the "20-somethings in great underwear and no discernible cellulite."

Even after fulfilling her lifelong dream of becoming an author, Manning couldn't separate her self-esteem from her weight. In fact, her public success made matters worse. She imagined "autographing books and regaling television and radio hosts with my witty remarks—I am wearing high-fashion, hip-hugging, thigh-skimming skirts with impossibly high-heeled shoes that accentuate my long legs. My makeup and hair are perfect. But most important of all, I am always, always, thin." Manning's struggle with self-esteem seems at odds with her remarkable professional talent. "My childhood goal of becoming brilliant," she says, has "eased into a pleasure and peace with being pretty smart. Those adjustments have been relatively painless. But where my weight is concerned, there is no such acceptance. The little kid in my head is stuck in a conflict that traps so many women."[1]

59

As Manning has learned, body weight is not entirely determined by diet and exercise. We are born with genes that greatly affect our body size and structure, predisposing us toward a range of body weight. Self-discipline and lifestyle can adjust our weight, but they cannot determine it. Males and females alike are caught between accepting the way God made them and being the kind of people that society tells them to be. Men spend more than one hundred million dollars annually on hair coloring and well over a billion dollars on hair transplants, toupees, and other products to counteract baldness and graying.[2] But no matter how much we spend, no matter how hard we work, we simply cannot create the physique of our choosing.

Just as we fret or fantasize about body image, we often wonder about our ability to communicate. We see in the movies and on television perfect relationships in which people interact effortlessly. We imagine ourselves conducting a superb job interview or writing an inspiring novel. In thousands of ways we envision ourselves as gifted communicators, but deep down we all also know that we suffer from real limitations.

Our personal communication rarely meets the cultural ideal. Most of us are scared to communicate, especially in public. In fact, public speaking is the most-feared human activity.[3] Like Martha Manning, we sense a gap between the way we are and the way we would like to be. And it is not easy to accept our human weaknesses.

We are truly remarkable communicators with amazing creative power; still, we are inept amateurs at best. This chapter looks at some of the limitations of human communication.

First, I look at the ambiguity of symbols. Language, for instance, is merely an approximate means of communicating, clouded by ambiguity. In fact, symbolic ambiguity burrows deeply into our self-identity. Sometimes we feel as though we hardly know who we are. Manning fantasized about who she wanted to be by imagining herself in a different body. Because we all fantasize about projecting a self identity that others will like, rather than communicating openly who we really are, we present ourselves to others ambiguously.

Second, I examine how it is that many scholars are losing hope in their ability to know truth and to communicate it to others. Postmodern philosophy emphasizes the subjectivity in all human communication. It stresses the idea that human beings are invariably trapped in their own cultural definitions of reality. How could Manning find her true self in a confusing world of rapidly changing images and meanings? St. Augustine offers an age-old antidote to these postmodern blues.

Third, I consider how we can easily fail to identify and develop our God-given communication abilities. Instead of celebrating the unique gifts that God gives each of us, we tend to focus on our own misguided dreams, which are often shaped by the wider culture. When we battle to know our God-given paths, we too often focus on what we want to be, not on what God created us to be.

Finally, I discuss two crucial limitations on all human communication—time and space. God's Word is eternal, but human symbols are temporary; our communication disappears over time. Similarly, we cannot communicate everywhere at once, even with new globe-shrinking technologies. Unless we communicate wisely, our culture experiences entropy: It tends to weaken and disappear.

As symbolic stewards, we face the daunting task of managing communication for community. When we identify and develop our God-given communication gifts, we help preserve cultural memory, create lasting wisdom, and reduce symbolic ambiguity. Like symbolic gardeners, we have to figure out which symbols to plant, where to plant them in space and time, and how to nurture them so that they will bear the fruit of shalom.

Symbolic Ambiguity

Swarthmore College once faced a mess—literally and symbolically. Students found what appeared to be excrement and vomit on the floor of the campus intercultural center. Some students immediately concluded that the incident was symbolically charged. They believed that someone had left the mess intentionally as an insult to minority and gay students on campus.

Soon hundreds of people showed up for a campus rally organized "to condemn this crime" and to support the center and its values.[4] One speaker told the crowd, "When you violate that space, you violate me." Another speaker said that he had cried all night, but that the rally gave him "tears of hope."[5] Although not all of the facts of the case had been established, the incident sparked a campus-wide movement. Various campus groups quickly defined reality according to their own assumptions. Within a week, however, the college learned that although the vomit was real, the "excrement" was chocolate cake. Officials did not uncover who was responsible.

As the events at Swarthmore illustrate, communicators must interpret what symbols mean. Symbolic meaning is arbitrary, not fixed, and sometimes symbols carry multiple meanings. If the vomit was a message, what did it mean? We all sometimes misconstrue the meaning of symbols. An estimated 1.3 million Americans are injured annually by medication errors because of the similarity of certain drug names.[6] Two people might see the same film and yet come to widely different conclusions about its theme. Complex terms such as *democracy* and *spirituality* are linguistically imprecise. Sometimes a scholar writes an entire book to define the meaning of a single idea or concept—like communication! Even dictionaries, which attempt to capture the standardized meanings of words, change over time and never reflect the full diversity of interpretations. Communication is interpretive and dynamic, not fixed in static symbols.

Sometimes even our most careful communication produces miscommunication—contradictory interpretations of the same symbols. One company asked a culturally sensitive translator to add the phrase "family-size" to the packages of its popcorn that were to be marketed in France. The concept was so alien to a culture in which people shop for groceries every day that the translator refused the project. Unwilling to listen, the company got a different firm to translate the phrase. But the product still flopped.[7] We all face the challenge of understanding others and making ourselves understood. Much of our daily communication seems to work well because it does not require careful crafting to be effective. But even seemingly minor symbolic confusion can create arguments, heighten personal anxiety, and injure relationships.

While I was writing this book, I shared sample chapters with students and professors. One class of twenty students discussed the entire manuscript over a three-week period. The students' insights made this a much better book with far less symbolic ambiguity and many more concrete examples and illustrations. My careful listening and the students' openness enhanced the quality of the manuscript. But even many drafts later, some sentences still confused readers. No matter how hard I worked, ambiguity was a problem.

Symbolic ambiguity has always plagued ecumenical dialogue among members of different Christian traditions. Each Christian group establishes its own interpretations of Scripture. Some groups allow members to interpret the Bible for themselves. Other groups insist that their members use a particular translation. Bible scholars face confusing historical information, contradictory archeological findings, and incomplete fragments of early handwritten texts. A group of scholars, The Jesus Seminar, decided that the best way to determine which words in Scripture were actually uttered by Christ was to take a vote among the organization's membership.[8]

We overcome some symbolic ambiguity by forming communities of interpretation in which people agree on the meaning of various symbols. Each Christian tradition has a paradigm for how to interpret the Word of God in the face of ambiguity, but even within these communities people sometimes disagree. For instance, believers might disagree about whether Adam was a historical person or only a symbol for all people (the name *Adam* is often interpreted as "mankind" or "humankind"). People on both sides of this debate might agree that the story of Adam and Eve's fall from grace is historical truth, but they might define "history" differently.

The history of the church is the history of an interpretive community that overcame much ambiguity by carefully viewing both Scripture and the world through the lens of the gospel. Today Christians agree on certain historical truths: They concur that the Son of God was born and lived on earth, that he was killed on the cross, and that he was resurrected from the grave. Most also agree that Christ will return again to earth. Over time these interpretations of Scripture have become some of the nonnegotiables of the faith that are expressed in historic documents such as the Apostles' Creed.[9]

But ambiguity still seeps into specific biblical interpretations. Believers disagree about baptism, predestination, and the meaning of the sacrament of communion. They also argue about whether women should be ordained ministers and how to understand homosexuality in the light of the gospel. Even if they generally agree on the redemptive purpose of the gospel, people within individual communities of Christian interpretation also quarrel over many "non-gospel" issues.

Augustine versus the Postmodernists

A story in *Smithsonian* magazine tells of an irresistible Civil War photograph that has been published and republished so often and for so long that journalists now simply pass along each other's erroneous interpretations of it. The soldiers' young faces and dashing uniforms create an enticing image that few periodicals can ignore. Well-intentioned public communicators repeatedly misidentify the men in the photos as Confederate soldiers. Moreover, one of the men looks enough like John Wilkes Booth, who assassinated Abraham Lincoln, that publications wrongly conclude that the man in the picture is Booth. According to historians, however, the people in the photo are not Confederate soldiers, the setting is not the Civil War, and Booth is not in the photo. "Despite all the misrepresentations," *Smithsonian* concluded, "the picture will continue to survive because it is a compelling image."[10]

The photo fiasco might make us wonder just how precarious our interpretations of human symbols really are. Are we able to extract our communication from the mire of symbolic ambiguity long enough to get a solid grasp on the reality behind our symbols? Can we experience reality directly, or are we always dependent on someone else's opinion? This concern about the subjectivity of human symbols is one of the most important issues in nearly all scholarly disciplines, from history to physics to communication.

Contemporary communication theory is influenced by *postmodernism,* which is based on the philosophical idea that people use symbols to create their own, subjective versions of reality. Postmodern thought tends to relativize culture, community, and communication, arguing, for example, that people will invariably interpret the photo differently over time, and that no one can know the truth behind the image. As one scholar put it, we live in "a quicksand of ambiguity, a *melange* of artificial images, flickering from the TV and screen."[11] French philosopher Jacques Derrida, one of the first proponents of postmodern thought, argued that none of our symbolic interpretations are settled or stable.[12] According to some postmodernists, we all need texts, or messages, to make sense of the world, but we can never know if *any* texts, including the Bible, are ultimately true, right, or accurate. All we can do is subjectively "deconstruct" the ambiguous texts, peeling back layers of symbolic interpretation that ultimately lead us only to additional layers of subjectivity. Just as we may never know all the facts surrounding the Swarthmore incident, we can never fully reconstruct the truth behind any message (if there *is* a truth behind the message). We are forever mired in irreconcilable symbolic ambiguity. We might as well accept chaos and welcome Babel.[13] This is the human condition, say many postmodernists.

Postmodernism suggests that the meaning of any message is whatever people say it is. Readers of a book cannot know what the original author intended, so they might as well interpret the book according to personal interest. A film viewer's interpretation of a movie is as correct as the director's or screenwriter's. Under this kind of subjectivity, all interpretations are created equal. According to postmodernism, people are free to conjure their own self-seeking interpretations and have no obligation to seek the right, intended, or truthful interpretation. Freedom replaces responsibility to the text, to the author, or to the community—let alone to the Creator.

St. Augustine (A.D. 354–430) explained how the church might deal with ambiguity in communication, including scriptural interpretation. In some respects, his argument is the opposite of postmodernism's strident subjectivity. Augustine identified three crucial steps for reducing ambiguity: (1) know the *author*, (2) know the *text*, or message, and (3) know the *context* for the message. And he emphasized the importance of communal rather than merely personal interpretation.

Augustine anchored the interpretation of Scripture in the context of the faithful Christian community, not in the public's fickle opinion or even in experts' views. He also implicitly affirmed the role of *communities of interpretation* as a check against the unleashed will of individuals who would conjure up personalistic interpretations. For example, there is probably a community of archivists and Civil War buffs that has traced the roots of the "Civil War" photo to a particular photographer, a probable location, and even actual families whose forebears are in the image. Perhaps magazine editors should listen to that community of Civil War interpretation before publishing the photograph! To this day, Augustine's approach to biblical interpretation offers significant wisdom for anyone who wishes to interpret even highly ambiguous symbols.

In *De Doctrina Christiana,* Augustine's major contribution to the history and theory of rhetoric, he applied these three principles to the church's task of interpreting Scripture. He argued that when a literal interpretation is not possible, Christians should turn to the "more open places of the scriptures" and to the "authority of the Church." He suggested that "interpretation must be based on an understanding of the context in which a word or passage occurs and also on the overall meaning or structure of the work in which it occurs."[14] The church is a community that is responsible for knowing the author of human history, for knowing the sacred text, and for collectively interpreting Scripture in its historical context.

The Christian doctrine of the fall explains our current condition. Broken from perfect fellowship with God and with the community of believers, we are all "lost in the cosmos."[15] Once our communication with God was disrupted, the vessel that would take us to truth and reality was cast adrift; we are trying to navigate with an ambiguous map, a weak engine, and little gas. To paraphrase the apostle Paul, we are cast about by the winds of all kinds of doctrines (Eph. 4:14). All communicators are broken communicators. We all live in symbolic ambiguity. The church's voice is crucial for our collective wisdom, but even the church does not see all truth and all reality. Postmodern philosophers are partly correct: Communication with each other and with God is a subjective activity fraught with opportunities for misinterpretation and self-delusion.

We desperately need an anchor, a single person or community whose words we can trust. When the apostle John says, "In the beginning was the Word" (John 1:1), he claims that God predated human culture and the creation itself. Christ, the Word, not only proclaimed the Word of God but actually was and is the Word of God. To put it differently, God is not subject to human understanding or to any particular symbols. We do not create God or even the meaning of God. God is God. As the Old Testament writers express it, God is "I AM" (Exod. 3:14). All of our symbolic ruminations about the Creator do not change God; they merely alter our understanding of God. Belief in Christ changes how we think about God, but it does not transform who God is or what God does.

Augustine's theory suggests that the church cannot completely embrace a philosophical position that asserts that all truth is a mere delusion of communities of interpretation. Postmodernism itself demonstrates that our alienation from God turns our symbolic creativity against our desire for truthful interpretations and shared meanings. Living in what C. S. Lewis called the "shadowlands," we *do* sometimes misinterpret even God's Word. To adapt rhetorician Kenneth Burke's phrase, we are "rotten with symbolic *imperfection.*"[16] Too often we rely on fallen interpretations of messages and even of the meaning of life. We not only misunderstand each other but also misconstrue God's truth and God's reality. Thus, the nature of communication in a fallen world is a crucial philosophical and even cosmological issue, so it should not surprise us that some scholars question not only humankind's ability to communicate but also the existence of God.

As Augustine recognized, our ability to communicate always depends on God's grace. Just as journalists misinterpreted the meaning of the "Civil War" photo, we daily misinterpret one another's communication, but God graciously uses even our symbolic entropy for good purposes. As long as we cannot communicate perfectly, we are unable to establish a single evil empire on earth. But whereas postmodernism concedes victory to symbolic entropy, Augustine embraced the pursuit of truth. And although truth can be elusive, the gospel is God's unambiguous word to the wise: "I am." First God, as represented in Scripture, and then the church community becomes our anchor in a sea of symbolic ambiguity.

Recognizing Our Communication Gifts

After twenty years as editor of the first edition of the legendary *Oxford English Dictionary* (OED), a phenomenal lexicon with nearly 415,000 definitions, James Murray decided that he had to meet one of the project's greatest contributors, American surgeon William Chester Minor, who had submitted thousands of precise, neatly handwritten definitions. Professor Murray set out on the short journey to Minor's home, only fifty miles from Oxford. The trip was the revelation of Murray's life. He discovered that Dr. Minor's home was England's harshest asylum for the criminally insane: Dr. Minor was not only a wonderfully gifted wordsmith but also a lunatic murderer.[17] Human talent sometimes comes in surprising packages.

Although we are all created in the image of God, our ability to communicate effectively varies by person, situation, and medium, and while we should certainly identify and use our gifts, none of us will fully master any medium. The Creator enables us to communicate adequately for the tasks before us and for the needs of our communities, but not always as well as we dream or desire to do. God can use anyone—even murderers and people with severe mental illness—as symbolic stewards of creation. But first we must recognize and develop our gifts.

Communication is both a gift from God and a learnable skill. The scholar who developed the *communibiological* perspective of communication, which highlights the importance of genetic traits in determining how people interact, argues that "differences in interpersonal behavior are principally due to individual differences in neurobiological functioning."[18]

Whether or not he is correct, our God-given gifts are very important in communication, and we would do well to develop them. For instance, some people are born with the capacity to become talented writers, actors, and filmmakers. They have God-given abilities and remarkable talent that can be deeply cultivated through proper instruction and hard work. Gifted listeners or negotiators have, like born athletes, an innate capacity to perform well, but countless hours of hard work are required to translate capacity into actual skill.

Augustine recognized two crucial communication gifts—the ability to craft messages and the skill in delivering them. He suggested, for example, that a godly life is not enough to make a minister an effective preacher. A minister must be able to prepare and deliver sermons as well. Both substance and style are important in sermons. Augustine suggested that it is better for eloquent preachers to read other people's sermons than to deliver their own, poorly crafted ones. In the face of Roman sophism, which often valued delivery over truth, Augustine championed thoroughly good communication. He rightly saw that an orator's gifts are crucial for all truth tellers, not just for sophists.[19]

In fact, Augustine almost single-handedly persuaded the church to value rhetorical gifts. Philosophers before and during Augustine's life had emphasized method, or eloquence. They argued that communicators' impact was more important than their ethics, and that method was more important than truth. Augustine, on the other hand, taught that Christians need to combine eloquence with a knowledge of the truth. In his view, the church must use the best possible means to advocate truth and dispute falsity. He argued that eloquence should not abandon wisdom.[20] Once Augustine combined truth and eloquence, the giftedness of the communicator became a crucial concern for the Christian community. Christians could no longer focus just on the veracity of messages. Believers were obligated to look also at their messengers' rhetorical ability.

Augustine's view of rhetoric shaped communication theory for centuries and still influences the ways that some people teach the craft. We can hear Augustine's words today when a Christian communicator says, "The message never changes, but the method does." While not all methods are justified, how we communicate does affect how people will interpret our message. Some evangelists who rant and rave on street corners probably make it harder for listeners to hear the love of God. Eloquence should never substitute for truth or ethics, but Augustine's logic does require us to consider how our method affects our message.

When we live in shalom, we encourage and support one another's efforts to identify our communicative gifts and to exercise them on behalf of God. We must be honest with each other about our strengths and weaknesses, and we should avoid jealousies and petty squabbles over giftedness, recognizing that God uses the variety of our gifts to advance the kingdom on earth. We do not all need to be great orators or marvelous performers. Instead, we need to serve our neighbors according to our gifts. Dr. Minor was deemed a lunatic, but his talents contributed significantly to the greatest etymological dictionary in the history of the English language. Martha Manning used her literary talent to serve others who, like her, suffered with low self-esteem because of body weight. Our value as God's image bearers does not depend on whether or not we possess particular communication gifts, but God does expect us to identify and use our gifts to serve others.

God can foster communication among people who are not gifted communicators. Moses was not a splendid orator, so God appointed Aaron to carry Moses' words to the people, and those words convicted many people of their wrongful ways and led Israel back to righteousness (Exod. 4:12–15). The apostle Paul was not an elocutionary giant either, but God granted him such wisdom that his words, inspired by the Holy Spirit, became part of the sacred text of the Christian church (Eph. 3:7–12). Writer Elisabeth Elliot tells the story of her family's nearly deaf housekeeper, who communicated through the way she lived her life. Family members had to shout into a small microphone that she wore pinned on her collar. But as Elliot recalls, the housekeeper's demeanor and her servant's heart brought "peace to our house every day."[21] God gives special grace to people who need it to communicate the Lord's purposes.

Our fall from grace hides and distorts the truth about our communication gifts. Many communicators never recognize that they are equipped with gifts from God. Others recognize their gifts but fail to develop them. Still others develop their gifts but do not place them in the service of the Creator. Augustine opened the door in the church for all of us to love God by communicating according to our gifts. If we do not determine and use our gifts as a community, pursuing our own gifts and helping others recognize theirs, we will lose some of the best talent that could be used to bring peace, comfort, and reconciliation to the world.

Creating Legacies in Time and Space

Librarian of Congress James Billington compares modern society with personal insanity. Looking at the rapid cultural change and people's sense of rootlessness, he wonders if we have taken history too lightly. Our pasts, he says, should inform our present. Without a sense of our personal pasts, we may lose our self-identity to a "world of motion without memory, which is one of the clinical definitions of insanity."[22]

Billington's observations point to a fourth limit to our communication. Not only are we restricted by the ambiguity of symbols, by postmodern subjectivity, and by our failure to recognize and use our gifts, but we are also born with limited ability to build community across geographic space and through generational time. Although we are all called to be symbolic stewards, we are far from being omnipotent and omnipresent communicators. In fact, we are always on the verge of losing our culture and our identity as we drift into a kind of memory-less insanity.

Media technologies can extend our cultures through time and across space. Satellites instantly carry our images and voices around the world. Recording devices enable us to replay messages from long ago so that people can reexperience the rituals that once gave their community its identity. Telephones enable us to conduct business or build relationships with people in distant locations. European cathedrals maintain Christian communities' architectural presence long after the buildings were first constructed. In many ways, technology has made us increasingly powerful communicators both across space and through time.

In spite of technology, however, we can easily lose our ways of life. Canadian scholar Harold Adams Innis suggests that the effects of space and time on human communication are inversely related.[23] When our communication strengthens community through generational time, it weakens communication across geographic space. If we focus more of our time and energy on interpersonal communication within our families, for instance, we will be less connected to the worlds of national news and international entertainment. Conversely, as we spread popular culture around the globe, we weaken local, proximate community from generation to generation. Whenever we conquer geographic space, we weaken cross-generational bonds. We lose our particular "sense of place."[24] When developing countries rapidly import American popular culture, for example, they can lose their distinctive local traditions. If Innis is correct, we must balance our communication in time and space so that we will not destroy our traditions.

We must all make tough decisions about how much of our time, energy, and other resources we will invest in widespread culture versus local culture. How much of our lives should we commit to neighborhood friends, local business associates, and members of our congregation? Without local commitments we will likely lose touch with our own pasts. If we live entirely in a media world we will probably develop unstable, superficial identities and shallow communities. On the other hand, we should spend some money and time on books, recordings, and live media. If we don't, we could easily become parochial and narrow-minded.

Decisions that seem insignificant today can powerfully affect our future culture. "It is precisely because of the eternity outside time," writes Dorothy

Sayers, "that everything in time becomes valuable and meaningful. Christianity teaches us that 'eternal life' is a sole sanction for the values of this life."[25] We should incarnate the gospel in both time and space. As cocreators of culture, we must consider the eternal significance that our communication has for future generations whose identity will be shaped partly by our present-day decisions. Christians should strive for a legacy grounded in the eternal gospel rather than in transitory cultural fads.

Many scholars recognize *orality* as the basis for strong local community life that survives through generations.[26] Orality includes speaking and listening, which form the basis of all highly relational activities. Orality was at the center of Jewish life during the Old Testament era. In *Fiddler on the Roof*, the father celebrates tradition and decries its decline. He recognizes that orality has always been the primary way that families maintain traditional culture from generation to generation and from place to place, and he wonders how he can keep his family's Jewish faith alive when his daughters marry nonbelievers and move to other communities.

Orality is at the heart of prayer, at the center of disciple making, and at the core of organizational leadership. Speaking and listening to each other is the most intimate and personal way that we commune with each other. Orality opens us up to each other and builds trust. As philosopher Martin Buber puts it, orality is the basis of our "I-Thou" relationships, in which we treat each other with holy reverence and respect.[27] Relationships formed in orality are the most enduring form of interpersonal interaction and are the cross-generational glue of culture in any place.

Mass media threaten local community life when they challenge orality. For all of the entertainment and information the media provide, they are never an acceptable substitute for rich, interpersonal communication among friends, family, and fellow believers. In fact, people who live in a media-rich environment can feel terribly lonely. Soap opera viewers, for instance, sometimes substitute the fictional intimacy of the characters on the screen for real intimacy in their own lives. Some Internet users engage in commitment-free "cybersex." Most of us sometimes avoid the stress and pain of broken relationships by substituting vicarious relationships for real ones. In contrast, a healthy community is a "neighborhood of humans in a place, plus the place itself: its soil, its water, its air, and all the families and tribes of the nonhuman creatures that belong to it."[28] This type of local community "lives and acts by the common virtues of trust, goodwill, forbearance, self-restraint, compassion and forgiveness."[29] The media can threaten community life when they eclipse such relationships.

Orality also produces accountability among people, whereas mass-mediated communication easily becomes propaganda. Orality can safeguard ethical accountability by fostering dialogue, identification, and trust, but ironically, in many countries orality is being challenged by the growth of consumer-oriented mass media.[30] The killing fields of Cambodia and the Stalinist purges of Soviet Russia would probably not have occurred in communities of trust and mutual respect. When mass media are the conduit of revolutionary ideas, people are much more likely to be demonized, victimized, and exploited.[31] Without orality, mass-mediated societies can self-destruct.

The effect of digital technologies on the quality of communication is not clear. Cybercommunication can facilitate or weaken shalom, depending on how we use it. Digital technology disrupts familiar networks of direct association and marginalizes people around the world who lack access to online media because of high cost or inadequate infrastructure.[32] On the other hand, digital media can facilitate strong friendships between people who cannot easily get together in person.

None of us fully understands this world of rapidly circulating sounds, images, and texts that we have created in our quest to conquer time and space. We have the technical skill to create technologies and compose messages, but we lack the critical, interpretive ability to make sense of the media world and to guide it toward shalom. In fact, the growth of media empires seems to weaken our ability to understand the world. Just when the cost of our mistakes could be especially high, we are lost in heavy "data smog."[33] Perhaps we have ingested too much of the "silicon snake oil" that causes us to praise new technologies without assessing whether they can live up to their promise to build community.[34]

Because our communication is always anchored in time and space, problems in communication are also problems in community life.[35] Without strong face-to-face relationships we cannot cocreate strong communities. We have an amazing international system of communication that can transmit a mind-boggling array of information around the globe. But technology and information do not automatically create a global village.[36] Community does not come easily. Ethnic, religious, and territorial conflicts divide people and nations around the world. No matter how advanced our technology is, our communities will be unstable if strong local communication is not stabilized over generations.

Unless we cultivate a legacy of strong local communities that maintain culture from generation to generation, we will all eventually lose our identity; we will become memory-less people. Unless we act for posterity as symbolic stewards of God's world, we will plunge ourselves into cultural insanity. Instantaneous media will not produce shalom. On the other hand, unless we interact with the wider world we can easily become ethnocentric, bigoted, and parochial. We must cultivate our community's ability to understand communication as a God-given gift for maintaining the wisdom of the

71

Christian faith from generation to generation. After all, the Word transcends both time and space.

Conclusion

Our ability to communicate reflects not only the image of God in us but also our humanness. Among the reasons for our poor communication are the ambiguity of symbols, the self-defeating relativism of postmodernism, our failure to develop our giftedness, and the trade-offs between space and time. Our communication is gloriously creative but also often distressingly weak. Grace will carry us through, but we also have to make wise decisions about using the gifts that God gives us.

Each of us lives in a particular place and time. We cannot redeem the world overnight, but we can invite others to join us in creating communities of shalom. We can help to breathe life into our local communities, beginning with our families and congregations. Shalom does not emerge in a crazed media frenzy but in the orality of our daily lives. God equips us with communication gifts and with the Holy Spirit. In communities of grace we overcome some of the symbolic ambiguity of our lives, we live the truth of the gospel, we discover and exercise our communicative gifts, and we balance the various media forms as we pursue tangible peace and justice.

FIVE

Slaves to ·Sin

The Effects of Sin on Communication

In his book *Secret Life,* prize-winning poet Michael Ryan tells the story of his lifelong obsession with seducing women. After recounting his experience of being repeatedly abused when he was five years old, Ryan describes his adult life as a predator who was "drunk" with his own sexual compulsion. "All of my talents," he recalls, "all of my good qualities as a human being, were devoted to serving it, and I was willing to sacrifice any-thing to it."[1] Although he regularly felt deep shame, guilt, and self-loathing, Ryan lived for each new sexual conquest. Dominated by a perverted erotic identity, he developed his gifts of communication for the purpose of becom-ing a talented seducer. Over the course of his life, Ryan increasingly sub-mitted to the hellish bondage of his own sexual slavery. Then Princeton University fired him for conquering female students.

How could Ryan fall so deeply into the pit of evil, unable to control his gift of communication? Ryan's autobiography is a parable for all of us who recognize that we are not the kind of persons we would like to be. Perhaps we are all "seducers" who use communication to get what we want but should not necessarily have. Like Ryan, we abuse others by misusing the gift of communication.

This chapter addresses humankind's fall from grace. I argue that the most complex and devastating reason for our breakdown in communication is sin—our breaking of relationship with God.[2] Sin spoils shalom and fundamentally corrupts our communication.

First, I examine the scope and nature of our sinful communication. All people rebel against God. Filled with arrogant pride, we engage in sins of symbolic commission and sins of symbolic omission. Instead of accepting our position as symbolic stewards of creation, we slavishly cling to distorted desires—just as Michael Ryan did.

Second, I explore how communication spreads sin throughout organizations and across entire cultures, so that sin becomes an intrinsic part of the fallen fabric of community life. Like Ryan, who spread his own childhood abuse to others, we become evil tempters, carrying sin into human relationships.

Third, I suggest that our fall from grace leads us to practice symbolic domination. Rather than using symbols to serve our neighbor, we communicate primarily to control others for our own selfish purposes.

Finally, I show that as a result of the fall we all squander our communication resources and talents. Mesmerized by technology, satisfied with poor quality, and ignorant about truth, we cocreate poor communication.

Recognizing Our Fallenness

Michael Ryan finally perceived the depth of his sexual addiction one day while he was driving to his friends' house in another state. He had already lost his teaching position and destroyed his marriage. Nevertheless, all he could think about during the trip was how to seduce his friends' fifteen-year-old daughter. Gripped by fear and panic, he glimpsed his own fallen condition, his deep loneliness and despair. Rescued by what he calls "the grace of God," Ryan turned his car around and drove home.[3] Ryan's fear of himself helped him to recognize his own fallenness, and that was enough to cause him to reverse his life's direction. He began traveling from the folly of hell to the wisdom of shalom.

Sin is not a popular idea in either the academy or everyday life. Because the concept of sin seems so old-fashioned and negative, many people dismiss it. Some communication scholars talk instead about such problems as interference, bias, relational instability, conflict, vagueness, and code switching.[4] Humanistic scholars might replace sin with "errors in ethical judgment" or "poor ethos." In the field of communication, there is hardly mention of evil let alone sin. So in this section, I offer a language for identifying and discussing sin in human communication.

When we break our relationship with God, our hearts and minds are more susceptible to evil. We do not just *do* evil, we *become* evil. Sin pervades all aspects of our lives. As C. S. Lewis says, our descent "begins with a grumbling mood," but soon all we can hear is the "grumble itself going on forever like a machine."[5] When we rebel against God, we become evil slaves to sinful intentions and actions.

Sin fundamentally corrupts our ability to communicate. When we sin, we do not merely misunderstand. Nor do we just inadvertently confuse others. We *cause* confusion and misunderstanding—and far worse. We become obsessed with using our gifts of communication to serve anything "besides God as our ultimate value and worth."[6] Sex became Ryan's god, driving his sinful seductions. He sacrificed his career and his marriage to satisfy his unquenchable thirst.

Our alienation from God radically corrupts our ability to communicate in ways that promote God's peace and justice. Using symbols selfishly, we pretend to be God. We listen to our own cravings instead of to God's commands. We ignore the needs of our neighbor. Our communication becomes a pervasive, destructive idolatry. Unless we recognize the reality of sin, we will wrongly assume that all we need for better communication is a bit more common sense, greater education, or additional practice. We will act as if there is nothing fundamentally wrong with us.

Blind to humankind's sinful condition, many scholars convey a naively romantic view of communication. They encourage us to believe that we all possess a wonderful ability to win people over, to persuade them, and to impress everyone with our rhetorical ability. One pair of authors even hopes to "promote a greater measure of communicative literacy for every human being on the face of the globe."[7] Unfortunately, human communication is not so easily repaired. Even after studying communication we struggle. Sin is a stubbornly pervasive part of the human condition. We cannot become superb communicators simply by working harder. Our *motives* need to be redeemed. We desperately need grace.

As sinners we sometimes communicate maliciously. We lie and manipulate as Ryan did to gain sex. We talk too much and fail to listen. We intentionally remain silent when we need to speak on behalf of others. We intimidate. We gossip. In fact, we often enjoy warping communication for our own ends. Some of us even silence powerless individuals and propagandize exploited communities. With our sins of omission and of commission, we are symbolic predators in the communication jungles of a fallen world.

We commit *sins of omission* when we fail to communicate what and when we should. Just as Adam and Eve hid from God and from each other after eating the forbidden fruit, we avoid our neighbor.[8] Living with a deep sense

SLAVES TO SIN

of personal sin and communal shame, we fail to accept communion with others as a gift of God. Uncertain and anxious, we withdraw from meaningful discourse.

We spend much of our lives designing excuses to avoid communication. Parents avoid speaking to their children about drugs, claiming that it is the responsibility of the media or the school. Witnesses to crimes thwart justice by remaining silent. Gripped by laziness or fear, we stay out of conflicts and awkward situations. Sometimes we even abusively refuse to communicate with people we consider inferior or unworthy. We repeatedly fail to speak when we should, blithely assuming that time will heal the injury or that communication is someone else's responsibility.

Sins of symbolic omission plague all levels of society. Professional communicators, such as publicists and speechwriters, refuse to confront corporate officials who sanction unethical actions. Employees keep quiet about illegal dumping of chemicals. Members of opposing political parties fail to compliment each other for doing something well. Governments hide important information from the public about illegal or covert activities. Editors refuse to run corrections to news stories that have regrettable errors. Students do not confront other students who repeatedly cheat on exams. Doctors fail to thank nurses for their excellent patient care. Victims of clergy abuse remain silent, because they don't want to get the pastor in trouble. We could create justifications for each of these omissions, and silence is indeed sometimes golden, but more often it reflects fear or callousness.

In Bible times, the prophets were the whistleblowers. They spoke the truth regardless of the potential costs to themselves. Stephen was stoned to death simply for professing his faith in Christ (Acts 6:8–7:60). Not all of us have the courage of prophets, so we should refrain from judging people for their silence, but selfish silence weakens communities and hurts individuals, especially those who are powerless and exploited. Our own silence can harm our neighbors.

Our communication also suffers from *sins of commission*—from intentional misuse of our gifts of communication. Sinful communication often stymies shalom, contributing to hatred, wars, divorce, suicide, and loneliness. We spread distorted, selfish, and manipulative information. We lie, defame, verbally abuse, and gossip. The apostle James rightly calls the human tongue "a fire, a world of evil among the parts of the body. It corrupts the whole person, sets the whole course of his life on fire, and is itself set on fire by hell" (James 3:6). The tongue is the "rudder" of our lives (James 3:4). Our communication proceeds from our hearts, from the course we set for our lives. As Michael Ryan discovered, we become slaves to our insatiable desires to do evil.

Sins of commission reflect our prideful selfishness. We love to listen to ourselves. We like to tell others what television programs to watch and which poetry to recite. We speak quickly and arrogantly. We are convinced that we are right when someone disputes the meaning of our words. How dare someone challenge our intentions! In some of our darker moments, we find prideful pleasure and spiteful relief in others' inability to communicate. Selfishness destroys many relationships because it offers little or no room for the grace of humble forgiveness.

We pridefully blame others for corrupting our communication. Adam blamed Eve for his own disobedience, and Eve then blamed the serpent (Gen. 3:12–13). Neither was willing to admit the truth to God. So it goes, on and on through generations of sin. Parents have "eaten sour grapes, and the children's teeth are set on edge" (Jer. 31:29). We are not just lazy or lousy communicators; we are self-promoting fools. Instead of harnessing our tongue to the joy of shalom, we delight in turning our symbols against our Creator and against other creatures—as if they are the cause of our evil. Puffed up with pride, we smugly challenge God and sew critical seeds of conflict and envy.

In our sins of commission, we act like we are the Creator; we try to elevate ourselves to the throne of creation. Just as Adam and Eve tried to deceive God after eating the forbidden fruit, we "fall back on one art learned from the serpent, that of correcting God, of appealing from God the Creator to a better, a different God."[9] Using the pen, the computer, the camera, and the stage, we launch ego-filled messages for others to appreciate and extol. Playing god, we communicate selfish agendas and personal pride. We glamorize our own communication. Advertisers create visual fantasies in order to build market share. Young lovers speak gloriously of the beauty of their lovemaking even though they are uncommitted to a life together. Symbols are often the tools with which we play God by selfishly redefining reality. We turn the gift of communication into a glamorous weapon of destruction.

In our sins of symbolic commission, we often purposely mislead others to advance our own interests. Scriptwriters stereotype members of a particular race to boost television ratings. Employees advance hidden agendas in the workplace to win a promotion. Children may lie to their parents to avoid punishment.

Our problem, then, is not simply ineffective communication. Nor is it lack of instruction. As Michael Ryan's life shows, even highly educated people can be spiritually sick and can communicate in ungodly ways, thwart shalom, and turn relationships and communities into a godless mess. Our endless variety of symbolic folly challenges shalom and subverts the truth about God and ourselves. We rebelliously turn God's cosmos into cultural chaos by trying pridefully to make a name for ourselves.

Communities of Corrupted Communication

When Kofi Annan became the secretary-general of the United Nations (UN) in 1996, he pledged to reform the organization. At that time the UN was torn apart by squabbling, poor funding, and ineffectiveness. Annan's task would not be easy, but nevertheless, he promised reform. After the first five months of Annan's leadership, the UN seemed no better off. A reporter asked the secretary-general why he had not made good on his commitment. After all, joked the reporter, God created the universe in only seven days. Annan responded, "The Lord had the wonderful advantage of being able to work alone."[10]

God graciously gives us the ability to cooperate; he enables us to care for the creation. But we are born into imperfect, fallen communities that spread evil. Sin is not only personal but also corporate. Our alienation from God infects entire social institutions. In everything from small groups to enormous organizations we institutionalize evil patterns of communication. One theologian suggests that sin is "more than the sum of what sinners do. Sin acquires the powerful and elusive form of a spirit—the spirit of an age or a company or a nation or a political movement. Sin burrows into the bowels of institutions and traditions, making a home there and taking them over."[11]

Both intentionally and unintentionally, we establish corrupted communities that promote evil instead of shalom. Human communication carries the viruses of despair, racism, hatred, indifference, and pride. We weave evil into life. Kofi Annan is right: Our collective efforts can weigh us down. Our social groups and organizations can become collective incarnations of evil, what Scripture calls "principalities and powers" (Eph. 6:12 KJV).[12]

Advertising agencies, for instance, sometimes collectively advance sinful symbols that glorify evil. The Virginia Slims slogan, "You've come a long way, baby," vigorously promoted cigarette smoking among women by appealing to their pride about the much-needed gains they had made in society. A Liz Claiborne ad pronounced: "A woman can't have too many affairs." The company celebrated the image of the promiscuous woman in places where religious traditions condemn adultery and fornication. These messages are created and promoted by large organizations, not just by a few managers or professional communicators. Men and women together champion such campaigns.

In a fallen world, social institutions of all kinds expect people to conform to their fallen values. Young professionals who join the ranks of communication organizations are sometimes asked to give up their personal standards of conduct and to live by the organizations' internal culture. One communication graduate was so thrilled to get a job with a publishing firm that she rationalized the company's participation in the soft-porn market by arguing that the book profits enabled the company to do so many good things. Professionals often become party to institutionalized evil because they willingly sacrifice their religious integrity in order to get ahead in the organization.

Theologian William Stringfellow tells the story of a graduating Harvard Law School classmate who accepted a position with a great Wall Street firm. The classmate married the summer before he began at the company. When he later reported to work, the employer told the new lawyer that he should have consulted the firm before marrying, but "since he was married, it would be advisable for him and his wife to refrain from having any children for at least two or three years. Furthermore, for the sake of his advancement in the firm, he should and would want to devote all of his time both in the office and in his ostensibly personal life to the service of the firm, and children might interfere with this."[13] The law firm wanted to own its employee's heart and mind, to control what he did in his personal life, not just in his professional practice. Social institutions sometimes have the power to dictate even personal ethics.

In the award-winning film *Network*, ruthless executives transform a major U.S. television network into a corrupt community. The UBS Network will do just about anything to boost audience ratings and generate advertising revenue. Profane managers broadcast all programs that will attract viewers and please advertisers: politically revolutionary programs hosted by militant Maoists, "prophecy" shows hosted by psychotic and deranged people, and dramas with explicit sex and gratuitous violence. Through the sinful actions of many people, the network becomes an incredibly evil community of arrogance and ambition. The story culminates in the executives' decision to murder a program host because his audience ratings have declined. Although it is highly unlikely that a real television network would kill an employee, commercial television executives do justify nearly any program that attracts a sizeable audience, even if the program might be bad for society. The networks are driven by institutional values that dictate how employees will think and act.

The Tower of Babel was built by a well-organized technological community fueled by selfish ambition. The citizens of Babel built the structure out of human-made bricks, and their work probably looked like a pyramid, reaching to the heavens. The construction of the amazing tower required a great deal of effective communication among its designers and builders. The arrogant Babylonians' goal was to "make a name for ourselves" (Gen. 11:4). They apparently wanted to be equal to God, to create an identity for themselves that would impress all others on earth. But the Lord scattered them, confusing their language and retarding the growth of Babel's institutionalized evil (Gen. 11:6–9). By interfering with Babel's communication, God was able to thwart the Babylonian menace.

Like the citizens of Babel, we use communication to create and maintain evil structures of oppression and deception. Elected leaders try to ride public opinion to victory by telling citizens what they want to hear, even when it is far from the truth. History shows that "principalities and powers" "require their members to surrender their lives in order that the institution be preserved and prosper."[14] Evil organizations have always invited people to institutionalized bondage.

Individuals often have to struggle to do well within systems of institutionalized evil. In the 1950s, music baron Berry Gordy of Detroit's legendary Motown Records used Italian-Americans to promote African-American recording artists on Caucasian radio stations, and Motown's album covers often depicted Caucasian couples instead of the faces of the African-American musicians. More recently, the African-American owner of a Detroit foodservice employment agency continued to use sales material that pictured page after page of smiling Caucasians even though her staff was about 98 percent African-American. At one time she even "pinched her nose and spoke nasally to make her voice more 'white' on the phone." Most amazing of all, she removed the word "owner" from her business card so prospective customers would not see that the business's owner was African-American.[15] These kinds of strategies help minority businesses address the symptoms of institutionalized evil, but they have little impact on deeply racist social structures.

Social institutions can be used for good or for evil. God's grace enables us to build collective structures of justice that advance God's name, combat evil, and communicate shalom. But institutions can represent the human fall as well as God's grace. They can collectively use people's gifts to give others a taste of hell instead of heaven on earth. Although we cannot blame institutions for our personal sins, we can hold them accountable for the pain and oppression that they cause. We can play a part in creating slavish cities such as Babylon, or we can work to build heavenly communities such as the biblical Jerusalem.

We need to accept the fact that we each have a larger obligation than maintaining a personally peaceful life. If we look only at our own personal communication, we are not being obedient caretakers of God's creation. Symbolic caretaking in the modern world is invariably a local, regional, national, and even global affair conducted through families, businesses, churches, schools, media, and other social institutions. We must discern the symbols of the public realm, seeking wisdom about how to shape the agendas and techniques of both private and public communities, from our local churches to the United Nations.

Symbolic Domination

C. S. Lewis's book *The Screwtape Letters* satirizes the devil and his diabolical minions. In a series of letters from the devil to one of his naive new recruits, Lewis portrays Satan's organization as a dog-eat-dog world of bureaucracy, deception, and exploitation. "My symbol for Hell," wrote Lewis in the book's introduction, "is something like the bureaucracy of a police state or the offices of a thoroughly nasty business concern. . . . Bad angels, like bad men, are entirely practical. . . . I feign that devils can, in a spiritual sense, eat one another, and us. Even in human life we have seen the passion to dominate, almost digest" our neighbor. We try to make our neighbor's "whole intellectual and emotional life merely an extension" of our own.[16]

Lewis's portrayal of devilish evil captures the human tendency to use communication selfishly to dominate others. Instead of serving our neighbor, we often use verbal and nonverbal symbols to advance our personal and collective agendas. Rebelling against God, we manipulate and control others. We practice *symbolic domination*—forcing our symbolic reality on weaker people or groups.

Often we do not admit that the church, too, is a fallen institution that can exercise dominance. Long ago the church adopted methods of manipulation and control. During the Crusades of the eleventh and twelfth centuries, the unequivocal message was: "Become a Christian or die." Christians recovered the Holy Land from the Muslims, but many people died in the tragic abuse of Christ's name. During the Reformation, some churches burned Anabaptists at the stake if they refused to renounce their view that the state was subservient to Christ. European and North American missionaries attempted to replace indigenous cultures with their own. Throughout history Christians have used force and cultural domination in the name of spreading the gospel.

Human beings have always used symbols to communicate manipulatively. The classical Greeks, defining communication largely as persuasion, launched two thousand years of Western scholarship and teaching that are based on the idea that people have the right to influence others. Clearly not all persuasion is symbolic domination, but the tendency toward evil domination is part of human nature. We all sometimes disrespect others and try to use them to serve our own, selfish purposes.

Symbolic domination exists wherever the few have power to control the many. Totalitarian governments create elaborate propaganda campaigns designed to convince the masses that fascism or socialism is for their own good. Stalin linked Soviet domination to the rhetoric of Marxist superiority. Nationalism and totalitarianism often go hand in hand, dangerously creating the symbolic superiority of one group over others. Similarly, ethnic pride has encouraged groups to propagandize and sometimes to annihilate other groups. Some cult leaders have even convinced members to commit group suicide. Jim Jones persuaded nearly a thousand members of his California cult to kill themselves in a horrible mass suicide in Jonestown, Guyana, in 1978. Similarly, Heaven's Gate cult leaders in San Diego convinced nearly forty members to commit suicide in 1997 as the Hale Bop Comet appeared in the sky. These kinds of self-righteous movements powerfully wreak hurt and devastation.

Gender relations are another staging ground for symbolic domination in a fallen world. In many cultures, including some religious groups, men have opportunities to gain status and power simply by virtue of their gender, not because they are more gifted or responsible. In North American society, men generally occupy the positions of power, from government and corporate management to church leadership. Men learn to communicate aggressively, and women are expected to listen. People have historically tended to symbolically associate masculinity with authority, giving men an enormous opportunity to dominate women at work, at home, and in the church. Michael Ryan's many seductions of women were possible partly because of the power imbalance between men and women. Our verbal and nonverbal symbols are loaded with implications for gender domination that stereotype men and women.

Dutch theologian Abraham Kuyper rightly argued that "all men or women, rich or poor, weak or strong, dull or talented, as creatures of God, and as lost sinners, have no claim whatsoever to lord over one another."[17] Unfortunately, our sinfulness drives us to dominate rather than serve our neighbor. Like the devil in *The Screwtape Letters*, we try to transform others' lives into an extension of our own folly.[18] The sin of symbolic manipulation characterizes the kingdom of death.

Squandering Our Symbolic Wealth

Management expert Peter Drucker sometimes asks executives how they spend their time, then he instructs them to record for a while how they actually spent their working hours. One chairperson was convinced that he spent about one-third of his time with senior management, one-third with important customers, and the remaining third in community activities. After the executive kept a six-week log of his time, however, Drucker discovered that he invested almost no time in any of these three activities.

Instead he spent most of his work hours acting "as a kind of dispatcher, keeping track of orders from customers he personally knew, and bothering the plant with telephone calls about them."[19] In fact, the executive's interventions usually delayed the orders. At first the executive refused to believe how he spent his time. Like us, he was self-delusional about how he squandered his symbolic wealth.

Sin corrupts how all of us use our time and energy. Like the busy executive we tend to squander our communication gifts. We often focus narrowly on technology, settle for poor-quality communication, and ultimately discount the importance of truthfulness. We overindulge in our communicative folly and reject God's call to be judicious, talented, and wise communicators. Our communication is a means of taking care of God's world, yet we simply do not give it the kind of care and attention that it warrants.

First, we are often preoccupied with technology, which becomes our means of communication. When we fill our lives with manufactured messages and technological processes, we often lose a sense of our own value as gifted communicators. We consume all kinds of sounds and images from packaged media, but we are not able to reach out to our neighbors. We lock ourselves into techno-consumerism, valuing the quantity of our technological toys rather than the quality of our relationships with our neighbors. Relying on others to communicate for us, we fail to communicate for others. We settle for a role as consumers of technology rather than accepting God's vocation for us as producers of shalom.

Novelist Jerry Kosinski suggests that even our infatuation with television can diminish our respect for life. In his novel *Being There*, he creates Chance, a fictional character who has no parents and is socialized almost entirely by television. Chance is ill-equipped to leave the security of the estate where he works as a gardener—the only task that he knows. But when the estate owner dies, Chance must leave. He walks out the front door of the house completely unprepared for the real world. At one point he tries to defend himself against street thugs by pulling his television remote control out of his pocket and clicking the buttons for a different channel. Chance is incapable of simple human interaction. All he can do is watch the world around him. Years of all-day television viewing have rendered Chance an "innocent" fool. He is incapable even of understanding that there is a difference between right and wrong. Chance has become a "videot" (a video idiot).[20]

Second, the quality of our communication is declining. In Hollywood, companies often are more interested in making business deals than in telling stories well. Producers pitch ideas to get funding for their projects, not necessarily so that they can create quality productions. Even in the church, we wrongly convince ourselves that only the message matters, not the method. We assume that God doesn't mind using schlock to accomplish great things. Certainly God has the power to use anything for peace and justice. Nevertheless, we must pay attention to the quality of the expression of our ideas. Our communication need not always be fancy or costly, but it should be well done. Big budgets and slick pitches do not guarantee that our communication will have lasting value, but well-crafted communication can please God and witness for the joy and harmony of shalom.

In the developed world, we often wrongly equate extravagance with quality, but the truth is that some of the most expensive communication is also the worst. Technological extravagance, in particular, is hardly a virtue: It is often a vice that leads to sloppy and superficial communication. Within the church, some of the most technologically sophisticated worship services and the most elaborate musical productions can contain lots of hype with little substance. Modern media create in us an appetite for products that are flashy, impressive, and stimulating, and meeting these criteria often requires large production budgets. But flashy presentation does not guarantee that producers have a worthwhile message or that they express their message well. Sometimes a simpler, more profound, and more compelling message is less expensive to present.

Our speech, prose, music, and drama should be characterized by joyful elegance, appropriate style, interesting composition, and all of the relevant marks of quality. Aristotle and other ancients included *invention* in their lists of the elements of rhetorical practice; they rightly saw that creative communication without careful reflection is often silly or ineffective.[21] God called his people to build the temple carefully and well; we should craft our communication with style and with delight in serving others.[22]

Communication is not merely a pragmatic means of building relationships and creating shared interpretations of symbols; it is also a means of aesthetically adorning God's world. Aesthetic judgments easily get us into trouble, however, when we simplistically categorize art and dismiss some styles or forms of communication. For instance, people sometimes naively condemn popular art while uncritically praising classical culture. We might wrongly condemn an entire medium, such as television, while naively praising another one such as the Internet. In the 1920s and 1930s, many churches rejected all jazz music. In the 1950s, some denominations condemned television altogether. When we make quick-and-dirty distinctions, we fail to exercise reasonable powers of discernment and we sometimes even blithely dismiss the careful work of gifted people. Says one theologian, "The disdain many Christian scholars show towards domestic popular religious culture is itself a theological defect, stemming from a failure to develop an adequate theological understanding of ordinary religious people."[23] Both evil and God are revealed through the narratives and metaphors of popular culture.[24]

Third, we forget that truthfulness in our communication is as important as effectiveness. In the industrialized West, we are overwhelmed by a flood of confusing images that we have neither the time nor the talent to interpret and evaluate, and truth seems so elusive. We are inundated by torrents of information, entertainment, and persuasion coming to us from the telephone, television, radio, fax machine, and computer. As a result, all communication seems badly inflated and devalued. The discernment of truth is a hassle that gets in the way of our pragmatic needs for success and self-fulfillment, and grow increasingly callous to the impact of our deceptive communication on our neighbors. In our fallen world, the gospel is evaporating from our hazy symbolic environment. Veracity is disappearing from public life. We emphasize effectiveness over truthfulness, impact over honesty.

We squander our symbolic wealth in each of these ways. Like the executive Peter Drucker discovered, we lose track of how we spend our time and how we use our communication gifts. We rely too much on our role as technological consumers and settle for third-rate quality, and we lose track of truth itself.

Conclusion

The concept of human sinfulness is virtually absent in scholarly discourse. We can take all the courses we want and even study with the best teachers and still fail to realize that sin affects communication. There are no quick fixes for the depth and scope of sin in our communication. Books, teachers, common sense, and hard work cannot fundamentally change our hearts. At best, they can only reveal our folly. Without grace our communication rots in our hearts and in our communities. Michael Ryan achieved success as a poet and teacher before his secret life as a sexual predator finally caved in on him. Grace ruined his evil plans while he was on the road to another seduction. We cannot create grace, however; we can only accept it from God.

In one sense, as the writer of Ecclesiastes might put it, our communication, like everything else, is meaningless (Eccles. 1:2). In another sense, our words and images can convey the goodness of the creation. Our symbols can carry life as well as death, shalom as well as violence. Communication can be amazingly powerful. When we recognize our fallenness, transcend our corrupted communities, reject the urge to dominate others, and stop squandering our gifts, we are on the road to shalom.

SIX

Incarnate Power

The Spiritual Component of Communication

In Massachusetts during the late 1990s, a seventy-one-year-old Jewish businessman rebuilt his family's textile mill after it had burned to the ground in a spectacular fire that left over three thousand workers unemployed. During the yearlong plant reconstruction, he continued his employees' benefits, kept many of the workers on the payroll for ninety days, and promised to restore their jobs as soon as possible. The businessman explained his unusual commitment to his employees in this way: "What's important in God's eyes is when there is a situation where there is no ethical grounding, do everything in your power to be a man . . . a *mensch*."[1] A mensch is an especially humane, sensible, and mature person whose actions speak powerfully to others.

In this chapter, I first explore the spiritual power of communication to breathe godly interpretations of reality into culture. Using symbolic power, we create interpretations of the world around us. The businessman's actions told his employees that he valued them not just as employees but also as persons. His benevolence testified to the entire community that business can be more than profits and market share; the practice of business can also serve people and inspire others to be virtuous.

Second, I consider the power of knowing. Generally speaking, people who know a great deal about the world have a powerful advantage over those who do not. Knowledge of God, in particular, breathes spiritual life into communication. "The knowledge of the Holy One is understanding" (Prov. 9:10). Our knowledge of the gospel frames all other information and contextualizes everyday life. Christians should all communicate as knowers of God.

Third, I briefly examine charismatic power as a reflection of a person's authenticity, God-given gifts, and spiritual character. In my view, real charisma is far more than a matter of audience perception. Charismatic power gives specially gifted individuals a potent advantage to define reality in light of the kingdom of God. The businessman exerted charismatic power by publicly demonstrating his servant attitude. His actions pointed to a godly world of truth and justice.

Each of these forms of symbolic power enables us to respond more effectively to God's call to care for and develop creation. Exercising our symbolic muscles, we powerfully fashion culture that reflects the justice and joy of the kingdom of God. Like the businessman, we can incarnate symbolic power in our lives in order to serve our neighbors. In the process, we cocreate signposts to a kingdom reality.

Using Communication for Life or Death

Theologian Richard Mouw recounts a childhood incident in which the school principal chastised him for uttering an ethnic slur. "But he threw a stone at me! He hit me!" protested a defensive young Mouw. The principal responded, "But Richard, you have done something far worse. He tried to harm your body. You responded by trying to harm his soul."[2] Symbols have the power to direct people to spiritual life or death. They can build our neighbors up or tear them down. Symbols can point people to God or lead them to a world of despair. By defining reality, communicators invariably shape the spiritual contours of people's lives.

Since the ancient Greeks conducted the earliest study of rhetoric, people have recognized the power of symbols to alter human perceptions of reality. The Greeks defined *rhetoric* as "persuasion" partly to convey the power of symbols to transform people's values and beliefs. Some sophists tainted this definition of rhetoric by separating persuasion from truth, encouraging people to define reality cleverly in their own, selfish terms. Two millennia later, the word *rhetoric* still suffers from these sophists' perversion of its meaning. Rhetoric often connotes self-serving communication filled with suspicious arguments and misleading appeals.

For good and for bad, symbols enable us to incarnate our longings in culture. When we communicate, we create particular definitions of reality.

Madeleine L'Engle writes, "God asked Adam to name all the animals, which was asking Adam to help in the creation of their wholeness. When we name each other, we are sharing in the joy and privilege of incarnation."[3] Using communication, we "name" the kind of culture that reflects our desires. Some of these cultural meanings are good and life-affirming. Others, like the ethnic slur that Mouw used, are evil and destructive.

Language enables us to name relationships, to define ideas and things, and even to create cultural groups with their own identity. Throughout Scripture, people's names often express the underlying reality of their spiritual life. Abram became Abraham, for example, after God gave him the knowledge of a new covenant (Gen. 17:5). When Simon recognized Jesus as the Messiah, Jesus called him Peter (Mark 3:16). Today, corporate logos define the identity of organizations. Job titles define people's work as well as their status within an organization. Vision and mission statements establish what organizations believe about themselves and whom they claim to serve. Unlike any other creatures, we use symbols to incarnate powerful definitions of reality that may or may not reflect the way things really are.

The reality that the phrase "Holy Land" conveys for Christians in the United States is different from the reality it conveys for Christians in Palestine. People use language to define the area as holy. They also use language to indicate who really owns the Holy Land—Christians, Jews, or Muslims. If we define the Holy Land as the Jews' own God-given territory, we disenfranchise some of the property owners who reside there. Our symbols shape what people believe about the region and influence how people will act toward those who live there. Our symbols can breathe life or death into people's perceptions of even the physical world.

Symbolic power is never spiritually neutral. It always favors particular people's view of reality and challenges others' views. Our communication invariably upholds some versions of spiritual reality and neglects other versions. When Alexis de Tocqueville visited the United States in the nineteenth century, he discovered that the nation's language was changing its spiritual life. Most of the new American words expressed "the wants of business, the passions of the [political] party, or the details of the public administration." Meanwhile, he said, the country's language was losing references to "metaphysics and theology."[4] The language, and therefore the culture, of the United States was becoming secular. De Tocqueville discovered that a nation's language reflects its secular and sacred desires.

When the apostle Paul wrote his letter to the church at Ephesus, he hoped to redefine the Ephesians' view of spiritual reality. At the time, the city was a center for magic and various religions reminiscent of today's popular horoscopes and New Age philosophy. As people converted to Christianity, they often introduced their old religious ideas into the church. In order to redefine reality for the new believers at Ephesus, Paul emphasized the sovereignty of God and the supremacy of Christ,[5] skillfully redirecting their view of the "cosmic forces" in the world and illuminating the Creator who made all people "to do good works, which God prepared in advance for us to do" (Eph. 2:10). Paul's rhetoric was meant to establish the spiritual reality of Jesus Christ as the one, true, sovereign God.

Symbolic power can also create definitions of reality that lead to physical violence and death. In fact, name-calling often precedes and sometimes instigates physical violence.[6] Conversely, "If you punch me in the nose," says one theologian, "you say something to me."[7] In the Old Testament, Cain and Abel defined life in opposite terms. Abel's view of reality included God; Cain's did not. Cain affirmed his own reality by killing his brother, and God later told Cain, "Your brother's blood cries out to me from the ground" (Gen. 4:10). Cain's actions spoke to God about Cain's sinfulness. Throughout human history, people have created their own, sinful versions of reality to justify physical violence, including murder.

Even without physical violence, our communication can injure listeners and speakers alike. Politicians speak the wrong words and their political campaigns crumble. When former U.S. President Jimmy Carter was on the campaign trail, his popularity dropped fifteen percentage points in only ten days according to the public opinion polls simply because he had told a reporter from *Playboy* magazine that he had lustful thoughts about women. Ironically, Carter had been trying to explain to the reporter that, according to the Christian faith, all people sin.[8] Carter had mistakenly thought the interview was over and that the reporter had turned off his tape recorder. All of us have uttered powerful words that we later regretted. Our symbols sometimes harm people even when we are trying to build them up and encourage them.

God intends for all people to breathe the power of spiritual life into their communication. When we use our gifts of communication to promote shalom in the name of God, we reduce alienation, strife, injustice, and disharmony. We help serve the world by communicating the reality of Christ's life-giving grace. Our symbols can powerfully change people's view of reality and even lead individuals to acknowledge God. Perhaps the virtuous actions of the businessman mentioned at the beginning of this chapter reflected his own righteous fear of God. If Mouw had sincerely asked his classmate to forgive him, he might have transformed the conflict into shalom. Clearly, human communication carries spiritual power.

Knowing God

In his "I Have a Dream" speech, delivered publicly in Washington, D.C., during the height of the civil rights movement in the United States, Dr.

Martin Luther King Jr. envisioned that one day all people would be judged by the "content of their character," not by the "color of their skin."[9] Most of us are familiar with that speech, but many people do not recognize that King's rhetorical power extended beyond well-crafted and persuasively delivered speeches. King's rhetoric of equality was anchored in his convictions about God. In fact, his public speeches were essentially sermons. He urged all people to "seek God and discover Him and make Him a power in your life." Without God, said King, "all of our efforts turn to ashes and our sun rises into darkest nights. Without Him life is a meaningless drama with the decisive scenes missing." With God, King concluded, "we are able to rise from the fatigue of despair to the buoyancy of hope." King agreed with St. Augustine that we "were made for God and we will be restless until we find rest in Him."[10] King's knowledge of God shaped his message of racial equality and gave his public oratory deep spiritual power.

In a Christian worldview, our knowledge of God should shape our understanding of everything else. As Scripture puts it, our "fear of God" is the beginning of all true wisdom (Prov. 1:7). Our knowledge of God has the power to alter our view of ourselves, of others, and of the entire cosmos. It is like a pair of glasses that changes our vision of everything, including how and why we communicate.

This theological truth mirrors a broader axiom about all human communication: Knowledge is power. Even when we reject God, our communication is a powerful means of gaining and using knowledge to create culture. We learn through communication what to know and how to know. Then we use that knowledge to cocreate culture according to our desired reality.

All forms of *knowledge,* from information knowledge to skill knowledge, provide potential symbolic power to those who possess them and can use them effectively. A college graduate who knows how to write an effective résumé and give a persuasive interview has more power to get a job than does a graduate who is less informed. And college graduates who know the people who do the hiring are perhaps in the most powerful position. We often underestimate the value of knowledge even in everyday life.

Our knowledge does not always need to be entirely true or trustworthy to be powerful. If a potential employer *believes* an applicant has the right experience, that applicant will be more likely to get the position than someone who lacks experience. So an applicant who knows what the employer seeks in a new employee might lie on a résumé to secure the position. Knowledge can help people deceive others and selfishly get what they want.

Knowledge is crucial in the military, which uses spies and technology to secretly glean intelligence. Specialists monitor telephone messages, satellite communication, and Internet traffic. They also use satellites to photograph the earth, hoping to capture the movement of people and materials. The best-informed countries have considerable advantage not just in military operations but also in political diplomacy. They know more about how best to persuade leaders of other countries, to form political alliances, and to take military action. Modern warfare is often characterized as much by propaganda battles over perceived knowledge as it is by physical conflict. When dissidents launch a coup, they attack not just the national palace but also the television and radio stations, which can control knowledge on behalf of political leaders.

Without a specific knowledge of God, general knowledge is often fleeting and merely a political tool. Knowledge without God may grant us only short-term gain, such as money, fame, and status. Albert Einstein's discovery of the relationship between speed and mass catapulted him to international prominence and guaranteed his position in history. But even history and history books shall pass away. Moreover, such knowledge could be used for good or evil. Without a fear of God, people might use the "secrets" of nuclear power to dominate and enslave others. Knowledge is often embraced and even owned by people who do not see it in the context of God's authority—sometimes with dire consequences.

Certainly many organizations overplay the mere acquisition of knowledge. Sometimes governments acquire far more data about the world than they could ever interpret adequately. In some scientific disciplines, scholars can get bogged down in journal articles and academic papers: There is far too much information to assess and to integrate usefully into existing theories. Communication scholars produce thousands of books and articles every year, making it nearly impossible for anyone to keep current. As an end in itself, knowledge can be a false god that offers as much confusion as wisdom.

All knowledge gains its ultimate value only in relationship to the Creator. This is why the Christian communicator should begin humbly with knowledge of God, which is the basis for all other knowledge. One theologian writes, "What were we made for? To know God. What aim should we set ourselves in life? To know God. What is the eternal life that Jesus gives? Knowledge of God."[11] Our knowledge of God should shape how we gain and use symbolic power. As stewards of the Creator's world, we recognize that "our" knowledge is merely a small part of what God already knows. As we commune with God and others, we merely taste fruit from the garden of the Creator's wisdom.

When they don't know God, power-seeking people may easily care more about the selfish value of knowledge than they do about the deeper source and greater value of wisdom. When Adam and Eve ate the forbidden fruit, they tried to extend their knowledge beyond human limitations, deceiving themselves and each other. They fell prey to the temptation to believe that human communication can make us omniscient and omnipotent.

Our quest for shalom should lead us far beyond the immediate or practical value of information. As we strive for godly wisdom, we must nurture our relationships with God, our neighbors, the creation, and ourselves. The power of knowledge can be used for good or for bad. Symbolic power based on knowledge can be used to thwart the powers of evil and injustice, or it can be used to advance our selfish, arrogant goals. Racists can use information to define their own warped reality, but we can use information to fight racism. We need to be ever mindful of how our communication fits into the larger picture of God's creation, the human fall into sin, and our redemption in Christ. Facts are easy to acquire, but true wisdom requires experience and careful cultivation in the light of God's Word and the collective discernment of the community of believers.

Charismatic Power

At six feet, four inches tall, Father Marcelo Rossi is not an average-looking priest. In fact, with his good looks and a chart-topping record, *Music to Praise the Lord,* the Brazilian cleric is almost a pop star. He regularly draws crowds of seventy thousand to the weekly masses he celebrates in a former bottle factory in São Paulo. Father Rossi's masses are followed by a *festina,* or little party, where he leads the congregants in "Aerobics for the Lord"—jumping, singing, and air-boxing. He is part of a new generation of Roman Catholic clerics that the local press calls pop-star priests. "Be a fan of God," Father Rossi told one interviewer. "I only want to bring young people to the Church." Some critics say Rossi's ministry is more marketing than religion, but regardless, he is among the first Catholic priests who can compete rhetorically with Protestant preachers who know how to attract a stadium full of eager celebrants.[12]

Father Rossi's popularity illustrates how important personality often is in communication. Not every priest can fill a stadium with enthusiastic worshipers. Created in the image of God, each of us communicates through our distinct personality. Although we can create a fictional personality—a *persona*—we still possess an underlying *personhood*—the way we are as created by God and the way that God intends us to be. Our godly personhood can be a powerful means of communication.

Communication scholars have long recognized that an audience's perception of a speaker influences communication. We are interested in the communicators, not just in their messages. Father Rossi's phenomenal ministry reflects the power of his presentation as well as the content of his homilies.

Through the centuries Christians have developed yet another angle on speaker presentation and audience perception. They have often viewed special communication gifts, or charisma, as evidence of the work of the Holy

Spirit in a speaker's life. The Greek language of the New Testament uses *charisma* to refer to spiritually gifted persons, including communication-gifted persons. Charisma is not just image or perception but a real, God-given gift.

Charismatic communication is authentic human communication that gains its power significantly from the God-given gifts of the communicator and that reflects the spiritual virtue of the communicator. If Father Rossi is an authentic, gifted, and godly communicator, not merely a media-created persona, he has real charisma.

First, charismatic communication is authentic communication; it is not merely the making of an image. A communicator whom an audience perceives positively is not necessarily an *authentic* communicator. Authentic communicators believe what they intend to communicate. The Roman philosopher Quintilian (A.D. 95) argued that the message and the beliefs of the real person should be the same: "The authors who have discoursed on the nature of virtue must be read through and through, that the life of the orator may be wedded to the knowledge of things human and divine. But how much greater and fairer would such subjects appear if those who taught them were also those who could give them most eloquent expression!"[13] In other words, person and message should be united so that what we say is a product of who we are and what we believe, not just a reflection of our eloquence. Later, Augustine made essentially the same argument for Christian rhetors.[14] Both scholars rightly argued that presentation alone is inadequate: Communicators should also be authentic, otherwise they might be mere sophists.

Entertainment industries manufacture celebrity and stardom but not normally authenticity. Media consultants design and promote images for politicians and even some corporate moguls. Televangelism so successfully generates pseudo-charismatic power that some viewers perceive television preachers as spiritual luminaries, even if they are not godly in real life.[15] Audiences often project their own desires and hopes onto celebrities, starting in the preschool years with television heroes and continuing during adolescence with rock stars and movie idols and even during adult years with sports figures, soap opera characters, and self-help gurus. In these situations, the audience's perception of a star may have little or no relationship to her actual personhood. We perceive image, not authentic self.

The apostle Paul used authentic communication to solidify his leadership and to build community. Friends and foes alike examined his life to see if he truly believed his own rhetoric. Not everyone liked what he had to say—especially the religious establishment. But his words reflected what he believed about the kingdom of God, not just the ethos that he could produce with his sophisticated rhetorical training.[16] Paul was willing to go to prison and even to die for what he believed and preached. His authentic rhetoric both garnered new followers and alienated him from religious leaders.

Second, charismatic power reflects the God-given gifts of the communicator. The human ability to communicate is itself a gift from God. But clearly some people are more gifted than others in particular forms of communication, and these specially gifted persons owe their ability to the Creator. God gave it to them for particular tasks and special circumstances. Their above-average symbolic power reflects God's creativity in their lives. Whether they use the power as good stewards of God's world is, of course, a different matter.

Scholars in the field of communication wrongly advocate a utilitarian view of symbolic power that fails to attribute communication gifts to God. In effect, they have separated the power of human communication from the authority of the Creator. Charisma points not only to the human communicator but also to God, who ultimately creates all human communication potential.

Third, real charisma always flows from the virtuous character of a communicator. Charisma requires goodness in the heart and soul of the communicator. Adolf Hitler received a tremendously positive public response among Germans. He was a gifted political communicator, but he was a despicable character. No matter how gifted he was as an orator, he was essentially an evil propagandist. In fact, he employed skilled propagandists to create his charismatic façade. Hitler's documentary film, *Triumph of the Will*, for instance, portrayed Der Führer as the German savior by associating him with Jesus Christ.

By the power of the Holy Spirit, God works in communicators, building their character. Charismatic communicators display fruits of the Spirit such as love, gentleness, self-control, and patience. These characteristics can be feigned in a fallen world, but when they truly exist in the heart of a communicator, they suggest that God has breathed grace into his or her life.

God can produce all of these aspects of charisma in unpredictable ways, sometimes bestowing charisma upon unlikely persons for particularly important moments and events. God can give charismatic power that defies attribution to natural causes such as genetics, training, and culture. We will never be able to explain charisma in purely human terms. Charisma reflects God's power to use mere persons to define reality for cosmic purposes.

Conclusion

Communication can be a means of gaining and using power. Knowledge and effective presentation enable communicators to create influential views of reality. News anchors, Hollywood celebrities, and sports stars use the media powerfully to establish their followings. So do leaders of religious cults, governments, and some corporations.

Charisma, on the other hand, is a special kind of power based on authenticity, giftedness, and virtuous spirituality. Unlike worldly forms of power, charisma is a uniquely Christian kind of influence anchored in the Triune God. The Creator gives us the gifts, the Savior reveals our authentic selves, and the Spirit grants us the spiritual character. God calls us to use symbolic power to serve others. Symbolic power is crucial for building communities of shalom.

SEVEN

Symbolic Power

Servant Communication

The film *The Elephant Man* tells the true story of John Merrick, who died in London in 1890 at the age of twenty-seven. Newspapers called him "the world's ugliest man" because of his repulsively deformed head, contorted face, and loathsome skin. A greedy circus owner had been charging customers five cents each to gawk at Merrick in a traveling freak show, and the compassionate Dr. Treeves was trying to free Merrick from the circus owner so that he could be used for medical research. Treeves took Merrick to a medical research facility, but according to policy, only patients who could care for themselves custodially were allowed to live at the hospital. Merrick would have to go back to the freak show unless he could demonstrate to the hospital supervisor that he was indeed human.

Dr. Treeves planned to teach Merrick how to communicate his humanness to the hospital administrators. The doctor struggled to teach Merrick how to speak lucidly and how to communicate with strangers—a daunting task for someone who had been treated as an animal and who likely thought of himself as a wretched creature. Treeves was making little progress, and the house governor was ready to dismiss Merrick from the facility. Then as Treeves and a hospital administrator were quietly debating Merrick's prospects in a hallway, they heard a strange voice reciting a psalm in a nearby room: "The

Lord is my Shepherd, I shall not want. He leads me in green pastures." Suddenly they realized that the elephant man could speak! Treeves had hoped to teach Merrick some rudimentary language, and now the doctor was hearing the truth that Merrick was able to communicate not only as a human but also as a child of God.

Treeves and the circus owner had both used communication to alter the course of Merrick's life. The circus owner had promoted Merrick's grotesqueness for personal financial gain, caring little for Merrick's own interests. Treeves, on the other hand, saw Merrick as a real person—at least as someone who could be used for medical research that might help others. Once the doctor confirmed Merrick's fundamental humanity, he knew that a hospital was an insufficient home for Merrick. Regardless of his physical appearance, the "elephant man" deserved a life worthy of a child of God. So Treeves invited Merrick to visit his house.

Everyone who communicates also cocreates culture and affects the lives of others. God gave to humankind the task of taking care of and developing the creation. Our symbols are powerful tools that enable us to glorify God and to serve our neighbor. No matter what our earthly title, each of us inherits this God-given responsibility to care for creation. Treeves responsibly recognized that Merrick was his neighbor. The circus owner did not. These contradictory responses reflect the range of people's options in life. Some of us serve others, but many of us prefer to dominate our neighbors. Most of our responses fall somewhere between service and domination, depending on the situation.

In this chapter I first distinguish between using symbolic power to exploit others and using it to serve our neighbors. Because of our fall from grace we are tempted to dominate people, just as the circus owner manipulated his freak-show star. God calls us instead to care responsibly for creation by serving others. Like Dr. Treeves, we should use symbolic power to seek justice and peace for our neighbors. Jesus Christ calls us to use our symbolic ability to serve those who are in need, to practice *downward mobility* by reaching out to those who have less symbolic power.

Second, I consider our responsibility to give to others out of our symbolic abundance, to practice "symbolic generosity." Just as Christ emptied himself on the cross, we must generously give our communication gifts to others to cultivate shalom. We can do this especially by praying for others, sharing our earthly authority with them, nurturing symbolically gifted people, and keeping alive the voices of those who have preceded us.

Finally, I look specifically at our responsibility to give our voices to those who have little or no symbolic power in society. As Scripture emphasizes, we are called to serve primarily the weak, not the strong (Matt. 25:31–46). We should all empower the voiceless—the people who do not have power in culture. Dr. Treeves became John Merrick's voice for justice and peace. To whom should we loan our own voices?

Downward Mobility

Father Henri Nouwen left his prestigious position at an Ivy League university to serve members of a community for disabled people in Toronto, Canada. He went from hobnobbing with the intelligentsia to bathing and dressing bedridden individuals who would never be well known or powerful. "The compassionate life," he later recalled, is "the life of downward mobility!"[1] Nouwen became a compassionate servant. "Compassion," he wrote, means "to suffer with." It is the "way to the truth that we are most ourselves, not when we differ from others, but when we are the same. . . . It is not 'excelling' but 'serving' that makes us most human."[2]

In the field of communication, the concept of *symbolic power* usually presupposes a purely human view of power. Scholars generally assume that we use symbolic power as a means to influence others: Successful communicators master their craft to get what they want from the world. This communicator-centric view of symbolic power emphasizes taking rather than giving.

A Christian focus on shalom turns our notions of symbolic power upside down. It emphasizes selfless servanthood rather than selfish masterhood. Dr. Treeves increasingly realized that he was serving one of God's image bearers. He recognized that his own words and images were on loan from the Creator and that God had granted him the authority to care for Merrick. As servant communicators, we are all created to communicate on behalf of others. Like Henri Nouwen, we are called to be downwardly mobile, not to elevate our own status at the expense of others. *Masterhood* is selfish domination of others. *Servanthood* is humble service to our neighbor.

As communication scholar Greg Spencer has suggested, God's Son, Jesus Christ, compellingly illustrated servanthood.[3] God became a human, granting us an opportunity to see and hear our Creator communicating as a human being. God had always spoken in and through creation: with voice and with fire, through the flood, from a burning bush, and through meteorological disturbances. But in Jesus Christ, God took the form of a human servant. God became incarnate in a human being, a shocking example of *downward mobility*.

God's incarnation in Jesus Christ was part of the Creator's plan for communicating with fallen humankind. The voices of the Old Testament had yearned for God and humanity to be reconciled, for Adam and all of his descendants to come home to their Creator. So God sent a personal Redeemer to reveal divinity to humankind. Jesus Christ is the Word who lived among us (John 1:1–18). God's incarnation in Christ restored communication between God and humankind. The incarnation is "not only the crowning event of God's communication with man but also that event in which all other forms of God's communication with man are embodied."[4] The Creator demonstrates through Christ how we can serve our neighbor with our own God-given symbolic power.

Christ teaches us, first, how we can serve others by being downwardly mobile. God's communication through Christ is a monumental reversal of how we normally think about the role and purpose of symbolic power. Christ did not exploit his status for selfish purposes. Instead, Christ "humbled himself" (Phil. 2:8). He took the position of a mere human being. As Greek scholar Gerald Hawthorne puts it, Christ "stepped down" from his high position and put "himself at the disposal of other people."[5] Thomas Aquinas wrote that God took to "Himself our littleness."[6]

Scripture shows how Jesus repeatedly used communication to serve some of the most despised and weak people in society. Jesus communed with the shunned Samaritan woman, with tax collectors, with prostitutes, and with the destitute blind man. Christ's ministry was not a quest for celebrity, it did not reflect a yearning for symbolic domination, and it was not a means by which to boost the authority of established social institutions. Jesus did not *take* symbolic power as much as he *gave* it to the powerless; his earthly ministry culminated in the cross itself, the greatest symbol of liberation in human history.

While imprisoned by the Nazis during World War II, German Lutheran theologian Dietrich Bonhoeffer discovered what it meant to serve. Stripped of his freedom, Bonhoeffer shared the Good News with Nazi guards and fellow prisoners. Recalling Christ's question at Gethsemane, "Could ye not watch with me one hour?" (Matt. 26:40 KJV), Bonhoeffer concluded that servanthood "is a reversal of what the religious man expects from God. Man is summoned to share in God's sufferings at the hands of a godless world. . . . It is not the religious act that makes the Christian, but participation in the sufferings of God in the secular life."[7] Bonhoeffer's prison writings, which were published after his execution near the end of the war, are still read by Christians around the world. Although he had no official power inside prison, Bonhoeffer served God faithfully by ministering to prisoners and guards alike.

Second, Christ's downward mobility should lead us to communicate humbly by listening to and identifying with our neighbors. Humble communication rejects self-righteous arguments, deftly styled put-downs, and opposition-squashing debates. Humility embraces responsive, sensitive, and patient interaction. We are to be humble, down-to-earth communicators (*humble* comes from the Latin *humus* or "earth"). Our identity in

100

Christ enables us to become less self-absorbed and increasingly attentive to God and to our neighbor. Bonhoeffer wrote in prison, "One must completely abandon any attempt to make something of oneself, whether it be a saint, or a converted sinner, or a churchman (a so-called priestly type!)." Instead we are to "throw ourselves completely into the arms of God, . . . watching with Christ in Gethsemane."[8]

Servant communication requires listening to others in society, especially those who have little symbolic power. Teachers must listen effectively to students. Stockbrokers should hear the voices of the people who are affected by the corporate policies of the companies whose stocks they trade. Playwrights and film directors need to tune in to the voices of the people who inhabit their stories, especially the voices of people who do not enjoy the privilege of direct media access. Advertisers should listen to the voices of the ethnic subcultures that are threatened by consumerism. Politicians must hear the electorate. Corporate leaders should listen humbly to their employees and customers. Parents need to listen to their children. Christ often spoke the truth boldly, but never without first hearing the needs of those with whom he communicated. Humble listening is the beginning of all real leadership. This is why the servant-minded communicator is "quick to listen, slow to speak" (James 1:19).

Third, Christ's servant communication should remind us of the insidious potential of symbolic power. Because of our capacity to communicate, we will be tempted to master others. When he was tempted by the devil in the desert, Christ refused to use his powerful speech to turn the stones into bread. Humankind "does not live on bread alone," Christ told Satan, "but on every word that comes from the mouth of God" (Matt. 4:4). Christ refused to believe the devil's rhetoric. His reply to Satan gives us a remarkable lesson in humility: Humankind lives on the words of God, not on the attractive sophistry of selfish people. Unless we listen to the Word of God, our symbolic power can become an insidious disease of the soul. Playwright David Mamet says, "The power of a person to serve is in direct proportion to the strength of his or her resistance to the urge to control."[9]

Alienated from God and from each other, we fight for upward mobility. We try to dominate others through myriad creative communication strategies. The circus owner used communication to restrict outsiders' access to John Merrick because anyone who came to know the elephant man as a real person would surely question the owner's motives. Hitler conspired with Nazi leaders to create charges against Bonhoeffer. Nouwen once felt the exhilarating power of communicating with the wealthy and highly educated members of the Ivy League establishment. None of us is above the corrupting power of selfish communication.

Symbolic power is subtly intoxicating. We enjoy it, and we aspire to become influential communicators. In J. R. R. Tolkien's *Lord of the Rings* trilogy, the creature Gollum becomes a slave to his desire for a magical ring, lowering himself gradually into darker beastliness in his yearning for the ring's power until there is no evil thing he would not do to possess it.[10] In various degrees, Gollum lurks within all of us, slowly corrupting us with the intoxicating desire for power.

We ought to recognize the potentially abusive nature of symbolic power in every area of life. As Ken Blue explains, some spiritual leaders "coerce their congregation through the skillful use of the language of intimacy and trust." The worst abusers use symbolic power to get money, time, or sexual favors from people by convincing them that they will go to hell if they refuse to oblige. Blue recommends that the first thing we must do when we find out about such victims is to "listen to their stories,"[11] beginning the process of restoring our exploited neighbors.

Our communication should manifest the love of God, who became fully human for us and for our salvation. Like Henri Nouwen, we become downwardly mobile to serve others and to avoid the corrupting power of upward mobility. Our communication continues God's redemptive plan when we offer the love of Christ to others. Christians are God's conduits, the Creator's eyes, ears, and voice on earth. Our communicative talents belong to Christ, not to ourselves. Human communication is a humbling responsibility demonstrated by the ultimate servant, Jesus Christ.

Symbolic Generosity

A dying woman stubbornly refused to obey the doctors' orders when she was in the hospital. As her husband recalls, nurses repeatedly discovered her "out of bed in the night, sitting beside some other patient who was suffering, soothing her, holding her hand, praying for her." The doctors appealed to the husband to persuade his wife to remain in her bed. He tried. His wife would "look guilty and grin and promise—and then she would hear a sob or a cry in the night." After his wife died, the man discovered what she had been doing during those late nights in the hospital. He received "dozens of letters, some almost illiterate, from people who had been in the hospital with her, saying that she had helped and sustained them. One said she was like an angel of God."[12]

God created all of us with the potential to give out of the abundance of our symbolic power. I suggest four ways that we can serve our neighbors with our symbolic power: (1) praying for our neighbors, (2) sharing our earthly authority with them, (3) nurturing their symbolic giftedness, and (4) keeping alive the voices of those who have gone before us. In the last section of this chapter, I discuss one more, deeply biblical form of servant communication that transcends all others: giving our voices to our voiceless neighbors.

First, in prayer we can commune with God on others' behalf. Although we rarely think of it in these terms, prayer enables us to use our symbolic power on behalf of anyone else on earth. Living under the priesthood of all believers, we do not have to overcome the principalities and powers of earth to petition God on behalf of others. Prayer is probably the most democratic form of human communication. Anyone can pray for anyone else. When we petition God, Jesus intercedes on our behalf, and God promises to listen. The hospitalized woman recognized this and prayed diligently for others even as she grew weaker.

Psychiatrist Robert Coles tells the story of David, a dying ten-year-old boy who started asking the doctors and nurses attending him whether they prayed for their patients. The medical staff called in Coles to find out what was troubling David. Coles spoke with David and initially concluded that the boy's talk about prayer reflected his fears about his impending death. But the longer Coles listened, the more he questioned the diagnosis. David said of his prayers for the medical staff, "I ask God to be nice to them, so they don't feel too bad if us kids here go meet Him. . . . When I meet God I'll put in a good word for the people [who work] in this hospital." Coles finally recognized that this ten-year-old boy was a faithful petitioner of God. "In retrospect," writes Coles, "I realize that the boy David was an important teacher of mine. . . . His spirituality enabled me to contemplate the spirituality of other children."[13]

Prayer opens heaven's doors for all people, no matter their age, income, profession, or situation. Dietrich Bonhoeffer's prayers filled him with hope while he was in the Nazi prison. He prayed that God would take care of his family, the German nation, and the world. He was not naive about the political realities of the time, and from prison he even helped to devise a plot to kill Hitler.[14] But he recognized that power on earth is not limited to political force. He prayed for his friends, just as they could pray for him. No one could stop them from lifting their voices to God. Humble, honest prayer empowers all of us to serve our neighbor.

Second, we can give away symbolic power by sharing our earthly authority with our neighbor. Every position that we attain in this world can be used appropriately on behalf of others. Teachers can share knowledge and discernment with students. Media professionals can use periodicals, broadcast stations, Web sites, and civic speeches to serve others. The authority that we gain in life is not just for our own pleasure but also for others' shalom. Within the reasonable opportunities that our position in life affords us, we can serve others.

When school administrators invite students and parents to participate in developing school policies, schools can be transformed into service-minded educational institutions. Research shows how important parental involvement is for students' academic success. At one successful Atlanta public high school where over 95 percent of the graduates go on to four-year colleges, parents are "as integral to the life and performance of the school as math instructors and football coaches."[15] By sharing symbolic power with parents, the administrators and teachers tap an amazing source of talent, energy, and money. As parents accept the administrators' invitation to share symbolic power, they become servants of the school and the community, not just of their own children.

Third, we can give away symbolic power by investing our time, energy, and financial resources in nurturing gifted communicators. We are all differently gifted people. Each of us has a distinct place in cocreating culture as stewards of God's world. Unfortunately, we often focus too easily on our own gifts and forget to wisely care for and develop the creation by nurturing our neighbors' gifts.

We are called to enable and empower one another. Churches can nurture gifted communicators by giving them scholarships, providing housing for them when they are in college, mentoring them, sharing information about people and positions in communication-related fields, recommending helpful books and periodicals, and equipping them with appropriate technology. We can nurture our neighbors' gifts with every genuine compliment and every word of encouragement, support, or loving correction. These kinds of nurturing activities should be second nature to those of us who worship in communities of shalom.

Finally, we can keep alive the voices of the deceased. Throughout the history of the church, Christians have retold the stories of Scripture. They have copied and distributed Bibles, published biographies and autobiographies, and orally passed along memories from generation to generation. They have used all of these media to tell the stories of the many saints whose voices have been silenced through persecution and strife.

We all have an obligation to help keep the past alive, especially the traditions that are central to the faith. Culture disappears unless people constantly recreate it through time and across space. The husband of the dying woman who helped others in the hospital eventually compiled a book of the couple's correspondence with C. S. Lewis—a fitting remembrance of both Lewis's and the couple's faith in God.[16] As Scripture says, we are "nothing but dust and ashes" (Gen. 18:27). If we fail to recall the glorious past, we might even lose important Christian wisdom. If we forget the tragic past, we will likely repeat it.

A Polish Catholic who was a member of the underground resistance during World War II was forced to witness the kinds of Gestapo actions that we should never forget. As he recalls, the soldiers ordered the assembled Jews to strip naked and jump into a pit of quicklime, a caustic substance that would slowly dissolve their skin. Some tried to get out, but soldiers beat them back down. Mothers jumped in holding children, while others tried to throw their children out of the pit. Yet others gave up and simply threw their offspring into the liquid at the bottom. Finally, as the people wailed and cried, the Germans started pumping more liquid into the pit. The lime began slaking, boiling the people alive. "The cries were so terrible that we who were sitting by the piles of clothing began to tear pieces off the stuff to stop our ears. The crying of those boiling in the pit was joined by the wailing and lamentation of the Jews waiting for their perdition. All of this lasted perhaps two hours, perhaps longer."[17]

Long after the killers are all deceased, we must recall again and again what unrestrained power does to human beings. We should be the voices of people who have died at the hands of evil killers and despotic regimes. History, which often reveals the darkest sins of human beings, is always on the verge of disappearing. Each generation must keep alive the cries of deceased people so that we might learn from the past and avoid future episodes of terror. Aleksandr Solzhenitsyn's novels will long remind us of the Soviet death camps under Stalin.[18] Letters sent home from soldiers during the American Civil War can help all Americans to recall what the nation had to go through in order to be reunited. In South Korea a historical museum was built recently to recall the tens of thousands of women, mostly Korean, who were forced into sexual slavery by Japanese soldiers during World War II.[19] Books, recordings, pictures, and orally transmitted stories are all important. The past disappears without new generations of messengers.

Of course, we should re-create positive memories also. History is filled with the good work of saints, the heroic acts of soldiers who fought valiantly for freedom, and the great writers of each generation who illuminate the human condition. We are on the verge of losing memories of beauty, goodness, and especially wisdom. Do we want to risk losing the great joys and wonderful triumphs of the past and literature and films that powerfully capture the human spirit? We should make special efforts to retain for future generations the gems of our own religious traditions, such as the writings of Augustine and C. S. Lewis. When we rekindle Christian tradition, we also reinvigorate our faith.

In the information age the need to lend our symbolic power to past generations that have lost their voice is perhaps greater than ever. Bombarded daily by thousands of short-lived messages, we find it difficult to keep our minds attuned to history and directed by wisdom. We can all sing advertising jingles galore, but we can barely list the Ten Commandments or accurately tell the story of one faithful saint. Life goes on with a tornado of symbols rushing through our tired minds, and the past is a distant echo barely gaining our attention. But God gives us the gift of lending our symbolic power to people whose voices left this planet long ago. Do we listen? Do we share their stories? Do we care?

Empowering the Voiceless

In the late 1990s, researchers in Atlanta inserted into a person's brain a tiny implant the size of the tip of a ballpoint pen. The recipient of the implant, an alert and intelligent man, had been connected to a ventilator because of a devastating stroke that had paralyzed his limbs and silenced his voice. As one neurosurgeon put it, "Of all things people lose, the ability to communicate is the most frightening thing—to know what you want to say and not be able to say it."[20] Six months after receiving the implant, the recipient began using new technology to communicate directly from his brain through a computer. He could "think" particular words and ideas and cause a computer cursor to point at message icons on a screen. "It's like we're making the [computer] mouse the patient's brain," said one of the doctors who had developed the amazing, though rudimentary, technology, which has enhanced many people's ability to communicate.

In a fallen world, the voiceless include all people who have no means to communicate, have no audience, or are afraid to speak. Certainly this includes the young and the unborn, perhaps one of the largest groups of voiceless people in every age. Although we are all born with the capacity for communication, physical and cultural limitations regulate who can participate in public discourse. We do not all have equal power even in matters that affect us directly. No matter how much we know or how gifted we are as communicators, without an audience of listeners we cannot fully exercise our symbolic power. A preacher without listeners will have little impact. Even those who speak silently through quiet vigils and candlelight protests need an audience. In society after society, voiceless people are wrongly denied the opportunity to respond to God's mandate to care for and develop the creation. Forced into silence, voiceless people suffer because of others' indifference or exploitation.

In the 1970s, Scott Turow, who later became a best-selling author and an attorney, wanted to know what it was like to be a first-year female law student. He noticed that most of the twenty or so freshmen women rarely spoke in class. "I know how this sounds," one of the women told Turow, "but a lot of the women say the same thing. When I get called on, I really think about rape. It's sudden. You're exposed. You can't move. You can't say no. And there's this man who's in control, telling you exactly what to do." Turow concluded that the "law world has been rigidly patriarchal." He even suggested that women's "refusal to participate in these traditional and often unjust relationships was to me one of the happiest portents I saw all year."[21]

In Central America, some indigenous groups have been denied access to both government and media. During the 1980s, military leaders backed at least partly by corrupt government officials killed thousands of native Guatemalans. Unable to get their stories of persecution into the public media in order to gain international publicity, these mountain people lived in silent fear. In fact, when some people did complain to public officials or speak with missionaries about the problem, their families were hauled off by masked bands of terrorists, never to return.[22] Amnesty International and other organizations try to give persecuted people a voice by writing letters of protest directly to the offending governments on their behalf and by publicizing the offenses.

Voiceless people can be children, college students, or elderly people. The case of a child raped in a Chicago housing project received little publicity in contrast to the media attention lavished on the case of a wealthy white victim.[23] Employers occasionally force voiceless employees into criminal or unethical activities. On some public university campuses, Christian staff and students are marginalized because they lack an approved public forum for addressing the relationship between faith and learning. When actor Ed Asner helped an Alzheimer's care facility raise funds, he decried the media stereotype of older citizens as "doddering fools" and explained that he could help "bring attention to the fact that there are not enough of these centers out there."[24] Sometimes victims of sexual harassment are silenced by the organization against which they file a lawsuit, knowing that it will be difficult if not impossible to stay on the job even if they win the case.

Christians who seek justice should be alert for evidence of oppressive domination and should then find appropriate ways to give oppressed people a public voice. Christians should be whistleblowers, local and international media gadflies, and tireless critics of unjust communication. In and out of church, Christians are called to give their voices—their talents, technology, and relationships—to those who do not have their own voices in society. Our voices belong to God to serve our neighbors.

On college campuses, Christians should be the first to speak up for minorities, freshmen, nontenured faculty, female professors, secretaries, maintenance crews, and other relatively powerless persons. But at some Christian colleges the students ignore non-faculty staff such as landscape workers and dining-hall cooks and servers. Christians can dedicate pages in the campus newspaper to needs and concerns of the voiceless, or represent their views in the official channels of campus politics. A student at one college joined with a faculty member to offer a course on how disabled people are portrayed and stereotyped in popular films. The student co-teacher made a powerful impact from his lectern, a wheelchair. Academic institutions often pretend to be bastions of free speech, when in fact they create classes of voiceless people according to their own cultural standards of upward mobility.

107

Millions of persecuted Christians around the world suffer silently. The authors of *Their Blood Cries Out* estimate that around six hundred million Christians are being persecuted throughout the world. Three-fourths of persecuted Christians live in the third world, where persecution is much more common than in the developed West. The authors further suggest that American Christians are far too silent in the face of the widespread persecution. Generally speaking, the media—and perhaps most Christian audiences—are uninterested in human rights violations. Most people would much rather enjoy sitcoms and soap operas than be informed about suffering people around the globe. But when our fellow Christians are being persecuted, we must not "conclude that no news is good news."[25]

Only a few nations have a significant worldwide voice in news and entertainment media. The global flow of media content is largely "from the North to the South, from the developed countries to the developing nations."[26] The United States exports films and television programs to over a hundred nations, but few of these countries' media products flow into the United States. North America has a hand in shaping cultural styles, worldviews, and musical tastes around the globe, but few nations have a cultural impact on North America. Worldwide media are remarkably dominated by a few powerful voices in the industrialized West.

Christians can address how the media decide which people get a public voice. Contemporary journalism tends to rely too much on official sources that represent recognized public organizations, especially governments. Sources such as academic experts and political officials have influential voices denied to most people. The public may not always believe officials, but how can the public express dissent? Many urban ethnic groups have formed organizations to project their own voices in the public sphere. African-Americans, for example, have founded groups to speak publicly to the media about such things as police brutality; the lack of police, fire, and paramedic services in urban areas; and political gerrymandering. Not surprisingly, such groups are often sponsored partly by Christian congregations that legitimately seek to give oppressed people a voice. These groups can reveal inequalities and call for justice.

Journalists should give a voice to the voiceless by writing stories about the rights of the oppressed and downtrodden. As one Christian critic of news reporting suggests, "All reporting in fact has an elitist bias. . . . Journalists must report on the activities of heads of state and highlight the inane statements of the powerful. If there is reporting without reference to the hierarchy and without an eye on institutional interests, it is a very rare thing indeed."[27] A radio commentator challenged the news system by giving two African-American teenage boys tape recorders to cover local stories in their Chicago neighborhood. When a little boy was murdered, the teenagers

108

held local officials accountable for their political rhetoric about cleaning up the crime in the housing project. Politicians "keep sweeping the dirt under the rug and it just keeps piling up," they said in one of their reports, which were later published as a book.[28] These young reporters spoke up for their community, and many people have heard their voices.

We become compassionate voices for the voiceless only when we first listen to our neighbors. We must hear them express their own stories. Without visiting a nursing home, for instance, we cannot know firsthand what its residents feel and what they would like to say to others. As we begin to hear others and to identify with them, we should become warmhearted, sensitive listeners. Only then might we appropriately speak on their behalf.

But even the most compassionate listening is dangerous without a commitment to knowing the truth. The truth stabilizes our symbolic action and keeps us from straying into our own self-interested rhetoric or moralistic crusades. For Christians, truth is both the gospel itself and viewing the world through the lens of the gospel. Our view of the voiceless in society must be shaped not by our own prideful penchants or petty causes but by the facts and by the wisdom of Scripture as interpreted faithfully by the broader Christian community. Our communities of faith give us the resources of experience and fellowship to discern what is right, and the courage to act on wise counsel.

Without a firm grasp of the truth, we are easily caught up in the latest fashionable campaigns to reform society. Too often we listen only to the claims of one political party or social group. We allow ourselves to be propagandized by narrowly focused ideas and half-truthful fund-raising gimmicks. We all find it easier to listen to the voices of people who are like us than to the voices of those who are different. Social critic Jacques Ellul says that people today have lost a sense of "objective reality." We are "plunged" into stereotypical abstractions "not only with regard to facts, but with regard to [people]." Instead of knowing the human condition, we speak narrowly of "the consumer, the workman, the citizen, the reader, the partisan, the producer, or the bourgeois."[29] In short, we look at people not in their common humanity or in their particular need but only in their cultural categories and stereotyped abstractness.

We cannot be silent in the face of the domination of others. We must use our symbolic power as caretakers of God's world—as voices for the voiceless. We should see symbolic power as a resource for serving others. We can take care of God's world partly by protecting others' voices and partly by giving our voices to those who are silent and oppressed. Communities of shalom recognize that every voice is important because each human being is a valuable creature made in the image of God. Like the technologists who gave the speechless man a brain implant so he could communicate, we lend our knowledge and abilities to others so that they, too, can participate more fully as caretakers of God's creation.

Conclusion

Symbolic power is necessary for each of us to care for creation. We should study symbolic power, enjoy it, and excel in it. We can accept Aristotle's famous claim that the power of communication is "discovering in the particular case what are the available means of persuasion,"[30] but we know that there is far more to it than that. We are called to be caretakers of our symbolic power, using it only under the Creator's authority. Our power under God enables us to serve our neighbors responsibly by listening to them, by helping them express themselves, and by sharing our earthly authority.

Symbolic power is intoxicating. As Alice learned in Wonderland, communication offers us the power to define reality.

> "When I use a word," Humpty Dumpty said, in a rather scornful tone, "it means just what I choose it to mean—neither more nor less."
>
> "The question is," said Alice, "Whether you can make words mean so many different things."
>
> "The question is," said Humpty Dumpty, "Which is to be the master— that's all."[31]

Like Humpty Dumpty, we should all ask who our master really is— whom we serve with our symbolic power.

We all regularly need a reality check. Do we define symbolic power in our own, parochial ways? Or do we have a real sense of the scope and depth of God's power to communicate through all people? We read in Revelation that the church at the end of time includes people of all tongues, tribes, and cultures (Rev. 14:6). This picture of the ultimate shalom in heaven clearly shows that truth and justice are not the province of only a few powerful people.

We tend to be more like the circus owner in John Merrick's story than the doctor. We marshal symbolic power on behalf of our own pet projects and programs instead of for the wider purposes of shalom. Without humility, we can become victims of our own insidious power schemes. In a world of true shalom, there would be no reason to dominate other people because God's Word would guide the way. We would all humbly seek to be downwardly mobile in the service of our neighbor.

EIGHT

Blessing or Curse?

The Role of Media

British film producer David Puttnam wanted to make a movie about "winning on your own terms."[1] For "the past ten years," recalled Puttnam, "my career has led me to behave rather expediently." He hoped that *Chariots of Fire* would enable him to "exorcise" his expedient ways. Puttnam imagined himself as the film's major character, Eric Liddell, an evangelical Scot who refused to run the one-hundred-meter Olympic race on a Sunday—the Lord's day of rest. But he recognized that his own life was more like that of Liddell's competitor, Harold Abraham, a "somewhat aloof, unpopular figure who ran in order to satisfy his personal ambition."[2] Puttnam felt that, like Abraham, he was living as a pragmatist rather than acting in accord with his higher ideals. He hoped that the making of *Chariots of Fire* would put him on higher moral ground.

Puttnam's dream of producing *Chariots of Fire* soon turned sour. Financiers refused funding, and media moguls humiliated Puttnam for trying to produce a movie with limited audience appeal. One studio executive held a draft of the screenplay over a wastebasket as he told Puttnam what he thought of the project: "You must be out of your mind. I don't understand you. You get an opportunity to produce mainstream commercial movies, and you bring along *this*." The executive dropped the script in the trash and offered these words of wisdom: "Go away and *grow up*, and don't waste our time again in the future."[3]

In spite of the obstacles, Puttnam persisted. He raised the necessary money, worked closely with a screenwriter on five drafts, and cast a little-known pair of actors for the lead roles. Along the way, Puttnam made what he considered to be acceptable compromises. He even added an expletive so the rating would be boosted to PG, potentially increasing the adult audience in the United States.[4] Puttnam seemed to know how to manipulate the Hollywood system without selling out. *Chariots of Fire* eventually won the Academy Award for best picture in 1981, and five years later Puttnam became head of Columbia Pictures.

But Hollywood was not excited about Puttnam's rise to power. In the industry's eyes, he was too principled—too much like Olympic runner Liddell. Puttnam refused to pay stars and their agents outlandish fees. He turned down fat-cat deals that would guarantee whopping salaries to producers even if their films failed at the box office. Worst of all, he simply declined to give the Hollywood elite royal respect and the attention they expected. Within a year, Columbia's board ousted him. The system had axed one more naively altruistic filmmaker.

The story of Puttnam's rise and fall raises troubling questions about the potential for justice and peace in Hollywood. Perhaps a principled and peace-loving person cannot survive morally amid the deal making and power struggles. The entertainment industry appears to forego conscience in favor of the almighty dollar, to shelve shalom in favor of ego and self-interest.

In this chapter I examine the part the entertainment industry plays in American and global culture. I first examine how American media seek to fuel increasingly international consumption communities. Popular entertainment tends to flatten traditional cultures and to build a superficial culture based on branded products and services. If we allow ourselves to be seduced into these consumption communities, we become spiritual amnesiacs, losing sense of our religious roots and our relationship to God.

Second, I explain how the media function as both God-given technologies and fallen social institutions. Mass media require not only equipment but also capital, personnel, and organizational structures. Puttnam apparently thought that he could change the system of Hollywood movie-making, when in fact the institution strangled his power to affect change. Puttnam found himself in the midst of principalities and powers that are driven by Mammon.

Third, I consider our misconceptions about what media technologies can accomplish. We tend to think that the latest medium is either going to save

112

the world or doom it. We associate media technologies with either God or the devil, but they actually reflect our own mixed motives. Some supporters saw Puttnam as a media prophet who would save the industry. Perhaps they naively believed in the power of the media to greatly improve the world.

Finally, I address our tendency toward technophobia. We at times wrongly assume that technology itself is inherently evil. Instead, we need to remember that media technologies are part of the unfolding of God's creation that offer opportunities for both good and bad—for promoting peace and joy and for spreading conflict and oppression.

Consumption Communities

Brian Warner became rock star Marilyn Manson in 1989 when he took on the first name of sex symbol Marilyn Monroe and the last name of mass murderer Charles Manson. Having grown up in a conservative Protestant home and having attended a Christian school, Manson might have identified with the evangelical faith. But the apocalyptic expressions of the faith scared him, and the Christian community intimidated him. Desperate for attention and acceptance, he eventually formed a rock group. As Manson recalls, the applause from fans gave him "a sense of pride, accomplishment and self-satisfaction strong enough to eclipse my withering self-image and my punching-bag past."[5] His rock group criticizes the church and offers troubled kids both acceptance and identity. In order to be accepted, fans consume Manson's products, attend his concerts, imitate his clothing, and celebrate his way of life. Manson and his fans can create anti-Christian culture while building their own consumption-oriented community.

Manson's popularity reveals how consumer culture can replace religious faith and community, especially when religious people are not practicing what they supposedly believe. Manson's fans buy and display his products to tell the world who they are and what they believe. They freely adopt Manson's pop theology about "saving ourselves," exuberantly enjoy his frenzied performances at concerts, and scour music magazines for photos of their idol to display on their bedroom walls. Even if fans do not completely accept Manson's Satanism, they might identify with his cynical religious attitudes and join their peers in creating new personal identities. Over time fans can become, like Manson, spiritual amnesiacs who have forgotten their religious roots.

Media begin shaping consumer identities long before kids enter school. Preschool children listen to rock radio stations and play their older siblings' CDs. Animated television programs blend consumer identities into kids' imaginative play, creating a marketing bonanza for branded products, from toys to school supplies to clothing.[6] As children start reading, they

113

also have access to consumer-oriented magazines and comic books. Younger and younger children think that they have to join an adolescent consumer culture that dictates choices about clothing, body image, and media usage.[7] They believe that they will not be loved and accepted unless they conform. Out of misdirected love, parents sometimes provide money for their children to join even self-destructive communities of consumers.

Manson's popularity illustrates how mass communication restructures our communal lives by inviting us to ignore our religious communities and to identify instead with people who consume the same goods and services that we do. We sometimes feel as though we have more in common with strangers than with members of our own families and local communities. Like spiritual amnesiacs, we rush to keep up with cultural fads and lose sense of our religious past. Unlike the church, the media always accept us and entertain us; advertisers and filmmakers never reject us. Manson accepts every adolescent who purchases his products or attends his concerts. In Hollywood, everyone can be a neighbor.

The commercial media encourage us to form superficial communities of consumption. Beginning in the nineteenth century, first with magazines and later with radio and television, the media connected people across geographic space with consumer products that symbolized attractive lifestyles and the American dream. People began replacing local, ethnic, and religious connections with consumer-oriented lifestyles, forming what historian Daniel Boorstin calls *consumption communities*.[8] These shallow communities are many people's substitute for shalom.

Consumerism invites us not only to purchase particular products but also to identify with people who have the same lifestyle. Advertisers direct people's need for clothing into desires for particular name brands. In the late 1940s, advertising encouraged millions of people to use installment loans to purchase automobiles, even where public transportation was readily available.[9] Radio and television commercials helped create new middle-class fads in games, toys, and leisure pursuits. North America had its Chevy drivers, Lucky Strike smokers, and Pepsodent toothpaste users. Later it had clothing by the Gap, Abercrombie and Fitch, and Ralph Lauren. Suburban malls replaced neighborhood markets. Consumption communities increasingly became a substitute for ethnic neighborhoods and religious enclaves. Eventually American society gave birth to the worldwide Lexus community, the global Barbie-doll community, the transcontinental Marilyn Manson community, and thousands of other consumption-based cultures.

Consumption communities can be either bad or good for traditional religious communities. They can weaken valuable traditions or infuse them with new life, facilitate shalom or foster love of Mammon.

The church is far from immune to consumerism. Cult heroes such as Marilyn Manson are easy to identify, but what about consumption com-

THE ROLE OF MEDIA

munities within the church that promote superficial expressions of faith? Christian consumption communities encourage the rise of influential parachurch celebrities such as Christian broadcast personalities who are more interested in selling their products than in nurturing faith or building local community. Christian broadcasting sometimes champions a kind of sentimentalism where faith is little more than being a fan of a mass-mediated religious personality who pretends to be our neighbor.

The church's consumption communities transform mundane products into superficially "holy" icons. They promote Bible trivia games, Jesus paintings, W.W.J.D. bracelets, wallpaper and pencils inscribed with Bible verses, bumper stickers and evangelistic T-shirts with catchy sayings. Advertising copywriters compose slogans to create demand for special Bible translations and annotated Scriptures, including gender-specific Bibles, student Bibles, and Bibles for single people. Sometimes publishers wrongly promote their books as though they will provide complete solutions for complex personal and spiritual problems.

On the positive side, however, consumption communities can help members of religious traditions to strengthen their faith. Consumer goods can meet real needs while they generate a profit. Some products can and do make faith relevant for many people and provide an alternative to mainstream consumer culture. They go beyond entertainment to substance, offering practical parenting advice, insightful Bible study materials, informational reviews of contemporary culture, and discerning discussions of political issues. Some of the best religious products revive traditional religious practices even if the products are not extremely popular.

Supporters of contemporary Christian music know that it has edified many younger church members who otherwise might have joined consumption communities such as Marilyn Manson's. Moreover, it has renewed worship music with fresh styles and meaningful lyrics that even enliven the faith of older members. Some congregations have encouraged younger members to write music for the local body of believers and to publish it for the benefit of other churches. Religiously inspired consumer products can help build Christian community.

The value of contemporary Christian music for many believers reveals how popular religious culture can avoid love of Mammon and facilitate faithful community. Jesus' early followers used popular artifacts to communicate the gospel and to build new communities of belief. When the apostle John wrote of Jesus as the Logos, the Word, he borrowed language from the Greek culture of the day, using a popular metaphor to communicate the incarnation to unbelievers. At Mars Hill, Paul used a familiar statue and words to a popular song in his presentation of the gospel. Popular communication can invite people to consider a deeper relationship between themselves and God. It is an important means of introducing the faith to nonbelieving cultures.[10]

115

Indeed, commercial mass media learned many of their marketing lessons from the church![11]

In our fallen culture, however, it is sometimes difficult to know where faith ends and consumerism begins. The contemporary Christian music industry has both helped and hurt many local churches. Christian rock music has bothered pastors and music leaders who believe that contemporary music is not appropriate for worship. These concerns are valid when Christian artists treat the church setting as a worldly entertainment venue, with spotlighted singers in cocktail dresses at ten o'clock in the morning. Popular Christian music has also made it more difficult for those who are trying to maintain or revive traditional hymnody. While contemporary worship styles may help keep some believers in the church, they also may make believers indifferent to church traditions and inflexible about worship preferences.

Consumption communities can foster spiritual amnesia within the church so that we become "people without the kinds of memories that nurture and enrich our lives."[12] The church is God's historic community, not merely a faddish consumption community. The Christian faith is far more than temporary experience. It is more than vague relationships with people who wear the same bracelets, carry the same version of the Bible, or spout the same religious slogans. Christian community must be anchored in our shared belief in God's redemptive work throughout history.

Shalom, relationships of godly justice and peace, requires us to form communities of memory in which we both share our contemporary life stories with one another and identify with the historic church. In real Christian community we frame our lives in the historic stories of Scripture, the richness of a Christian tradition, and the communal bonds of local fellowship. We all need a community that is anchored in its past, not floundering in faddish enthusiasms, material anticipation, and happy feelings. Shalom is never fully achieved through media-inspired consumerism.

Christian community is always grounded in a particular geographic place and anchored in the cultural activities of generations of faithful people. Consumer culture tends to replace our historical connections and our sense of place with faddish events and mass-produced products. As writer Wendell Berry puts it, without the salt of faith and shalom, an industrial economy is "unable to distinguish one place or person or creature from another."[13] This is precisely the problem with Hollywood. Rootlessness makes the entertainment industry a fertile culture for superficial neighborliness and deep-seated love of Mammon. The love of fame and fortune replaces the love of God and neighbor.

Consumption communities are part of a larger social trend that wrongly encourages us to see ourselves primarily as consumers. Mass-mediated communities focus on people as mere buyers and users of consumer goods. At their worst, consumption communities reject God's cultural mandate in Genesis that we take care of and develop the creation. They seductively invite us to become what we buy, rather than to produce and purchase products that reflect what God wants us to be. We are called to be caretakers of all of the resources at our disposal, including consumer products. Our gifts, talents, and possessions should foster deeper communities of shalom.

Fallen Institutions

When David Puttnam became the head of Columbia Pictures, he had to make some difficult choices about the rules by which he would guide the studio. He wanted to serve audiences in addition to making a profit, so he began planning to make films with socially redeeming value. Soon, however, he recognized that Columbia was merely one part of a larger, deeply entrenched social system made up of banks, talent agencies, movie critics, film exhibitors, and guilds. He could not fully re-create Columbia as an independent institution. In fact, studio owner Coca-Cola would not let him.

All mass media are forged by social institutions—human organizations that collectively create culture. Social institutions are communities with their own values, practices, and beliefs. Puttnam became part of a social institution when he took over Columbia Pictures. He inherited employees who were already conducting business according to the company's own, internal culture, which mirrored the culture of other commercial media organizations.

People in commercial media create popular culture to make a profit. Commercial media institutions include broadcast networks, media conglomerates, and the Christian music industry. God's gift of human communication enables people within these organizations to work together as coordinated institutions. Newspapers, for example, coordinate editors, reporters, and printers to publish newspapers. Similarly, it takes screenwriters, lighting technicians, directors, scene designers, actors, and producers to create motion pictures. Because the media require so many differently skilled people to operate, they need organized systems to function. Without the ability to coordinate their activities through social institutions, people could not produce mass communication; society would have only individual artisans.

In a fallen world, however, all types of media institutions can exploit the people they supposedly serve. In totalitarian nations, for instance, state media often abuse citizens by advocating and promoting official values and beliefs that serve the government more than the people. These nationalistic media

117

sometimes appeal to people's racism or ethnocentrism, and some governments restrict public access to media in order to control political dissent. In countries with market systems, on the other hand, media can exploit people by pandering to their basest instincts, giving consumers whatever they want, even if it is not good for them.

All media institutions contribute negatively to culture in some way. The normal ways that newspaper editors select and present the news can hide the bigger truth about a story. Newspapers sometimes censor the voices of members of groups that do not buy many papers. Broadcast networks give audiences melodramatic television shows that glamorize sex outside of marriage. People say of television news stories: "If it bleeds, it leads; if it's sex, it's next." The people who run community playhouses often select scripts that will pack the house without serving the needs of the community. Christian music artists might equate market share with ministry.[14] In a fallen world, there are no perfect media institutions.

As social institutions, many media implicitly discourage creativity and individuality. Like Puttman, Christians who try to improve the media often learn that worldly success requires them to imitate other media professionals. They, too, homogenize media content and reject alternative points of view. Followers of Christ should instead find ways of re-creating media institutions bit by bit until they are open to practices that better serve society.[15]

Media Idolatry

Both the media and consumers often demonstrate a naive hope in the power of technology to improve society. French scholar Jacques Ellul concludes that people in industrialized societies idolize media technologies. They have a technological mindedness that leads them to emphasize the values of efficiency and control over all others. Values such as love, compassion, justice, and fairness have little place in technological society.[16]

Throughout history, humankind has practiced *media idolatry*—a belief that the latest media can solve practically all of our social and individual problems. In the United States, the rise of the telegraph in the 1850s elicited strong public pronouncements about the "universal" new medium that would usher in "worldwide peace" and lead to the Christian conversion of pagans everywhere.[17] Later, radio, television, videocassette recorders, and eventually the Internet produced the same kinds of mystical predictions. One Christian called broadcasting one of the "major miracles of modern times." He argued that electronic media were returning the church to its early roots in household worship by "breaking down the walls of tradition" and "ushering in a revolutionary new form of the worshiping, witnessing church that existed twenty centuries ago."[18] This sanguine view of media technology is deeply rooted in American evangelicalism.[19] Still, studies show that most people are converted to Christ through the personal efforts of friends and family, not through the mass media.[20] Being a real neighbor in the biblical sense is splendid communication and an effective witness.

We might wish that the media had such magical power to spread the gospel and to rebuild community, but imperfect social institutions always reduce the real value of technology. The fact that the church calls various religious programs "missionary television" does not necessarily make them so.[21] Once we actually use a new technology, we find that it never lives up to the hype about its evangelistic value. Technology can be no more effective than the people who use it.

History reveals our technological folly. At one time the videocassette recorder was going to save education by delivering marvelous curricular content directly into all classrooms, making master teachers available in the inner city and the suburbs alike.[22] Later, public excitement about the "Information Superhighway" elicited the same utopian rhetoric.[23] Uncritical advocates of the Internet assert that it will connect all students to high-quality educational materials. Millions of education dollars have been spent, but none of the grand technological predictions have come true. When we convince ourselves that salvation from our problems is a few fonts, images, or nanoseconds away, we idolize media.

We could accomplish far more with the media if our efforts were not diverted by our false hopes. Many organizations in Christian broadcasting, for instance, invest very few resources in programming and production. Because they are transmitting messages across geographic space, they create the illusion that they are communicating effectively with audiences. International Christian broadcasting is sometimes so ethnocentric that non-Anglo cultures do not find it particularly intelligible, let alone persuasive. Many overseas broadcasts are translated directly from English scripts, with no sensitivity to how the receiving cultures understand the Scriptures differently.[24] Producers wrongly assume that all cultures are like North American, middle-class society.

Jacques Ellul's biting critique of the media may be overstated, but it illuminates how difficult it is to use media technologies to promote peace and justice. When we idolize technology, we put too much faith in the media and our attention is diverted from our own fallenness. Our optimism about redeeming the media has to be tempered by the stark realities of a sinful world with broken institutions. Many media are part of billion-dollar, multinational empires based on love of Mammon. Others are anchored in ideological movements or controlled by authoritarian governments. We cannot alter the core values of media institutions by writing a few letters to stockholders, calling for a couple of flashy boycotts of advertisers, or congratulating a Hollywood company because it hires a handful of Christian employees. As long as we idolize technology, we will be easily sidetracked by naive, short-lived reform campaigns, and we will fail to see the difficulty of transforming the media. As Ellul argues, we need not only vision but also biblical discernment and collective wisdom.[25]

Technophobia

If we sometimes expect media technology to accomplish too much, we also fail to see its potential. *Technophobia,* or fear of technology, obscures the ways that God works through even unrefined technologies to bring grace and peace to humankind. Just as our communities can fall prey to the latest media fads, they can unnecessarily rue every new technology as the possible end of civilization. Christians, too, sometimes turn the media into the lone cause of all evil in society. News anchor Tom Brokaw rightly wonders, "What or who was blamed for the flaws of the world before television. It has become a handy, all-purpose scapegoat."[26] We focus so narrowly on the faults of television that we deny the power of God to work through us to use it appropriately for the good of humankind. Each new media technology is both a source of social and spiritual problems and also a reservoir of opportunity.

We should listen humbly to technophobic media critics even as we reject their knee-jerk negativism. We will likely find some enlightening ideas in their critiques. Malcolm Muggeridge wonders if moving-image media are inherently dishonest because they pretend to capture reality as if no one is behind the camera,[27] and Neil Postman argues persuasively that television promotes amusement, stifles reading, and eclipses viewers' rational thought.[28] Even if Postman overstates the case against television, he raises important issues that we should address. We need to determine the appropriate place for television in society, church, and home. We must consider how to push media institutions to create edifying programs, and we must challenge the ways that people uncritically use television in their lives. Media critics such as Muggeridge and Postman can help us to formulate questions and to perceive media-related issues that we might otherwise overlook because of our own laziness or our naive enchantment with technology.

But we must caution ourselves against believing with some critics that there is no place for the media in our communities of faith and hope. Even though there are real problems with existing social institutions, we must not give up all hope. The best media critics realize that often in human culture the devil is in the details. Rather than large generalizations about the value of the media, we need nuanced, discerning insights into the good as well as the evil.

The growth of cable and satellite TV opened up channels for historical, educational, and artistic productions. The video and DVD technologies gave parents much more selection for themselves and their children. All online publishing can hardly be called pornography or labeled trivial. The digital explosion has opened up new ways for teachers, pastors, and parents to find news and information about their world. If critics are not addressing these positive developments along with the dangers of new technologies, they are not serving their neighbors. The most helpful critics distinguish between naive condemnation and fair-minded criticism. They know that even media behemoths come and go. With governmental regulation and fickle audiences, today's media guns may be out of ammunition tomorrow. Decent people do manage by grace to gain influential positions. Moreover, new media are always emerging, and there are opportunities for godly people to shape them. We need to listen to the media critics but avoid technophobia.

Conclusion

The mass media are communities of mixed motives that produce mixed blessings. On the one hand, they can reflect the good found in life. On the other hand, the media can highlight some of our weakest tendencies to love money, to express destructively our own egos, to seize power over others, and to pretend that we are serving or even saving people when we are really exploiting them.

Although we often think of the media as mere sources of entertainment, they are really extensions of our God-given ability to cocreate culture. In spite of their limitations, the media are potential resources to help us serve our neighbor by telling the truth and building communities of shalom.

NINE

Prophet, Priest, or Demon?

Mass-Media Mythology

In *A Fistful of Fig Newtons,* novelist Jean Shepherd depicts a future in which archaeologists are excavating the remains of New York City. Hoping to understand what led to the decline of "Fun City," the archaeologists carefully unearth treasured artifacts in the basements along Manhattan's Madison Avenue, the heart of the advertising world. They discover tin canisters holding old film of television commercials—a "cosmic" archaeological find.

The archaeologists feed the antique reels of film into a projector to view firsthand the remarkable artifacts. Image after image flickers on the screen, revealing past icons of American culture. Finally, they view a commercial that appears to be the ultimate discovery, the nexus of American belief. A stern man clad in an authoritative uniform stands in front of small, white, apparently sacred scrolls. "Ladies, *please* don't squeeze the Charmin!" he says. Amazed at the apparent significance of the archaeological find, the leader of the excavation says, "If we can find out what was on those Charmins, or what they were used for, I believe we would know what their civilization was all about, what they believed in. Do you follow?"[1]

Shepherd's tale suggests that advertising is at the heart of American popular belief. If Shepherd is right, products of the media, especially advertising, are sacred texts. Americans derive popular values and beliefs not just from organized religion or the sacred Scriptures but also from the mass media.

Shepherd's theory challenges the views of most communication experts. Media scholars often describe four major roles that mass communication plays in society: informing the public, entertaining audiences, persuading consumers, and educating citizens. They say, for example, that news informs, advertising persuades, prime-time television entertains, and public television and film documentaries educate. If Shepherd is right, these four roles are less important than media's underlying function: Perhaps the media are modern society's mythology—its public expressions of what most people truly believe and value.

In this chapter, I argue that the consumption of mass-mediated stories has largely replaced "tribal" storytelling. Instead of sitting around the fire recalling tales of our own cultural tribes, we gather around the television, read newspapers and magazines, attend movies, and listen to the radio. Shepherd's tale satirically captures the media's ability to tell "sacred" stories. Increasingly, the media serve a kind of religious role in society.

Second, I illuminate what I call the media's priestly role. As priest-like institutions, the media do not try to challenge the tribe's values and beliefs. Instead, they primarily confirm people's existing beliefs and values. The commercial media in particular affirm our culture more than they try to change it. After all, they have to attract audiences for advertisers. As priests, the media offer society an uncritical portrayal of itself. They "hold us up" for us to see. These media represent the tribe to itself.

Third, I discuss mass media's demonization of certain individuals and groups. As they tell priestly stories, media reflect the kinds of morally good and morally evil characters that already exist in the tribe's imagination. The media stereotypically assign the evil roles to members of certain groups, affirming the tribe's belief that evil resides only in evil people, not in all of us.

Finally, I examine how the media can also function as prophets by challenging society's existing beliefs. Reporters, documentary filmmakers, media critics, and playwrights are among the people who sometimes serve this prophetic role. Shepherd's story about discovering old commercials in New York City is essentially a prophetic tale that reveals American dependence on superficial consumer culture.

Creating Myths

Noel Gallagher, leader of the rock group Oasis, once said, "We're more popular than Jesus Christ now." He added, "Some of the pop stars I like are more important to me than God. I would hope we mean more to people than putting money in the church basket and saying ten Hail Marys on

Sunday."[2] Gallagher captured a strange truth about modern society: Some media celebrities *are* more popular than religious leaders. Pop stars *do* create a popular mythology that competes with religion. Some fans even worship celebrities.

Aristotle used the term *mythoi* to refer to a culture's stories that people use to understand themselves.[3] Today we think of "myths" as fictional stories, but for Aristotle and many others, it was irrelevant whether the events in the stories had actually happened. The purpose of myths is to create shared experiences and beliefs among people, to capture a particular community's beliefs and feelings about life. Often the most popular rock groups achieve mythical significance. They do far more than entertain audiences; they connect fans with one another through common media experiences.

The key to understanding the mythological role of the media is the relationship between story and tribe, or community. God created us as creatures who use stories not just to entertain but also to bind people together in a common life. Our mythical tales enable us to express and share assumptions about life. Jesus taught primarily by telling stories that dealt with the culture of the day,[4] and his stories became part of the larger collection of stories known as the Bible. Inspired by God, the church recalls the stories of Scripture time and again to remind believers that their own lives are now part of the story of God's redemption. All cultural groups forge identities partly through *tribal storytelling*.

Popular media, then, are like a secular "bible" for contemporary culture. Their stories reflect how and what we believe, even the commandments that members of the tribe are expected to obey. Sitcoms remind us to believe that we can overcome the complications of life. "Hang in there!" is the message. "Be positive!" Millions of people turn to their television sets night after night to see and know that people can overcome the difficulties of life. They use comedies to confirm their hopes.

One Canadian editor says that news is "a daily journal of moral conduct." A newspaper, he adds, is "a vehicle for parables about people and how they make moral decisions."[5] News teaches us about the trials and triumphs of sports heroes, criminals, politicians, and everyday people. Each of these kinds of stories instructs us about tribal beliefs. We shake our heads about the tragedies and celebrate the occasional victories.

In some respects, this media "religion" challenges the Christian faith. Commercial television and traditional Christian faith, for example, compete culturally.[6] We learn through commercials that our external beauty will determine our popularity among other people, whereas Scripture emphasizes the importance of what is in our hearts (1 Sam. 16:7). Sitcoms teach us repeatedly that things will work out in the end, whereas the Proverbs emphasize the consequences of our wisdom or foolishness. Biblical truth is a "story of what God has done."[7] Media stories, on the other hand, usually tell us what humans can accomplish without God. Whereas the gospel focuses on God, the media focus on people, virtually excluding any mention of a transcendent Creator. The Bible tells Christians how to find salvation and how to cocreate shalom. Television programs offer little more than temporary amusement.

In a sense, we worship *mass-media mythology*. Scholar Gregor Goethals calls television viewing in particular a "ritual at the TV altar."[8] She does not mean that we view distinctly religious programming. Rather, she argues that the tube has become one of our major sources of popular mythology. Television programs package our common cultural beliefs in ways that appeal to us and attract millions of viewers even for low-rated shows. Some people go to church to worship with a community of believers, but millions more go to the television set to commune with the invisible tribe of like-minded viewers. Some celebrities even function as saints for true believers of television fare.

The media, then, are far more than entertainment. They invariably support one mythological version of reality over another. Slimness is sexy; chubbiness is not. Violence solves problems; turning the other cheek does not. Mass media give us shared maps of reality in a chaotic and often confusing world.[9] Like sermons and Bible studies, popular entertainment offers what rhetorician Kenneth Burke calls "equipment for living."[10] When Noel Gallagher of Oasis said that his group was more popular than Jesus Christ, he implicitly suggested that popular culture is the source of inspiration and meaning for many people. Today's Christians are like the ancient Jews in Egypt; we are aliens of the dominant culture.[11] The idea that we can just disregard the media and live our own holy lives is naive at best. "It may be comforting to believe that flipping a switch or turning a dial allows independence and freedom of thought and action," but it is "impossible to turn off a whole culture!"[12]

Priestly Propaganda

Writer Philip Yancey recalls the time that he presented to students several dozen slides showing the way that Jesus is portrayed in a variety of cultures. He then asked the American students to describe what *they* thought Jesus looked like. Nearly the entire group suggested that Jesus was "tall (unlikely for a first-century Jew), most said handsome, and no one said overweight." Finally, Yancey showed them a BBC film featuring "a pudgy actor" playing Christ. Some students found the film offensive. Yancey concluded that our "glamorized representations of Jesus say more about us than about him."[13]

In a fallen world we seek media that confirm what we want to believe, not necessarily what is accurate or truthful. Perhaps the media have their greatest impact not in changing what we believe and value but in affirming what we already believe and value. Especially in a market system, in which large audiences are required, the media accept us as we are and encourage us to be even more that way.

Priestly media powerfully confirm and exploit what a tribe wants to believe. I use the term *priest* because the media perform symbolic rituals for a group of people. The word *priest* comes from the Latin *pontifex,* which means "bridge builder." Media build bridges that connect us to one another and to the broader beliefs of our culture. A real priest performs absolution and pronounces people married; the priestly media tell us that everything will work out for good and pronounce blessing on our lifestyles.

Priestly media perform secular rituals that affirm a tribe's beliefs. Because the media depend on the tribe's faithfulness, they need us to believe that stories will deliver what they promise. We expect comedies to end happily. From the very beginning, television programming was dominated by comedic shows with happy endings.[14] We want lovers to meet and fall in love. We want to believe the advertisers even if we do not fully trust them, because we desire products that will make us attractive. Priestly media require effective storytellers and a faithful audience in order to create a tribe's culture.

The media repeatedly say to the tribe, "This is who we are. This is our name. Join our rituals and believe." They thereby enable us to participate in popular rituals about forgiveness, success, grace, revenge, morality, and all of the other mythology of contemporary culture. As a tribe, we turn to media stories for confirmation of our beliefs. The media priests offer us one major doctrine: All things work together for good for those who believe in themselves and in the tenets of the tribal culture.

The market system typically encourages priestly mass media to embrace the broad community, not to address specific traditions or identifiable cultural groups. As historian Martin Marty once said, the gospel is an "improper opinion" for the media to express.[15] The heart of the Christian faith is too particular, too specific, and too exclusive for the vast tribe of North American culture. So the media create broadly defined "gospels" that resonate with the wider culture's beliefs.

Although the media do not offer the tribe a coherent worldview, they do survey the range of human triumphs and tragedies—almost like a full-orbed theology. Teen movies confirm that it is normal for teens to consider their parents stupid and to be obsessed with the opposite sex. Television cartoons comfort young people of all religious backgrounds by depicting good triumphing over evil. Newscasts present negative news that wears us down, then end doxologically with an upbeat, often humorous tale of good cheer. Magazine shows such as *60 Minutes* confirm what mainstream America believes about the triumph of individuals over evil organizations.[16] Adver-

127

tising confirms—often falsely—that if women lose weight, dress attractively, and color their hair they will be popular and loved. This market-driven mythology reflects believers' faith in themselves and their culture.

From a Christian perspective, priestly media are *propaganda*. French scholar Jacques Ellul argues that modern propaganda tells people what they want to believe more than it tries to change their beliefs.[17] His theory differentiates between the ultimate truth of the gospel and the day-to-day realities that we accept as truth. In Ellul's view, all of our attempts to find truth solely in the media are naive. Public opinion surveys do not determine truth any more than do audience ratings or Academy Awards. Commercial media are interested not in truth so much as in exploiting audiences' existing beliefs.

Contemporary media gain audiences by carrying messages that resonate not only with people's beliefs but also with their emotions. Often the priestly power of the media is not in stories or words but in images and music. Using these emotive tools, propagandists can affirm a tribe's feelings about love and religion, and confirm a people's nationalism and patriotism. Commercials and rock videos, for example, can provoke feelings that "stand in the way of self-examination."[18] Using emotive techniques, media connect directly with our hearts while short-circuiting our critical discernment. Sometimes there is a fine line between a multimedia rock concert and a contemporary worship experience. Both can use music and image to elicit such strong emotional responses that audiences feel as though they have at least momentarily transcended their mundane lives and achieved a state of blissful joy.

Perhaps the most effective priestly communication is produced by the persuasion industries: marketing and public relations. They combine emotion and belief in attractive stories, offering the tribe ways to satisfy its needs for popularity, prosperity, and happiness. They don't question what we want; they only tell us how we can get what we want. Advertising in particular is the high priest of consumer cultures, because both religion and advertising promise redemption, "one through faith, the other through purchase."[19] Commercials are the "aesthetic marvels of our age," presenting "glowing images of youthful beauty and athletic prowess, of racial harmony and exalted fellowship" designed "to persuade us that a certain beer or candy bar, or insurance company or oil-based conglomerate, is, like the crucified Christ or the defiant Lenin in other times and places, the gateway to the good life."[20] Not surprisingly, many of the founders of modern advertising were deeply religious people; advertising became their pulpit.[21]

The media often misidentify what the tribe really believes. Commercial propagandists frequently err in their attempts to say what their flocks wish to hear. Advertising and public relations campaigns sometimes misfire. The vast majority of new television programs and magazines last barely a year.

Most films disappear quickly at the box office. Radio stations change formats routinely. Public taste is fickle. Perhaps even the tribe does not always know what it values or believes. Media depend on imperfect priests to tell stories to unpredictable audiences in very competitive media environments. The process of garnering an audience requires a lot of faith in the storytellers.

Demonizing Our Neighbor

A Muslim man who had lived in the United States for thirty-three years observed that of all the world's faiths, Islam is the most widely misunderstood. Newspapers, television, and film, he said, foster the impression that Muslims are "a violent lot—a band of fanatics and terrorists who incite holy wars (Jihad) and are ruled by reckless men." He further observed that Muslims "are fearful because ignorance sometimes leads to violence against them, particularly when the Middle East is in the news." He concluded that since Islam is the second-largest religion on earth, people "must understand it."[22]

The media *demonize* groups by negatively stereotyping entire cultures or categories of people. They amplify a tribe's existing prejudices, confirming what audiences want to believe about their own superiority. Media propagandize by projecting evil and villainy on entire categories of people, members of particular racial, religious, or ethnic groups. Using images, sounds, and languages of peoples whom the media consumers do not personally know, the media tell stories that demonize many disparate groups. When demonization is at its worst, the media characterize groups of people as morally bankrupt.[23]

The popular arts in the United States have always demonized particular people. Circuses, vaudeville, film, radio, and TV portrayed immigrant groups and minority groups as evil people. Between roughly 1835 and 1940, freak shows divided people into two groups—"abnormal Westerners" and "normal Westerners." In so doing, they reflected how the dominant American culture determined who was a freak and who was a normal member of the tribe. Television and film later portrayed people with disabilities as villains. Evil characters had limps, eye patches, and ugly facial features. To this day, television's criminals are frequently unattractive or disfigured so we can easily identify their "evil" features.[24]

In one way or another, popular media use existing cultural stereotypes to gain audiences. As the North American population has become more multiracial and multicultural, the media have shifted to demonizing disabled people and even extremely religious people (depicted as "fanatics"). All of these types of demonizing tend to exacerbate existing conflicts and misunderstandings among people. Theologian Jurgen Moltmann suggests, for instance, that "our reactions to the disabled are often far worse than their disability."[25] Our media stereotypes of others shape how we act toward them in real life.

129

Journalists also demonize people whom the tribe fears or dislikes. News stories establish real-world villains. After the bombing of the federal building in Oklahoma City in 1997, the news media immediately began reporting that Middle Eastern individuals had been seen in the area before the bombing. Later they discovered that Midwestern Caucasians were actually responsible. Why would the media assume that the criminals were members of any ethnic or racial group? Such assumptions reveal underlying prejudices and invite further demonization of people in the denigrated groups. Sometimes reporters fail to conduct adequate research and to ask the tough questions; instead, they accept tribal stereotypes until they are confronted directly with reality.

Stereotypical demonizing is also common in news because of a lack of heterogeneity within the newsroom. The news business claims to value different perspectives, but it actually favors a kind of "journalistic correctness" that confuses objectivity with conformity. When the media speak of diversity, they are not talking about "diversity of opinion, only different faces and genders, delivering the same one-sided viewpoint."[26] A truly heterogeneous newsroom would include all kinds of different worldviews, not just ethnic, racial, or gender variety. The entire concept of "diversity" in contemporary society is itself rather parochial and stereotypical.

The role of media in demonizing particular groups of people is an extension of fallen human nature. Just as Adam blamed Eve and Eve blamed the serpent for their misdeeds, we all look for scapegoats to make us feel better about ourselves. As the media oversimplify reality and feed existing stereotypes, they satisfy our desire to confirm that we are members of a superior tribe. Demonization fulfills our arrogant drive to victimize others. Rhetorician Kenneth Burke wrote during the Cold War, "In keeping with the 'curative' role of victimage, each [nation] is apparently in acute need of blaming all its many troubles on the other, wanting to feel certain that, if the other and its tendencies were but eliminated, all governmental discord . . . would be eliminated."[27] In every historical period, the tribe's culturally engrained pride leads the media to confirm the tribe's own goodness and to illuminate neighbors' evil.

Demonization contrasts starkly with biblical truth, which stresses that evil lives in the heart of every person, not just in the hearts of members of specific groups. Like every individual, each tribe has certain strengths and weaknesses. One values monetary success; another values generosity. One exhibits excessive vengefulness; another exhibits excessive greed. Every society must consider its own faults, and every religious group must consider its own evil ways. All of us must avoid scapegoating—assigning guilt to others for our own misdeeds. And we must also avoid stereotyping—attributing to each member of a group traits that we assume to be characteristic of the group as a whole.

Throughout Christian history, adherents to certain Christian traditions have publicly demonized other traditions. Protestant luminaries such as Martin Luther and John Calvin demonized other groups in their day. Lutheran professor and historian Martin Marty admits that "Luther said horribly horrible things. Lutherans are all but sworn not to defend him."[28] Luther spoke against Turks, papists, and certain fellow Protestants. Long before modern broadcasting arrived on the scene, Christians used pamphlets, books, and sermons to demonize one another. The human fall from grace affected the church as well as the rest of society. Every tradition must address its tendency to sacramentalize its own beliefs and to demonize others' beliefs.

Shalom requires us to go beyond mediated experiences of other cultures and to forge living relationships with our neighbors. Missionaries from the United States often return to their home churches to report that other cultures are very different from the popular stereotypes. Missionaries, people who do business internationally, immigrants, people who live in the city or in rural areas, members of various racial or ethnic groups—all are people we should seek out at church, in school, through friends, and in our communities because they are valuable interpreters and storytellers for us to know and hear. Without firsthand relationships, we can depend too easily on stereotypes of Muslims and members of other groups that we too easily demonize.

Finding Prophetic Media Voices

A Middle Easterner visiting the United States was asked what he thought about American television shows. The visitor said that he was quite impressed because the bad guys always got caught and punished, and the good guys always won. Then he paused and said, "Now they just have to work on the news."[29] Indeed, news often presents depressing stories of conflict and despair. Even with the doxological, upbeat tales at the end of each broadcast, the news hardly reflects a world of shalom.

A culture with only priestly media is a dangerous place filled with arrogance and ignorance. Jacques Ellul says, "Day after day the wind blows away the pages of our calendars, our newspapers, and our political regimes, and we glide along the stream of time without any spiritual framework, without a memory, without a judgment, carried about by 'all winds of doctrine.'"[30] Without critical discernment, a tribe implodes with its mythological self-delusion or explodes with its own conflicts.

Prophetic media truthfully challenge a culture's beliefs. Throughout history, God-fearing prophets have challenged tribes' mistaken beliefs. Often these prophets are courageous and cogent observers of contemporary culture. As Jacques Ellul puts it, the prophet must refuse to "accept appearances at their face value, and information for information's sake."[31] Instead, prophetic media need to "rediscover the meaning of events, and the spiritual framework which our contemporaries have lost. This will be a difficult enterprise for it is new and humble."[32]

When we lack biblical discernment, Christians ignore a wide range of important cultural issues. The church has generally overlooked materialism, gluttony, ethnic stereotypes in films, sexism in soap operas, and violence in sports. In the late 1980s, Christian media were among the last to expose the fraudulent practices and heretical beliefs of certain outrageous television evangelists.[33] Christians should have cleaned their house long before the mainstream media had to do it for them. Christian media can be just as strongly priestly, and just as weakly prophetic, as mainstream media.

Prophetic media are less-visible alternatives to mainstream media institutions. Specialized magazines attract small audiences of contrary thinkers. Christian magazines such as *First Things, Sojourners,* and *The Other Side* offer perspectives at odds with those of priestly Christian periodicals. Similarly, nonreligious journals such as the *New Republic,* the *Atlantic Monthly,* and the *National Review* critically evaluate culture, politics, and economics—sometimes even with a Christian perspective. On public television in the United States, *American Playhouse* presents some of the finest television dramas ever produced, and the dramas frequently have a critical edge. Some mainstream newspaper columnists are passionate, fair-minded, and self-critical observers of contemporary society who transcend the typical liberal-conservative distinctions in search of a deeper truth.

Here and there, prophetic voices are struggling to make sense of a complex and exasperating world. Some, like African-American intellectual Cornel West, claim the "prophetic stream" of the Christian tradition.[34] Prophets are humble enough to recognize that the deeper truths about our state of affairs are not easy to grasp. Their message is, "You might not like it, but things are not as good as we want to believe." Christians know why: We are fallen people who are trying to refashion the world in our own image, rather than in the image of God's kingdom.

The World Association for Christian Communication (WACC), an organization made up of Christians who care about communication in society, is one example of a prophetic media voice. WACC's statement on communication says, "Prophetic communication stimulates critical awareness of the reality constructed by the media and helps people to distinguish truth from falsehood, to discern the subjectivity of the journalist and to disassociate that which is ephemeral and trivial from that which is lasting and valuable."[35] WACC runs leadership workshops in developing nations, publishes books critical of mainstream media, issues public statements about such things as media abuses of human rights and media monopolies, and engages in other activities designed to heighten awareness of media's impact on poor and voiceless people around the world. Many Christian traditions have their own organizations that are similar to WACC.

Prophetic Christian voices have emerged from Christian communities around the world. A small community of committed believers in Chicago started *Sojourners* magazine in the 1970s. Later the *Sojourners* community established residence in Washington, D.C., and began to minister in one of the poorer areas of the city.[36]

Christian schooling in North America is a means for communities of faith to nurture prophetic viewpoints. Using special textbooks, videos, computer software, and other media, Christian schools and colleges try to cultivate an alternative worldview and to provide a critique of the media culture. These schools should be among the most vibrant critics of the media.

Deeply prophetic media voices anchored in the gospel instead of fame or fad are essential for the Christian community. Prophetic media voices bring light to the darkness in media and society. Media prophets reveal what others do not see so that people might perceive things the way they really are. They never seek merely to massage their ego or to cause strife for others. Supported by their own community, media prophets love their neighbors enough to risk their standing in society to make the truth known. Love, not just anger, drives the prophets in a media world, just as it did the prophets of old.

A prophetic media voice is faithfully committed to applying biblical truth to the real world of sin. The prophetic news reporter, for example, seeks to understand contemporary events through the lens of God's Word rather than merely through the fads of popular opinion or the formulas of professionalism.[37] In the twentieth century, one of the most prophetic Christian voices addressing the media was that of Jacques Ellul. Although he was deeply pessimistic and elitist at times, Ellul left a remarkable legacy of dozens of books and many more articles about the role of media technology and propaganda in modern life.[38] The kind of prophetic critique of media and society that gets beyond inaccurate information and hazy facts, said Ellul, is possible only "under the illumination of the Holy Spirit."[39]

Voices such as that of Jacques Ellul represent a culture of resistance to mainstream society. The prophetic voice not only illuminates what is wrong with the world but also provides a perspective that is in contrast to popular opinion and everyday assumptions. Prophetic resistance calls us to take the world more seriously than most people do. Writes one critic, "It seeks to escape not the world but the trivialization of the world by which other persons become instruments of one's self-will rather than temples of the living

God."[40] The media prophet follows the rhetorical way of Jesus, turning popular wisdom on its head and standing up for the victims of society.

Without a community for accountability, however, prophetic critics can become self-seeking and destructive priests of their own small tribes. Christians can wrongly claim direct wisdom from God. Some savvy media professionals know how to create their own cottage industries by telling besieged subcultures what they wish to hear. Most columnists in the United States, for example, have become predictable complainers who follow standard ideological rhetoric from the political right or left. High-profile Christian media celebrities often engage in the same narrow-minded criticism that puts ideology above truth. In some cases even local pastors establish cultic followings of people who hang on their every word. When this happens, a tribe's prophets become its propagandists.

Prophets must possess deep personal humility and a strong sense of responsibility to the Christian community. They must serve not themselves but the Creator and their neighbors. True prophets are not self-serving negativists who simply enjoy criticizing others or tearing down established institutions, but statespeople who care primarily about the common good. In order to give to their neighbors, prophetic professional communicators become moral agents in society, dedicated to "selfless service to . . . fellow human beings" and anchoring their actions in "conscience and truth."[41] Media prophets recognize that we are all self-delusional, that power can corrupt the Christian, and that listening to others is a crucial means of evaluating their own rhetoric. They see, as did the Middle Eastern visitor, that media folly is deeply cultural and broadly institutional. Evil has a tenacious hold on every human heart. Darkness festers in deeply rooted principalities and powers. "Let us finally endeavor," Václav Havel told his colleagues in Eastern Europe, "to get rid of not only our fear of lies but also our fear of the truth."[42] In one sentence Havel captured the mission of the media prophet.

Conclusion

Christian faith is a radical call to discipleship, not a comfortable trip to the movie theater or a forgettable evening in front of the tube. As Jean Shepherd suggests in the story about the discovery of the Charmin commercials, we are usually blind to our cultural biases and prejudices. We fail to perceive how much we idolize movie stars and rock groups—even those who proudly proclaim they are more popular than Jesus Christ. We create culture in our own image, just as Yancey's students created their ethnocentric versions of Jesus Christ. Jesus calls us all to be wide-eyed, discerning archaeologists of our mass-mediated society. When we do that, we might even dig up some unethical garbage in our own backyards.

TEN

Radical Discipleship

Responsible Communication

Joanne is the head of information technology at a small Christian college. She has spent ten years helping faculty, staff, and students use computers and has developed the campus computer network, which includes even off-campus connections for commuters and homebound students. Joanne has done a terrific job and is highly respected by people across the entire campus.

One day she receives an email message intended for a small group of students but wrongly addressed to her. The male sender put her email address on the note by inadvertently transposing two letters. As it turns out, the message is a note to a small group of male students who apparently are sharing Internet addresses for pornographic online materials. What should she do?

Joanne's situation reflects the tough ethical dilemmas we face as people who must live responsibly in community. She could simply do what feels right to her—pretend that she never saw the note. That option might enable her to avoid relational conflict. But as a Christian she recognizes that God calls her to radical action, not to the easy way out of the situation.

This chapter addresses our responsibility as God's symbolic stewards to strive for ethical communication that is grounded in our radical call to live the gospel. Christians are called to be fundamentally different communicators who are less prone than non-Christians to thoughtless conformity and self-serving symbolic action. We are freed by the gospel, and God expects us to strive to do what is right, not merely what is easy, popular, or persuasive.

First, I argue that human communication is action, not merely behavior. Animals respond instinctually, but people communicate intentionally. We decide what, when, why, how, and with whom to communicate, although not always with great forethought.

Second, I suggest that symbolic action should always be evaluated within the context of community life. Human communication is not an individual enterprise but a collective activity. Through communication we cocreate culture in the midst of relationships, obligations, and expectations. Our symbolic action always carries responsibilities to other people in our personal and professional communities. As a member of the Christian college community, Joanne has to decide which individuals or groups should be part of her radical action.

Third, I review three major concerns facing radical communicators: truth telling, privacy, and representation. Joanne faces tough decisions both about respecting students' privacy and about telling the truth. She might also have to decide who should be represented in discussions about a possible institutional response.

Fourth, I offer two biblical standards to help all of us navigate the turbulent waters of ethical communication: liberation and grace. Each of these standards can help us to be radically faithful and courageous disciples.

Ethics is perhaps the most important issue in the field of communication. None of us can serve our neighbor and glorify God without making radical decisions about when, why, and how to communicate. Our symbolic action must be right, not just persuasive. Many communicators reduce ethics to a question of what is most expedient at the time—an ethic of pragmatism. I believe instead that God calls all people to an ethnic of radical discipleship with which we responsibly cocreate shalom.

Communication as Radical Action

Every year journalists are murdered around the world simply because they report the facts. Between 1987 and 1997, 173 journalists were killed in Latin America after they tried to publish truthful news stories.[1] In Mexico, reporters at the paper *La Prensa* spoke the truth at the risk of death. Drug runners feared journalists more than they feared the police. In his daily column, "Unconfirmed," journalist Benjamin Flores suggested the possibility that the police were involved in the drug business, reporting that half a ton of cocaine had been "stolen" from a local federal police office. Soon afterward, Flores was murdered by a blast from an AK-47 rifle as he entered the newspaper's offices. The killing was one in a string of murders of journalists who were courageous enough to crusade against the drug industry in their homeland. After Flores's death, someone pasted a ballad about the courageous reporter on the wall in the newspaper's offices. It said, in part, "He knew it might be coming, because he never sold out to anyone."[2]

Those of us who live comfortably in safe communities forget the sacrifices that some people make on behalf of truth and justice. Lutheran pastor and theologian Dietrich Bonhoeffer, who was held for several years in a Nazi prison before finally being executed, called radical discipleship a complete break with evil, secular authority. "When Christ calls a person," wrote Bonhoeffer, "he bids him come and die."[3] The radically responsible communicator becomes a new person with loyalties in heaven as well as on earth. She gives her life to glorifying God and to serving her neighbor. This kind of radical discipleship leads the Christian to do what is right regardless of the cost. Like Bonhoeffer, we become discomforting prophets as well as comforting priests.

Radical discipleship calls us from worldly authority, from allegiance merely to the organizations and people of this world, and leads us to declare our allegiance to Jesus Christ. Our communication is not merely on behalf of corporations, governments, or even churches; it is under the authority of our Creator and Redeemer. We might need to resist fashionable norms by rejecting offers of jobs that would require us to communicate deceptively or to treat others as less than God's image bearers. Radical action may even put us in conflict with our churches. When the official German church acquiesced to the demands of the Third Reich, Bonhoeffer secretly founded an alternative seminary in order to communicate to students the call to radical faith.[4]

According to the cultural view of human communication, people commune dynamically, creatively, and even unpredictably. People's symbolic actions spring from their desires and intentions. Our communication is willful action, not merely the passive behavior of animals.

Radical communicators recognize that all human communication is symbolic action. We act with our tongues, ears, hands, and eyes. We act when we listen. Television audiences act as interpreters of aural and visual symbols. During a physical examination, a doctor reads the symptoms by actively observing the patient, listening to the patient's complaints, and interpreting the results of various tests. In myriad ways, human communication is symbolic action, not passive behavior.

As a form of action, human communication reflects our God-given freedom. We decide what, when, why, and with whom to communicate. We decide when to listen and which mass media to use. Because of this freedom we enjoy life's spontaneous and robust discussions, conversations, and storytelling sessions. But also because of our freedom we must communicate responsibly. Human freedom "does not in the least solve all the problems of human life and even adds a number of new ones."[5] Every day we freely make thousands of decisions about our communication. Sometimes we face tough ethical dilemmas, such as Benjamin Flores's decision about whether to risk his life by reporting the facts about the drug business in Mexico. Flores could have acted differently. Communication ethics is predicated on our freedom to act.

Our words, like our silence, can foster life or death. Our symbolic action breathes heaven or hell into the world. When communication is badly misconstrued, people can literally die. Yet silence itself is dangerous. Perhaps Benjamin Flores recognized that the media's silence about the drug cartels gave them license to kill thousands of addicted people around the world. The apostle James places a heavy burden of accountability on teachers because they influence others through their words and deeds (James 3:1). We all must monitor our symbolic action with great sensitivity and care. As it says in Proverbs, "When words are many, sin is not absent" (10:19).

Communication is like the plumbing of every community. It should deliver fresh water and flush out the waste. When we do not take care of communication, the system becomes contaminated, explodes, or shuts down. Flores recognized how crucial his symbolic action was for the good of his community and his country. When we also breathe life into our communication, we radically serve others and please God.

Responsible Communication in Community

Living in a Christian campus community, Joanne recognizes that her freedom to communicate about the email incident also carries responsibilities. In her heart and mind, she feels the need for what Wendell Berry calls "beloved community."[6] She cares about the students, and she worries about the impact of Internet pornography on the people she loves and serves. But she struggles to know how to act responsibly as a member of the campus community.

Radical communication requires us to form communities that incarnate the gospel so that all people may taste shalom. Instead of conforming our communication to the world, we should constantly and radically renew it through the inspiration of Scripture, the Holy Spirit, and our community of faith. Radical communicators are symbolic stewards, not individualistic critics with self-serving motives.

Some communities try to force ethical communication by limiting freedom, for instance, using screening software to block community members' online access to pornographic materials. Of course, someone has to decide for the community which kinds of materials, if any, will be unavailable. Sometimes autocratic leaders dictate standards. In Joanne's case, a public forum might help the school's leadership democratically establish criteria for censorship. Perhaps the issue merits campus-wide discussion and decision making.

The democratic tradition is grounded in a *negative* view of freedom; that freedom means freedom from restrictions.[7] Communities that operate according to this view hold people responsible only if they abuse their freedom. The principle of freedom of speech assumes that communities should err on the side of freedom, not on the side of restriction. Citizens are free to defame others' character, for example, but they might have to face the consequences in a libel suit. If a college discovers that certain students have violated the community's standards by downloading unacceptable materials, the students might be disciplined by college officials or by a jury of their peers. But usually no one's freedom is restricted up front.

Ethical dilemmas cry out for a community of wisdom, not just for individual discernment. Sometimes we are inclined just to muddle through these situations on our own, but often we feel paralyzed by personal freedom. We face tough decisions and have too little time to review all the possible responses. The consequences of our decisions are impossible to predict. Sometimes community standards restrict us too much, crushing unpopular ideas that should be considered. But communities can also help us to deal more reasonably with the daily surprises and ambiguities of communication. Joanne might find that a committee would help her to make the tough decisions wisely.

In the midst of our frenetic world, we need the time and the courage to look discerningly beyond our own selfish motives to the wisdom of others. Our sinfulness pushes us to act merely in our own interests, but God calls us to community responsibility. The love of God and the responsibility to neighbors are the very fabric of shalom. Symbolic freedom is not an end in itself or a license to pursue fame, fortune, and fun. God gives us freedom so that we can act responsibly in and for community.

Truth Telling, Privacy, and Representation

Radical Christian communicators will make hundreds of different communication-related ethical decisions each year, in everyday situations that generally fall into three major categories: (1) *truth telling*—when to tell the truth and when we might justify a lie, (2) *privacy*—when to maintain confidentiality and when to reveal what we know, and (3) *representation*—

139

who should have a voice in particular situations and when we can ethically exclude someone.

First, the radical communicator avoids deception and normally tells the gospel truth in love. She also knows that the truth can be much more complex than the facts; the full truth is all of the facts viewed in the context of the gospel. The radical communicator also recognizes that telling the truth without love is self-serving and deeply evil. She nevertheless assumes that truth telling is the norm, not the exception. Truth telling may be much more difficult than lying, but truth telling is the basis for all godly relationships, even in a fallen world.

Lying is common in a fallen world. Rahab lied, and arguably God was pleased that she did (Josh. 2:3–7; 6:17). Jacob lied to Isaac and received his father's blessing (Gen. 27:1–29). In some cases, deception is a survival tactic for people who have little symbolic power in society. Some Jews living under Nazi rule, for example, lied for their own survival. Lying seems to be necessary sometimes in a world in which ethical dilemmas are often horribly complex.

In a technological society, the very concept of truthful communication is problematic. Deception is built into many technologies and institutional forms of communication. Is it truthful for a television camera operator to point his camera upward at an evangelist, creating a sense that the preacher is larger than life? What about the veracity of touching up photos for advertisements in order to make the models look flawless and as attractive as possible? Is there any ethical basis for a person to process a singer's voice electronically so it no longer sounds exactly like the actual voice? How about a television news editor who decides which video clips about a news story will get on the evening news and which will not? Does editing itself deceive the viewer? These are complicated issues.

Although truth telling has its detractors, most ethicists agree with one another that lying, or intentional deception, reduces trust.[8] Recent polls understandably show, for instance, that the public's confidence in journalists is on the decline. Journalists' shenanigans weaken the public's trust of the media. Staff from one journalistic television show deceived a trucking company and one of its drivers by describing the program for which they were being interviewed as a look at the "positive side" of the profession. In fact, the program reported on national television that the driver had falsified his driving log and had driven from Chicago to Boston without sleep.[9] A jury awarded civil damages of $350,000 to owners of the trucking company and $175,000 to the driver. When journalistic deception becomes public, people lose trust in journalists—even if their stories are accurate.

Unethical communicators try to win trust by manipulating people's perception of the truth. As one scholar suggests, "Trust is a co-operative, life-preserving relationship that often depends upon the adroit management of deception, sometimes even lying, for its very sustenance."[10] One major airline gained more than $1.5 million in after-tax profits thanks to what it called a "recent involuntary conversion of a 727 aircraft." The airline failed to mention that the "involuntary conversion" was the crash of one of its airplanes, that three people had died in the crash, and that it had received more insurance money than the airplane was worth. As long as customers knew nothing about the reason for the financial bonanza, their trust in the airline was probably unshaken. In fact, the good financial report may have increased stockholders' inflated trust in the company.[11]

Church leaders sometimes drop denominational affiliations from the names of local churches in an effort to build community trust and to broaden membership. One minister says that some "people mistakenly associate the Baptist name with an angry, judgmental kind of fundamentalism."[12] So-called community churches are popping up all over North America. Sometimes these kinds of name changes are deceptive marketing gimmicks that give a community a false impression about a congregation's allegiances and beliefs. At other times they are genuine attempts by congregations to distance themselves culturally from stereotypes that do not fit their identity. In the former case, the nondenominational name is deceptive and can destroy trust. In the latter, the nondenominational name can build trust.

Even in a broken world, radical responsibility assumes that deception is the exception, never the rule. Although lying is sometimes the best of a number of bad choices, it can progressively erode trust and foster more deceit. A husband who lies to his wife, and parents who lie to their children are destroying the trust necessary for family life. Democratic governments that deceive citizens are sowing seeds of anarchy or authoritarian control. Sales persons who intentionally fail to tell customers about a product's liabilities are not only practicing bad public relations but are also risking the loss of a reputation for integrity. Students who cheat on papers are tearing down the school as a community of trust and goodwill. Although we can certainly imagine particular situations in which a lie may seem to be the best decision, deceit generally erodes community life. Shalom requires trust, and therefore assumes truth telling.

But the radical Christian communicator realizes that truth telling is more complex than mere factuality, accuracy, or knowledge. The full truth in any situation is wide, deep, and rich. The *gospel truth* reflects our real condition, not just the "letter of the law." This is what St. Augustine meant when he argued that rhetoric should be not only knowledge-producing but also truth-producing.[13] When we say the gospel is truth, we mean that the gospel sheds light on everything that we do and believe. The gospel story is not only historical truth but also life-giving truth. The gospel is the *living* truth that changes our view of all reality.

The radical communicator is motivated by charity, not simply by nit-picky truth telling. When we make a statement that is factually true but is not the whole truth, our words might not be kind to others. Much gossip is like this—technically truthful but lacking the bigger context of people's lives. A lie that is motivated by love and is spoken courageously and with great charity to protect others is not the same morally as a lie that is used to get oneself out of a speeding ticket or to trick someone into buying an overpriced product. In the bigger picture, our motives are as important as the things we say. When we act with charity, we are slow to speak and quick to listen so that we can speak not only the facts but the truth as well.

The gospel illuminates not only facts but also motives. For the Christian, gospel truth is the core or essence of something, not merely the details. This truth is the biblical picture, the facts *with* discernment. The Christian truth teller has to be wise enough to get beyond a superficial understanding in order to focus on the story as the gospel contextualizes it.

A Christian journalist should penetrate to the gospel-illuminated heart of the story. Theologian Eugene Peterson writes, "If we get our theology—that is, our understanding of what is really and eternally God-important—from the journalists, we get a few facts, almost no truth, and nothing at all of God. But a biblically trained imagination accustomed to dealing with flawed leaders, discerns our sovereign God working out his salvation purposes in our history."[14] Peterson rightly calls for journalists to exercise a biblical imagination that gets to the crux of the matter.

Biblical teachers and preachers face the daunting task of knowing the truth before speaking it. They must discern the spirit of contemporary culture or they will become false prophets. Peterson says that most lies are "90 percent the truth. So you swallow the lie, and subtly, the edge of the gospel is blunted; you think you're preaching the gospel, and you're not. You don't even know it."[15]

Finally, there may be times when a lie is morally justified, but these are always rare exceptions rather than the rule. Weighty situations, such as harboring Jews during the Nazi Holocaust, protecting national defense during war, and maintaining privacy during sexual harassment proceedings, may be the only ethical routes. Nevertheless, we err on the side of truth telling, justifying lies in rare and abnormally extreme situations.

Second, radical communicators deeply respect others' privacy but are willing to break confidences for the good of a neighbor. Radical communicators know that without privacy society could not function. They do not violate the privacy of any person or organization unless they have compelling reasons that are grounded in love.

Every day we make important decisions about which information to keep to ourselves and which information to reveal to others. Should parents conceal their impending divorce from their children? Should journalists refuse to disclose news sources to the public? Should a college student lie to her roommate's parents at the roommate's request? Whom should Joanne inform about the male students who are accessing pornography via the campus computer network? We all struggle to know when it is ethical to reveal something that we have learned privately or that someone has told us in confidence.

Radical responsibility assumes deep respect for one another's personal and public reputation. We should care about privacy because we know that communication about people shapes how others will perceive them. Gossip is wrong, for example, not only because its content is sometimes untrue or exaggerated but also because it reveals private information with little or no respect for a person's particular weaknesses or personal problems. Part of our responsibility as citizens of God's community is to protect each other from harmful words and misunderstandings. We uphold our neighbors' names partly by protecting their privacy.

On the other hand, privacy is hardly an absolute right in a fallen world. We must love each other enough to seek help for those who need it. We might break a promise of confidentiality when someone we know is suicidal, taking dangerous drugs, or being sexually promiscuous. Nevertheless, we must be careful about whom we tell, how we tell them, and especially why we tell them. Joanne, the campus technology administrator, has to decide whom she can trust to maintain the students' privacy. As radical communicators, we love others enough both to protect their privacy and sometimes to humbly violate it.

Third, radical communicators include all relevant people in decision making and lovingly represent those who are unable to participate. They know that representation protects all people's right to speak and listen— including their own. The life of the entire community depends on the participation of its weak and inarticulate members.

As radical communicators, we care about who is allowed to participate in a community's communication—who has a voice, who can listen, who has access to the media, and so forth. In semi-democratic or authoritarian countries, representation is always an enormously important issue because powerful elites suppress people's voices. The government, the military, and other elites sometimes control public communication by intimidating the media, prohibiting public demonstrations, distributing propaganda, and silencing and even killing opponents. In these societies, leaders fail to rec-

143

ognize that all people are God's image bearers who have intrinsic worth. In democratic nations, citizens often presume that everyone has a voice, that we all have equal symbolic power in society. Unfortunately, this is not always the case. Money, privilege, and social standing can give some individuals special access to media. Often someone can gain a public voice merely because of his or her job title or education.

Brazilian educator Paulo Freire has powerfully addressed the ethics of representation, stirring the hearts of Latin American Christians who yearn for shalom. Freire led massive literacy campaigns throughout Brazil during the early 1960s to help less-educated people participate in public discussion about their society. Jailed after a military coup that overturned the popular government, he began writing on the importance of education as a way to "empower those who are dispossessed of their word, their expressiveness, their culture."[16] Freire saw that some groups were denied access to the media and other powerful social institutions. They were allowing powerful organizations to exploit them by creating laws and practices that benefitted wealthy Brazilians and foreign cultures more than they helped Brazilian peasants. As Freire put it, voiceless people "fatalistically accept their exploitation."[17]

Freire argued that powerful and powerless people alike must participate and seek mutuality in society. All citizens should have a real voice in the laws and policies of a nation. Public disputes are not truly resolvable, he claimed, unless all participants in the dispute act with intimacy and vulnerability.[18] Unless we can talk honestly and openly with each other, we are all part of an oppressive system that fails to recognize every person's inherent value.

Freire's radical view of representation insists that an entire community's quality of life can be measured according to the variety of voices that it enables to join public discourse. Freire's ethic is a radical expression of Christ's representational rhetoric. By listening to the tax collectors, prostitutes, and widows, Christ legitimized their voices in society. Just as Christ challenged the arrogant leaders of his day, Freire, in the face of political persecution, boldly asserted the value of powerless people. Freire saw that representation was a biblical issue about the nature of human persons. Because all persons have intrinsic value, everyone must be permitted to express that value publicly.

These three ethical considerations—truth telling, privacy, and representation—are part of the moral uncertainty that we face in a fallen world. Each of these kinds of ethical dilemmas becomes more complex as we build strong personal relationships and enter public life. We take such dilemmas lightly only at our own peril. Radical responsibility depends on honesty, confidentiality, and participation.

Liberating Grace

The editor of *Parade* magazine unintentionally offended a New York woman by describing her in a story as "an unmarried mother of five." The woman called the editor to complain after the story was published: "Why did you write that? Why is that anyone's business?" Of course, she was right. Even if the article was accurate, it was hardly fair to her. As one observer of journalism suggests, fairness is "the most basic value of the profession." But as long as "the language of values is spoken by press and public alike with a quirked eyebrow and a sneer, it will be impossible to carry out meaningful critiques of a profession that really needs them."[19]

Two biblical themes—*liberation* and *grace*—are road maps that can help us navigate responsibly toward shalom. Ethical standards help us to work our way through moral dilemmas. Instead of making ad hoc decisions as we hop from one ethical dilemma to another, we can follow standards of responsible symbolic action that reflect the Bible's teachings as well as the wisdom of the community of believers. Scriptural wisdom "starts in heaven but works at street level, where we bump shoulders with others. It isn't satisfied with information retrieval."[20] One way to get a handle on the many biblical stories and guidelines is to follow the themes of liberation and grace as they unfold throughout Scripture.

First, God has always called people to liberation. Sometimes we need to be freed from external oppressors as the Israelites needed liberation from the ancient pharaohs, but we always require deliverance from the internal sin that breeds our selfishness and breaks our fellowship with God. The gospel frees us *from* guilt and judgment and frees us *to* love and serve our neighbor, so we should have no problem embracing humankind's freedom to communicate, including freedom of the press and the right to free speech. Christians should advocate human liberation and support the right of people to exercise their freedom.

But liberation calls us to communicate responsibly. We are liberated by Christ to convey what we *should* communicate, not just what we *want* to communicate. Christians are liberated from bondage so that we can act responsibly toward self, neighbor, and God. Freedom of voice is not an absolute right; it is contingent on our responsible use of the gift of communication.

If we must err in our ethical decision making, it should be on the side of freedom. The Mexican government, for instance, should protect the freedom of dissenters such as Flores to castigate the government for permitting police to collaborate with drug lords. Similarly, *Parade* magazine should have the freedom to publish what it pleases about New York's citizens, even if the stories are not flattering. But it should also act charitably

145

and wisely, limiting its freedom out of deference to others and a commitment to ethical standards. Christians, too, should support others' rights to expression, even when those voices reveal painful truths, challenge the status quo, or use the freedom irresponsibly. Of course, there are situations in which people act so irresponsibly that their voice contributes nothing more than profanity or disrespect, or in which they shout so loudly that no one else can be heard. In these situations, we may have to ask others to communicate more respectfully or appropriately, or even to remain silent. In short, radical communicators liberate the truth and nearly always protect the right of others to communicate freely.

Second, all the moral codes of Scripture are fulfilled in Christ's work of grace on the cross. God has already won what we could not have won for ourselves—salvation. Today we live not under the condemnation of the moral law but under God's grace. In turn, we extend God's grace to others. The moral laws of the Christian faith help us to forgive and to reconcile, not simply to devote ourselves legalistically to rules and regulations. Paul claimed not mindless allegiance to rules but commitment to the gospel (1 Cor. 9:21). God's laws provide the direction for our lives; we must interpret them radically because they are the fulfillment of the call to love God and our neighbor.

Grace is a navigational standard that directs all biblical mandates toward one central task—reestablishing loving relationships with God and our neighbor. Telling the truth, protecting privacy, and fairly representing others can never be ends in themselves. We are called not to legalistically scrutinize everyone else's symbolic action but to accept the grace that God offers to us all. Christ cautions us, "Do not judge, or you too will be judged" (Matt. 7:1). We are to love our neighbor as ourselves (Mark 12:31). This kind of selfless love speaks God's grace in a broken world. Christian communication radically emphasizes grace over law. Christ challenged the Pharisees, who lived by the letter of the law instead of by the loving spirit of the law. Corrupt people can use moral and civil laws to exploit others and to champion their own legalistic self-righteousness. As radical communicators, we champion grace by loving God and our neighbor.

Moral issues such as justice and fairness may inspire laws that can be applied without reference to the moral spirit behind them. "No country can be happy," wrote Augustine, "while the walls may still be standing but the morals are collapsing."[21] Libel laws, for example, address situations in which people defame others' character, but they hardly address the evil spirit behind such things as gossip, rumor, judgmental attitudes, hatred, and indifference. The *Parade* magazine writer in New York may not have been officially guilty of libel, but he violated the spirit of the law by publicly harming the woman's reputation. Libel laws are guidelines to help society act on behalf of the public good by preventing adult name-calling, but speaking positively about others is far broader than just avoiding defamation. When they do not exercise radical responsibility, individuals and organizations easily violate the spirit of laws. The legalistic language of libel barely captures a few whispers of the language of grace.

At its best, radical responsibility emphasizes both legal rights and community responsibilities, both the *letter* of the law and the *meaning*, or *purpose*, of the law. When we are trying to determine whether a movie is appropriate for us to see, we cannot make a decision that is based purely on a legalistic rating scheme. No rating system can capture all the moral nuances and ethical dilemmas in a movie. In fact, the rating system might cause us to miss a worthwhile film that effectively communicates a good theme and contains only nongratuitous violence. All the laws of the land combined will not equip us to make ethical judgments. We need grace too.

Grace should make us particularly understanding and forgiving about others' communication. It reminds us that no human being is a perfect communicator and that all of us fall short of the will of God. We should be ready to forgive others who lie to us, invade our privacy, or silence our voice. When we cannot easily forgive, we should at least understand others' actions, knowing that we share the impulse to do evil. Grace leads us beyond legalism and into relationships of shalom.

Liberation and grace are important maps that we need in order to chart turbulent ethical waters. They help us think and act radically in difficult ethical situations. Liberation frees us to recognize our own responsibility before God. Grace reminds us that God loved us through Jesus Christ and that we are called to love others. If we apply liberation and grace judiciously to specific ethical dilemmas, we will likely do the right thing, even if it is not always the easy thing.

Conclusion

Radical responsibility is crucial for the Christian communicator. It steers our actions away from selfishness and back to the heart of the gospel. We begin every new day unaware of the dilemmas that we will face, and we cannot anticipate the consequences of our symbolic actions. Like Joanne, the college computer administrator, we navigate through a complex world of tough decisions, and sometimes the cost of radical communication will be high, as both Dietrich Bonhoeffer and Benjamin Flores discovered.

Radical Christians speak and listen carefully, delicately, and purposefully. We give up idle chatter and worldly deception because we realize that our symbols fly through our relationships with sharp edges and unpredictable results, and that our symbolic action shapes our communities. We work together to speak the truth in love, to protect each other's privacy, and to represent even the weakest people in our communities. We respect others and walk humbly with our Creator. These are big tasks in a world that has fallen from grace. But every time we exercise radical responsibility, we hold up one more signpost for shalom.

ELEVEN

Christian Virtue

Authentic Communication

Theologian Guillermo Cook once met with a group of Christian pastors, teachers, and scholars in a camp in rural Spain to discuss communication. When a stranger wandered into the camp one morning, some of the participants saw an opportunity to learn from this "gnarled old villager" and began questioning him about his life and culture. Suddenly the camp manager, who was a pastor, interrupted the discussion with a question of his own. "Sir, are you a born-again Christian?" When the villager mumbled an unconvincing reply, the camp manager pulled out his Bible and launched into a sermon, urging the villager to repent and believe in Christ. It was time for the villager to listen to the gospel.[1]

In his zeal to convert the visitor, the camp manager failed to listen to, and hence to respect, the stranger in their midst. Later the conference participants listened as the villager described how "rich city folk" had claimed his village's shoreline and polluted its water. Now the villagers had no place to fish. The participants also discovered that the old man had known nothing about the camp and the Christians who met there. The evangelicals who ran this camp had never invited him to visit. As Guillermo Cook and his colleagues cast their gaze on the camp's beautiful shoreline, they realized that the camp was "physically standing in the way of the gospel in its fullest sense, at least for the people in that small village."[2] They would not have known about any of this if they had failed to listen.

As Cook recalls, the camp meeting was supposed to be an opportunity for Christians to learn about communicating Christ, not about suffocating the gospel. "This experience taught me," says Cook, "that Christian witness should be done in a spirit of vulnerability, service, and openness to others." He concluded that Christians are often "motivated by a spirit of churchly pride which goes against the grain of the gospel." Furthermore, proselytizers like the camp manager often "do not take the time to find out where their hearers are."[3] We frequently fail to practice the kind of loving communication that we preach. We profess to love others, but we do not even honor them as God's image bearers. Once the conference participants recognized their mistreatment of the local visitor, they rightly invited him to tell his own story in their camp. The evangelists became empathetic listeners instead of overly zealous preachers.

Like the camp pastor, we are not the kind of communicators that we profess to be. We shuttle back and forth between studying communication and practicing it. We take courses, read books, attend workshops, and discuss communication with others. Then we launch into the surrounding culture, presumably to use our new knowledge. But before we get very far, we violate the principles that we just learned. We forget to listen. We express ourselves unclearly. We lie, exaggerate, or gossip. We embarrass others and ourselves. All the helpful things we have discussed in this book will make little difference in our lives unless we internalize them. Our communication is folly unless we become intrinsically virtuous persons.

In this chapter, I first suggest that it is not enough merely to study communication. We must internalize what we learn. We must be good communicators, not just know how to communicate well. We should strive to be virtuous communicators who incarnate the characteristics of good communication.

Second, I look at the conflict between virtuous communication and our professional calling. The camp manager was a professional pastor, but he was not a virtuous communicator. He failed to respect the villager. He preached a message of love but failed to live it. Often professional practices promote success or status instead of virtue. All professionals should be authentic communicators who say what they mean and mean what they say.

Third, I consider the importance of the virtue of civility. Like the disrespectful camp manager, we treat others in ways that we would not want to be treated. We tend to apply a double standard. Contemporary societies are often torn apart by uncivil symbolic action. The camp manager's ad hoc sermon bordered on incivility. Civil communicators treat all people with the respect and charity that they deserve as God's image bearers.

Finally, I encourage Christians to build communities of shalom by encouraging each other to become vessels of virtue. As the camp participants discussed what had happened, they agreed that they could be more Christlike communicators. As a group they nurtured repentance and encouraged one another to listen and love. They considered how the camp could be hospitable to the community. They began creating a community of virtue that would serve authentic soul food.

Loving Justice and Peace

Archbishop Oscar Romero of El Salvador learned to communicate virtuously in the midst of hatred and despair. In the 1970s, civil war was tearing his nation apart. Military death squads killed dissenters, and leftist guerillas terrorized supporters of the military. The only safe way to live was in silent submission. Romero eventually realized that the status quo was not acceptable to God. So he began speaking the truth publicly in love, calling the church to action on behalf of the poor and powerless. Romero criticized both the elite's death squads and the guerrillas' Marxist dogma. He increasingly defended the rights of peasants to break the terrible yoke of injustice until a death squad assassinated him as he said mass in San Salvador.[4]

As long as Romero kept quiet, he could affirm the gospel in safety. But as he internalized the gospel, Romero was compelled to live it as well as believe it. In the eyes of the military, he was then a dangerous communicator. His life became a threatening witness to justice and peace. By being a channel for the gospel, Romero also became a threat to the system of oppression.

Like Oscar Romero we should love what is right. Christians are called to be persons of virtuous character. Christian communicators are committed not only to *doing* what is right but also to *being* righteous people. C. S. Lewis once said that "you cannot make people good by law, and without good persons you cannot have a good society."[5]

First, *virtuous communicators* love justice. Archbishop Romero's homilies during the painful years of Salvadoran strife reflected selfless love for justice. He did not just preach justice; he embodied the fears and hopes of the Salvadoran people who yearned for shalom. Amid all the false hopes in worldly institutions, Romero called for ultimate justice. In one of his homilies he said,

> There can be no true liberation
>   until people are freed from sin.
> All the liberationist groups that spring up in our land
>   should bear this in mind.

151

> The first liberation to be proposed by a political group
> that truly wants the people's liberation
> must be to free oneself from sin.[6]

We are to be justice-loving people. In a fallen world in which sin and evil touch all aspects of everyday life, God yearns for justice. Plato said that rhetoric should always be used to "serve the ends of justice."[7] But even more, we are to *be* just in our symbolic action. Justice is not merely an end we seek but a virtue that motivates our communication. Romero so loved the Salvadorans that he spoke openly about the oppressed people and called for both economic reform and repentence on the part of all Salvadorans. He simply could not be silent about injustice, no matter what the cost. Because he loved God and neighbor, he deeply loved justice.

Justice directs our love to people who are oppressed, reinstating their status as full and valued members of society. Philosopher Nicholas Wolterstorff says that a society is just "when all the little ones, all the defenseless ones, all the unprotected ones, have been brought back to community."[8] Justice-loving communicators open public discourse to otherwise silent and weak humans; they challenge oppressive authority and call openly for fairness. The love of justice even leads people to use their symbolic power on behalf of others, especially the voiceless, so that wrongs can be made right.

If we love justice, we will demand that oppressors be held accountable. Sometimes publication of the truth both shames oppressors and punishes them by lowering their social standing or tarnishing their reputation in business or government. Normally the law must deliver justice. Occasionally the media expose injustice. One of the most unusual cases of media justice took place in South Africa. Under apartheid, the ruling officials repeatedly lied to the public about the government's outrageous and brutal acts of violence against its Black African critics. After apartheid ended, the new government formed the Truth and Reconciliation Commission. Victims publicly recounted episodes of torture, rape, abduction, and even murder. Because these hearings were not a trial, there were no cross-examinations. Victims were free to voice their fears and to tell the nation what they had lived through under apartheid. One young mother whose husband had been killed, leaving her alone with five children, recalled that she "wanted to kill all of my children and myself." Many of the victims testified to their faith by reading from the Bible, praying, and recalling stories of God's grace in the midst of oppression. The Truth and Reconciliation Commission hearings gave public voices to the "hard to see" in society and helped restore the victims' human and civil dignity.[9]

Second, virtuous communicators love peace. They echo God's yearning for a world in which all people experience the joy and delight of serving God and each other. They bless all peacemakers and celebrate peace wherever it exists.

When we communicate virtuously, we join God as agents of peace in a fallen world. Our voices must embrace the harmonious relationships God intends. We must write and produce peacefully. Like Oscar Romero, we must give our eyes and ears as tools for peaceful relations.

If we are not peacemakers, we are often catalysts of conflict. We seed symbolic conflict like bullies pick fights. We listen for conflict among others and enjoy sharing it through gossip and criticism. We use symbolic power to oppress others and to build up our own public image. We sow symbolic conflict with verbal violence and nonverbal harassment. Some of us even join organizations that breed conflict by institutionalizing arrogance and pride. In some of our worst moments, we pridefully stir up conflict by expounding ethnocentric, sexist, nationalistic, or racist rhetoric at the expense of other groups.

Christian peacemakers do not unrealistically oppose all conflict, but they do challenge people to address conflicts peacefully. In labor negotiations, for example, peacemakers try to get workers and management to listen to each other empathetically. By steering discourse toward real issues and away from inflammatory personal attacks, peacemakers can promote shalom between business and labor. To the peacemaker, symbols are primarily balms and comforters, not weapons. Even when they disagree, they do so with love and respect.

Peacemaking can be risky. Oscar Romero's work for peace angered his enemies and resulted in his assassination. As virtuous communicators, we must love what is right, not only what is comfortable or safe. We cannot predict what will happen when we speak positively about a coworker who wants our job. We may be afraid to ask forgiveness from people whom we have hurt unintentionally. Virtuous communicators trust that God will use them to usher in long-term justice and peace even when they see only short-term, self-sacrificial consequences. All personal and social transformation can be painful and even deadly; we can never know for certain how our actions will affect others. The process of peacemaking sometimes takes its toll on innocent people.

As peace-loving communicators, we embody God's redemptive path. We patiently seek reconciliation, we defuse anger, hatred, and violence. Our virtuous character tells the world that there is a way to shalom. Peacekeeping communication reflects the peace of God in the world and points to the complete shalom that the Lord will usher into the world when he returns. When Guillermo Cook and his colleagues heard the camp manager launch into an evangelistic sermon aimed at the confused villager, they sought a peaceful alternative. They quieted the manager and treated the old villager with respect, listening to his story. They recognized that a peace-

153

loving believer must first offer words of love, not condemnation, even when sharing the gospel.

Virtuous communicators love justice and peace. We work not for ourselves but for a Creator who cares deeply about the world and its inhabitants. We virtuously take care of and develop God's creation on behalf of our neighbor.

Authenticity

In his book *Playing for Keeps: Michael Jordan and the World He Made,* David Halberstam explains how two "basketball junkies" created a series of television commercials "that greatly enhanced Michael Jordan's fame and helped take it far beyond the bounds of sport."[10] One of the two was a young, irreverent copywriter from a small Portland advertising agency. The other was a struggling African-American filmmaker from Brooklyn named Spike Lee. As Halberstam recalls, the copywriter loved Jordan and the game of basketball too much to turn the talented player into "something he was not, an actor."[11] So the ad man asked Spike Lee to create a series of commercials that would honestly showcase Jordan's talent. "In a world where so many stars and heroes were inauthentic," concludes Halberstam, Jordan "remained remarkably authentic."[12] Like all virtuous communicators, Jordan said what he meant and meant what he said.

The Nike advertising campaign could have just as easily fabricated a Jordan persona built on Hollywood hype. Professional communicators often sacrifice authenticity in favor of status, money, and ego. Like other professions, advertising tempts communicators to sell their souls in the name of personal power and public glory. We too easily become mere "symbol brokers" who communicate whatever we think others want us to communicate, not what we truly believe.[13] In a sense, we prostitute our talents to benefit causes that we do not support.

Virtue is often co-opted by a superficial professionalism that encourages uncritical commitment to the values, beliefs, and practices of a profession. When we lack the virtue of authenticity, we worship our talents and our job. Our profession becomes our community, and professionalism becomes our doctrine. We do not profess our faith as strongly as we embrace our professional goals and aspirations; we fail to hold up our professional work to the light of the gospel and the demands of our faith.

Christian communicators are called to *authenticity—to saying what we mean and meaning what we say.* Authenticity is not merely truth telling but also deep personal integrity that anchors our communication in our faith. The Nike campaign reflected both who Jordan was and also what the writer and filmmaker believed about Jordan. We can be ethical and tell the literal truth, but it is much tougher to mean what we say, to stand behind the truth, to live the truth. In Scripture, the call to authenticity is reflected in the cautions about taking oaths. If we make promises, we should keep them. Oaths are unnecessary (Matt. 5:33–37). Authenticity carries an enormous responsibility to allow our faith, rather than just our career, to inform our symbolic action. Plato said that authenticity is when "all external possessions are in harmony with [the] inner man."[14] The Greek rhetorician Isocrates wrote, "Who does not know that words carry greater conviction when spoken by men of good repute than when spoken by men who live under a cloud, and that the argument which is made by a man's life is more weight than that which is furnished by words?"[15] The Christian, too, should communicate the truth rather than promote masks or facades.

Unfortunately, professional communication is not always authentic. Professional communicators often are paid to advance what other people believe. Colleges offer courses in advertising and public relations so students can learn how to become symbol brokers. The teachers tell the students that as professional communicators they will shed their own values and beliefs on behalf of their clients. Copywriters are expected to produce the most persuasive copy whether or not they personally believe the rhetoric or use the product. Students of public relations learn to pitch their clients' messages in a way that will attract positive press. Professionalism can be at odds with authenticity.

The field of political consulting perhaps best illustrates the dangers of inauthentic professionalism. When million-dollar consultants create persuasive election campaigns, almost "everything voters see and hear will be generated by people who have no direct responsibility for governing the country and no real accountability to the public."[16] Using polls and other market research, consultants determine how best to position their candidate's image in a political campaign. Their job is not to clarify where the candidate stands on the issues but solely to get the candidate elected. Political consultants sometimes even create a rhetorical fog that makes it difficult for the public and the opposition to figure out what the candidate actually believes. Along the way, they fling rhetorical mud at opponents, sometimes ruining their opponents' public reputation.[17]

Consultants need not personally support the candidates they promote. A consultant might quit one client in order to work at a higher fee for that client's political opponent. One news analyst said that such consultants are "driven more by the need to succeed than by any particular ideology."[18] Some voters get so discouraged about these symbolic chameleons that they choose not to vote and not to care. Democracy needs authenticity. God demands it.

On the other end of the spectrum are commendable columnists who tell their readers exactly what they believe. Nationally syndicated columnist Charley Reese, for example, annually writes a short newspaper essay on his personal beliefs—a kind of confession of his own biases. He informs readers what stocks and property he owns, his sources of income beyond the syndicated column, and where he stands on specific political issues. Usually he offers his religious beliefs as well. Authentic communicators such as Reese are the opposite of the symbol brokers who change their public stance with the winds of public support or the waves of income. Reese says what he means and means what he says. Even if we disagree with his views, we have to respect his virtuous authenticity.

Authenticity demands that we not use our communicative gifts to advance causes or to promote ideas and products that we cannot in good conscience support. Authenticity requires that as communicators we be true to ourselves, to God as the one who has gifted us, and to the community that we are called to love and serve. If we are not authentic communicators who believe our own messages, we are merely ghostwriters who say what needs to be said to satisfy a client and earn a paycheck. One communication graduate reported that every day on the job she faced ethical dilemmas. "I fight these battles, losing most but winning a few. But somebody has to be there to win the few." She is on her way to authenticity. Unfortunately, some Christians have been so influenced by the pragmatic demands of the marketplace, the lure of greater salaries, and the promises of enhanced social standing that they have abandoned authenticity.

Everyday professional routines make it difficult for many types of communicators to live authentically. Ideally, professional actors will have the freedom to shape the quality and the moral and philosophical content of the material they perform, their relationships with crew members, and the impact of their performances on audiences. Virtuous communicators know who they are and try to live their identity faithfully in the midst of daily pressures and temptations.

The term *profession* historically refers not just to work but also to belief. Our lives invariably testify about what we believe. In this sense, we are all professionals. Living in the shadows between heaven and hell, all Christians struggle to be virtuous professionals. Christians should *be* what they profess about Christ. Our professions, or beliefs, can serve us by helping us to live in authentic communion with God and neighbor. On the other hand, professions can encourage us to become misguided creators "of [our] own artificiality."[19] If we are caught between professionalism and authenticity, we had better choose the authentic route, which is also the journey toward an authentic profession of our faith.

Civility

In a Monty Python story, one guy asks another, "Is this the room for an argument?" The other one pauses and then replies, "I've told you once." Then the first gentleman disagrees, "No you haven't." Soon the two are firing salvos back and forth, contradicting each other to the point of absurdity. Before long, they are arguing about whether or not they are having an argument.[20]

We all laugh at such crazy situations, but life is a string of silly arguments laced with nastiness, arrogance, and personal attacks. Our symbolic action breeds disagreements and disrespect for others, causing common courtesy and decency to evaporate. Our impoliteness and rudeness become absurd.

Our virtuousness should lead us instead to *civility*—to politeness and respect for others. How we communicate is part of our witness to the world. Our symbolic action reflects what is in our hearts; it reveals whom or what we love. Uncivil communication springs from an angry and selfish heart. Civil communication flows from a heart filled with charity, patience, and kindness.

As new transportation and communication technologies facilitate cross-cultural interactions, we are increasingly likely to meet people who hold views that are very different from our own. Our interactions are multinational, multicultural, and multireligious. One observer has suggested that the United States will lose its cultural identity as it becomes a center for international trade and cross-cultural business.[21] We live in a world that requires civil communication among formerly separate cultures, nations, and religions. Whether our diversity will produce conflict or harmony depends significantly on the level of civility in our symbolic interactions.

Uncivil communicators engage in symbolic wars between cultures and among people. They arrogantly attack others with sarcastic put-downs, and they trample on others' rights to be heard, read, or seen. They do not listen enough to be able to identify with others. Uncivil communicators are ultimately interested not in loving their neighbors but only in advancing their own interests. We hear incivility in political debates, on talk radio, in the hallways of schools, and in the boardrooms of corporations. Sadly, we witness it even in Christians' public protests and economic boycotts.

Incivility flourishes during heated public arguments among contentious groups. Christians communicate rudely during public disputes over sensitive moral issues such as abortion and homosexuality. One Christian college professor concludes that Christians tend to adopt the uncivil tactics that are used by the groups they oppose. Instead of being peacemakers, Christians "fight ugliness with ugliness, distortion with distortion, sarcasm with sarcasm."[22] He suggests that Christians merely open their mail to discover the truth in what he is saying. They will find fund-raising letters that lack charity and that use hyperbolic rhetoric. In a single letter he found the following examples: "These shameful 'high priests' of the anti-virtue movement." "As God's people for this historic hour, we rise to the challenge and give whatever it takes to turn back the anti-Christian juggernaut which threatens our way of life." "Do not doubt that prayer will become a crime, the Bible off-limits, and sharing our faith in public forbidden."[23] This kind of nasty, alarmist rhetoric apparently increases giving to parachurch organizations that "successfully spin the dispute into a matter of honor or a point of identity,"[24] but it exacerbates the incivility between church and society. Like many people in the world outside the church, Christians often selfishly distort others' views and mischaracterize intentions. They wrongly declare rhetorical holy wars to advance legitimate causes.

In a fallen world, civility and truth often seem to conflict. Like the Old Testament prophets, we sometimes have to speak the harsh truth. Our critical message may seem to call for hatred and disdain, not humility and kindness. But we must learn to speak in love even when our message elicits hostility, slander, and hatred. We have no right to act uncivilly simply because we disagree with others. After all, we battle others' words and images, not their humanness as image bearers of God. If we do not speak the truth civilly and in love, we, too, will foster injustice and conflict.

Behind most of our incivility is the festering pride that has dogged the church throughout the ages, the pride that led to the torture and killing of the church's opponents and of members of rival sects within the church. Some of the most uncivil communication in the world takes place within the church—at congregational meetings. Frequent congregational and denominational schisms reveal to the world how uncivil Christians can be to one another. The church's incivility teaches youth to start uncivil holy wars when they become spiritual leaders.

Christians offer a very poor public witness when they speak of their opponents without common courtesy and mutual respect. We sometimes use hateful, derogatory terms to refer to people with whom we morally disagree, and we disrespectfully use the first names instead of the full titles of certain public officials. On some Christian radio talk shows, hosts unfairly demonize government employees and speak derogatorily to callers. Believers look and sound like the rest of the world, hanging out our dirty rhetoric for the world to see and hear.

When we do not love justice and peace, we communicate uncivilly. We stereotype and dismiss persons with whom we disagree. We disrespectfully condemn and belittle others without truly listening to them. In the Sermon on the Mount, Christ compares slanderers to murderers (Matt. 5:21–22). The apostle James urges us to be slow to speak and quick to listen (James 1:19). But we "think that we don't need to hear; we love to speak; and boy, are we quick to get angry."[25] We breed conflict instead of peace, arrogance instead of justice.

Christians should display a deep regard for the rights of others by respecting even our biggest detractors, by patiently listening to opponents, and by remaining humble in the heat of argument. The Rule of St. Benedict reminds us that humility is "facing the truth." The word *humility* comes from *humus,* earth. We should all "be earthed in the truth that lets God be God." Humility enables us to put God at the center of our lives and our neighbor before ourselves.[26]

Nurturing the Soul in Community

Susan Schaller writes about her efforts to teach rudimentary sign language to Ildefonso, a twenty-seven-year-old man who was deaf. Schaller spent many days trying unsuccessfully to convey the concept of "symbol" and the idea of "language." Then one day Ildefonso suddenly grasped the meaning of a symbol for *cat.* He sat up straight, and "the whites of his eyes expanded as if in terror. He looked like a wild horse pulling back, testing every muscle before making a powerful lunge over a canyon's edge." Ildefonso had "forded the same river Helen Keller did at the water pump."[27]

Years later, after Ildefonso had learned sign language with the help of other teachers, Schaller visited him. Now that Ildefonso could communicate more fully, she wanted to ask him an important question: What had life been like for him before he learned language? Ildefonso answered her question by recalling seeing children with books walking down the street when he was a young boy. "They were my height," remembered Ildefonso, "and I knew they were going to learn about what was in those books. I pointed to the children and begged my parents to let me go with them, to send me where they were going." Miming his own childish begging, Ildefonso "dropped to his knees and put up his hands in a prayish sign—a scene he must have seen many times in the Catholic church."[28]

For Ildefonso, language was food for the soul that assuaged his hunger for communion with others. As a languageless child he simply wanted to go with his peers to find out about books. Ildefonso was "communityless," says Schaller. As a language-using adult, however, he tasted deeper truths and more satisfying relationships. He could better nurture his neighbor, and his neighbor could better love and nurture him. In fact, Ildefonso eventually helped teach sign language to his adult brother, who was living in the same symbolic poverty that had dogged Ildefonso into his late twenties.[29]

Although virtue is a matter of personal character, it must be cultivated in community. With the gift of language we can nurture virtue in one another. It is possible that someone who privately reads and meditates on

God's Word will develop virtuous character. More often, however, virtue grows in us as we also experience the virtuous actions and attitudes of others. Rather than trying to cultivate virtuous character on our own, we should foster relationships that lead to peace and mutual edification (Rom. 14:19).

Shalom is a language of community that emphasizes harmony among people, God, the physical world, and the individual. The language says to the world, "Here is a foretaste of heaven. Enjoy this foretaste of what people and relationships will be like in eternal life." Shalom reminds us that God is with us, in us, working through us. We echo God's character when we are virtuous people in community, celebrating justice and peace and loving each other as God loves us.

Communities of virtue are soul food. They nurture godly character as a mother's milk causes her baby to thrive. The church should offer healthy role models and encourage members to dine on body-building values and nourishing beliefs. Virtuous communities fill us with goodness and grace, humility and love. We become healthy communicators as we "participate together with others in the community of the followers of Christ."[30] Much of communication theory can be summarized in one truth: We embody the community virtues that we savor.

The Eucharist symbolizes this truth within the church community. We eat the bread and drink the wine to remind each other and ourselves that God did not abandon us. The Creator of the universe loved us enough to save a small nation of misfits in the family of David, to incarnate himself in his Son, and to sacrifice that only Son on the cross. God broke down human hubris at Babel and empowered believers at Pentecost. He sent Jesus as the Christ, the living Word. He opened our ears to hear the Word. So we eat and drink as a community. We repent together. We celebrate together. We live together in gratitude for what God did on our behalf. The Christian community becomes virtuous soul food that God feeds to believers and to the rest of the world.

Communities of Christian virtue remind us that we live in the gap between heaven and hell. We do our best with symbolic action. We learn all we can, practice communication diligently, and try to live it as ethically as possible. But in the end, we fall short. We fail to become what we know we should be. The entire community falls short. So through faith the church communicates the hope that Jesus Christ covers the gap between what we know we ought to do and what we actually do. A virtuous community of faith feeds on the grace of Jesus Christ.

Much of Western culture today shouts at us to forsake virtue and to live for ourselves. If we do this, we also die for ourselves. God speaks to the world primarily through the community of believers. Jesus called the disciples together to begin the church. Those who were called listened. Soon the church became a worshiping, witnessing community. Two millennia later, the church uses the same communication gifts to build communities of grace-filled virtue.

Conclusion

As Christian communicators, we are called not just to work virtuously *toward* shalom but also to live peacefully *in* shalom. We need the encouragement, support, and discernment of others to live virtuously. Archbishop Romero needed a community of shalom in order to speak lovingly for peace and justice in war-torn El Salvador, and the virtuous community that Romero left behind is carrying his voice around the world long after his murder.

The pastors who met the villager at the camp realized that evangelism without virtue is foolish. They needed to invite their elderly neighbor to dine with them. They needed to listen to his story. They needed to commune with him authentically so they could share the gospel in love.

We can imagine the scene. One of the pastors hands the new friend some bread and perhaps some wine. "These are our gifts to you. Now listen to a gift from God. If you are interested in this gift, wonderful! If not, we still want to reflect the love of God for you. Either way, you decide. Please stay and share more stories of your village with us. If you stay, we can offer you justice and peace—a bit of heaven on earth." What would the man think about that offer? Would he wonder if the gospel is too good to be true? Would he at least want to hear more of the gospel story? Presented virtuously, the gospel would have sounded like real soul food.

TWELVE

Gifted Disciples

Communicators for God

Jesus Christ walked along the shore of the Sea of Galilee. He saw two brothers, Simon and Andrew, who knew him from at least one previous conversation. The two young fishermen undoubtedly had heard about Jesus' preaching in Capernaum and the other towns nestled around the shoreline. They probably talked regularly about Jesus with other fisherman as they readied their boats and nets each morning, speculating about whether Jesus was really the Christ, the Messiah, the expected savior of the Jews. This morning they would stop speculating.

While the brothers were casting their nets into the sea, Jesus called out, "Come, follow me, and I will make you fishers of men." We do not know what Simon and Andrew were thinking when they accepted Jesus' invitation that morning. Did they perceive the invitation as an honor for mere fishermen? Were they looking for something better in life than casting nets for fish? Did they believe that following the Rabbi would give them access to special teachings? Maybe they were simply bored or anxious teenagers with uncertain futures. In any case, Simon and Andrew immediately left their nets and followed Jesus. The Messiah called, and they followed (Mark 1:16–18).

As these three continued along the shoreline, they spotted two other brothers, James and John, who were in a boat with their father. Once again,

Jesus called, and the two brothers responded—leaving their father behind. They immediately gave up their livelihoods to follow Jesus (Mark 1:19–20). In minutes, they radically changed the course of their lives.

We can only wonder what others along the water thought about this turn of events in the lives of four average residents of the village. Were the four impetuous? Crazy? Why did they follow Jesus? Certainly the neighbors gossiped.

Christian communicators today do not primarily follow theories of symbolic action. Like the first disciples, we follow a person, Jesus Christ. Books, teachers, and ideas can help us greatly, but a Christian view of communication tells us that we must first follow the One who called the disciples on the shore of the Sea of Galilee. We must accept the call to become disciples of Christ, our leader and teacher. Then, as disciples of Jesus Christ, we also become students of communication.

When Jesus Christ calls, we put aside our personal agendas and follow the master Teacher. We begin to learn directly from the Word made flesh, · and only then do our efforts truly begin to transform lives and spread shalom.

Many scholars and teachers consider God's calling pure folly. So it probably was for many people who observed the first disciples. Jesus was obviously a student of Judaism, but he was also a mere carpenter. He was not respected by most of the Jewish leaders, and he lacked a good Roman or Greek education. He was known around parts of the pagan world primarily for his volatile, offbeat teaching. Jesus riled Roman leaders and seemed to endanger the lives of his followers. He owned literally nothing of earthly consequence. Who would reasonably follow this perplexing, shunned, and radical leader?

In this chapter I challenge you to love God and your neighbor with all of your heart and mind by becoming a disciple of Jesus Christ, an active member of a community of believers, and a wise and passionate communicator of truth. Surely these are strange requests in the academic world. But listen first, and then decide. Let the Holy Spirit call you. The music that you will hear may move your heart and capture your mind.

First, I suggest that truly good communication is a form of obedience to God's call. We are musicians in God's cosmic symphony. The Creator conducts all of creation, and he gives every one of us special gifts to cocreate shalom. But we must obediently take our assigned seats in God's orchestra, just as the first disciples did.

Second, I discuss the way God pours grace into our weak and flawed communication. We do not need to be perfect communicators. If we are faithful, God produces wonderful music with our limited symbolic gifts. The first disciples were not expert communicators, but God used them to build the foundation for the church.

164

Third, I emphasize that everything we do as disciples is a witness to the world. We truly cannot *not* communicate. Our entire lives speak what we believe and what we love. The entire creation hears our music. Residents of Capernaum undoubtedly watched the disciples, just as our neighbors see and hear us.

Fourth, I offer the simplest but also the most profound test for all of our communication. As disciples of Jesus Christ, we must care about the gospel-centric truthfulness of our symbolic action. Our symbolic action must reflect the Word and therefore the Spirit of God. Only then is our music harmonious and beautiful.

Finally, I conclude the book by considering the ultimate issue for all communicators: motive. Christ asks a penetrating question about our desires: Whom or what do we love? Every communicator is a lover seduced by particular ideas, desires, or people. Perhaps the most revolutionary aspect of a Christian view of communication is that Jesus calls us to love God and our neighbor with all our mind, heart, and soul. Our symbolic action is not just communication; it is also potentially a love ballad. As we communicate, we cocreate culture that is in tune with our desires.

Jesus Christ says, "Follow me." He invites us to make the music of shalom. When we accept Jesus' call, we venture far beyond merely imitating Christ's manner of communication. We place all our theories, models, and definitions of communication into the refining hands of our Leader. We become Jesus' apprentices, and our workshop is the entire creation. God gives everyone the ability to communicate so that we can cocreate shalom with Jesus Christ as well as with other people. Christ came to earth not only to redeem people from their brokenness but also to enlist and train new disciples. Our successful apprenticeship demands that we stay close to the Creator.

God calls us to use communication to claim the entire world in the name of Jesus Christ. We now follow in Adam's and Peter's footprints as cultural stewards of creation. We use the power of symbolic action to create a definition of reality that is in tune with God's Word. As agents of shalom, we are the Creator's ears and voice on earth, symbolic caretakers of a world entrusted to us.

Playing in the Creator's Orchestra

While he was in a Roman prison, the apostle Paul sent letters to new churches to help the believers know how to live. His epistles later became part of the New Testament. In his letter to the church at Ephesus, Paul penned one of the most amazing descriptions of the relationship between Jesus Christ and his disciples. Lying on the dark, damp ground of a Roman prison, Paul offered the Ephesians these words to live by: "For we are God's workmanship, created in Christ Jesus to do good works, which God prepared in advance for us to do" (Eph. 2:10).

No one knows precisely how the Ephesians responded when they read Paul's missive, but Paul's intent is clear. He wanted to assure the believers at Ephesus that God was performing great deeds with their efforts even while they lived under the oppression of the Roman Empire. God, he said, is a faithful artist who creates good works through all his disciples. God is the conductor of a cosmic orchestra that produces glorious music. Our task as disciples is not to make all of the music on our own but to cocreate the music obediently with a trustworthy Conductor. When Jesus Christ calls people to the orchestra, the score has already been written, the seats have been prepared, and the venue is ready.

As disciples of Jesus, we inherit one primary vocation: to make music together in God's cultural symphony on earth. Some of us are particularly gifted listeners, while others are writers, farmers, directors, carpenters, or speakers. But one thing is certain: Each of us has a place in this creation to cocreate culture. Our good works are ready to be "played." Do we dare take our seat in the orchestra? Do we dare not?

Human culture is a symphony in which we can all play either well or poorly. Every day we rise, wash, dress, and take up our communicative gifts. We enter the stage of God's creation and make our music. When we play well, in tune with our gifts and God's score, the music is magnificent. We pour spiritual life into a luscious creation. Our music attracts others who seek joy in peace and justice. Our communication calls more people to drop their nets and join the symphony. Grace abounds, and we say, "This is how we were meant to live." We accomplish good works together by cultivating life in our relationships with God, with others, with the physical world, and with ourselves.

On the other hand, when we stubbornly write our own score, we orchestrate dissonance, destruction, and despair. When we arrogantly fail to recognize the limits of our giftedness, or when we launch into sins of omission and commission, we make exploitative power plays and sow evil in social institutions.

No matter what occupation or profession we take up, we are called to use the gift of symbolic action to be caretakers of God's creation. Everyone is invited to accept and celebrate this role. God came to save the weak and lowly, not the self-righteous, arrogant, and proud. When Peter and his friends set aside their nets and followed Jesus Christ, they humbly declared whose they were. They trusted that God would produce good works through them. It was clear to everyone that they had a new calling as apprentices of Jesus. We also begin our journey of faithful discipleship by listening to the Rabbi from Galilee, and when we follow Jesus Christ, we put Jesus above all other teachers, and the gospel above all other stories.

God Makes Our Notes Perfect

The disciple Simon Peter claimed to love Jesus, but his actions suggested otherwise. After Jesus Christ was betrayed and arrested, Roman guards took Jesus to the house of the high priest. Peter followed at a distance, then sat down with the guards at a fire in the courtyard of the house. When a servant girl recognized Peter as one of Jesus' disciples, Peter denied it: "Woman, I don't know him." Later, Peter again denied that he knew Christ. Finally, one of the Romans challenged Peter for the third time to admit that he was a disciple of Jesus. Peter replied, "Man, I don't know what you're talking about!" As Peter was speaking, a rooster crowed. When Jesus looked into his eyes, Peter remembered what Jesus had predicted: "Before the rooster crows today, you will disown me three times." Then Peter "went outside and wept bitterly" (Luke 22:54–62).

God calls us to communicate faithfully, not perfectly. In spite of Peter's denials, Jesus did not reject his disciple. In fact, Peter became one of the leaders of the faith. We are all called to exercise our God-given gifts to the best of our ability, but like Peter and the other early disciples, we will never be perfect people. In God's symphony, we do not rely ultimately on our own talent but on the power of God's Word and the inspiration of the Holy Spirit. God perfects our symbolic action. Our job is to take our place in God's creation and play our best.

Jesus did not call rhetorically proven disciples. He enlisted a remarkably diverse and variously talented group of followers. At least five of them were fishermen, one was a tax collector, and the professions of the others are not certain. Peter was naively impetuous but later became a wise and bold preacher. James, son of Zebedee, was short-tempered, impatient, and judgmental. Before following Jesus, Matthew had been shunned because he was a tax collector. Many of the disciples had a poor public reputation, failed to listen carefully to Jesus, and even questioned Jesus' teachings.

God uses us according to how he has gifted us, not according to an idealistic standard of rhetorical perfection. Whatever symbolic abilities we possess, God has given them to us for a reason. If our gift is primarily listening, we should be good listeners. Like wetlands ecologist Cal DeWitt, we might be gifted listeners and passionate speakers who convey to others God's love for the earth. If we have a knack for encouraging others, we should exercise it like a priest who comforts the afflicted. If we are able to interpret and critique popular culture, we should apply that gift as prophetic disciples of Jesus and servants of the church. Our gifts are varied, complementary, and exciting. None of us is a perfect communicator, but each of us has a crucial place in the symphony of shalom.

We do not have to worry about whether we have *any* communicative gifts; instead, we should consider whether we have identified our gifts and are using them obediently. As we study communication, we can develop our gifts for service to others. In the end, however, we must put our trust in the master Teacher, not in our gifts. Our gifts are potential, waiting to be tapped, and as we develop them, God uses them for perfect ends that we cannot fathom. Although we may see ourselves as weak and ungifted communicators, God has places and purposes for our ears, our pens, and our voices. When we faithfully use our gifts, in whatever medium, God makes communication happen. Human symbolic action is serendipitous, unpredictable, and full of grace. Just as Jesus used the disciples, God uses us—sometimes when we least expect it. Our Conductor perfects our faithful efforts, enabling us to love our neighbors as ourselves. He builds on our gifts, our study, our practice, and our desire to serve.

The grace of the gospel of Jesus Christ liberates us from perfectionism and the fear of failure. Before Peter denied Christ, Jesus had invited him to walk on the water. As he tried to make his way across the water, Peter flailed and a hand grabbed him, and "like a drowning rat" he scurried back into the "frail safety of his life boat."[1] Through grace our Creator holds us above the water and accomplishes wonderful things with our limited gifts. The power of the Holy Spirit is able to overcome our weaknesses while we develop our gifts to the best of our ability.

God gives us communicative gifts and guarantees that by the power of the Holy Spirit we will be able to use them well. With study and practice, we can become increasingly effective communicators, carrying the gospel from person to person and generation to generation. God's call is to obedience, not perfection; we trust God to make the music glorious. And as he did in the beginning, the Creator turns the chaos of our broken communities and mixed-up lives into the cosmos of shalom.[2]

We Are the Music

Standing on a hill, Jesus spoke to a crowd, launching the most public part of his ministry. "Blessed are the poor in spirit," he began, "for theirs is the kingdom of heaven." He concluded hours later with a story about a fool who had built a house on sand, only to see it washed away by the rains. Between the remarkable opening statement and the concluding parable, Christ addressed many controversial topics: prayer, the perils of money, entering heaven, criticizing others, worrying, and lust (Matt. 5:1–7:29). As the disciples listened, Christ told each listener that his or her entire life is significant in the kingdom of God. And indeed, everything that we do should be done to the glory of God. As the Dutch theologian and statesman Abraham Kuyper put it almost two millennia later, "There is not a square inch in the whole domain of our human existence over which Christ, who is sovereign over *all*, does not cry: 'Mine!'"[3]

All aspects of culture have symbolic potential—our clothing, transportation, music, even our house and yard. We cannot turn our symbolic action on and off like a light switch. In the Sermon on the Mount, Christ showed his listeners that following God is not merely a matter of "religious communication," such as listening to sermons and participating in Bible studies. Following God is discipleship in every area of life. As the world listens, we are part of the music of God's symphony. All of our actions are words. Christ asks us to transform every nook and cranny of our lives into signposts for justice and peace. As we do this, our lives point to the eternal shalom of heaven.

Every aspect of our lives can be symbolic action that reflects the lordship of Christ. God's kingdom surrounds everything we do. We are inherently, incessantly communicators of whatever is in our hearts. If we love money, our actions will tell the world; we might be able to fool a few people some of the time, but in the end our greed will be revealed to ourselves as well as our neighbors. We can criticize others all we want, but as Christ said on the Mount, we will simply be judging ourselves. People will see our hypocrisy. We can break our promises, but we then will be saying to everyone that we are untrustworthy.

French writer André Malraux struggled intellectually to understand the value of life in a world where everyone dies after a short time on the planet. Like many communicators, he wanted his life to make a difference in the world, so he fought in the Spanish Civil War and the French Resistance, and he authored books about literature and politics. He did what he professed. But he concluded that the best we can do as death-bound humans is to turn our lives into works of art—to "sign" our lives as an artist signs a painting.[4]

In one sense, Malraux had it right. Our lives *are* like works of art—even like parts in a grand symphony. When the disciples decided to follow Jesus Christ, they began creating a very different musical score for their lives. Their lives became a new symphony in progress. But who was the author? Whose signature would grace the score? Just as Paul's epistles carry his signature, we should be willing to place our signature on our lives. As Paul referred to Jesus Christ as the author of his new life, so should we.

In another sense, Malraux had it all wrong. We might pretend to be immortal by placing our signature on our lives, but eventually we will be long forgotten as new culture replaces older culture. Sooner or later, everything we have cocreated will turn to dust. Our writing, movies, plays, and

169

conversations will disappear. All of life is meaningless, says the writer of Ecclesiastes (1:2). Can we gain eternal life merely by putting our own signature on our lives?

For the Christian, there is really only one signature that ultimately guarantees immortality: "Love, Jesus Christ." The final signature on our life is the name of the only one who turns our life into a work of musical majesty. Jesus Christ alone can work through us to reverse the effects of our fall from grace. And God's signature enables us to cocreate culture effectively with others in the orchestra of life.

Christ's revolutionary rhetoric redefined the scope of our responsibilities as symbolic caretakers of God's world. We do not define Christian communication narrowly as sermons, evangelistic movies, or novels sprinkled with Bible passages. Christian communication is every symbol that flows from a human heart that is anchored in Christ's discipleship and inspired by the Holy Spirit.

The Kentucky couple who at first sought revenge for the death of their son at the hands of a drunk driver eventually tasted shalom. Rather than letting the courts have the final say, they played the music of shalom in an unexpected place. They identified with their son's killer, prayed for him, invited him for dinner, and took him in as their own son. They rightly recognized that the call to Christian discipleship extends to all areas of life—not just to our religious duties or our church involvement. They didn't just give the hurting young man a Bible tract. They gave him their attention, their love, even their lives. And God signed their lives, "Love, Jesus Christ."

God's Word Makes Our Music Harmonious

Just before he called the disciples, Jesus Christ spent forty days and nights in the desert. Tired and hungry, he faced the devil. In the first of the three great temptations, Satan asked Jesus to transform stones into bread. Surely Jesus could have done this. He was God incarnate. But he refused. "It is written," Jesus told Satan, "Man does not live on bread alone, but on every word that comes from the mouth of God" (Matt. 4:4). Jesus refused to use his creative ability selfishly to thwart the will of God.

Recognizing the bigger picture of his role in saving humankind from sin, Jesus refused to go along with the devil's version of reality. Satan's music was seductive, but insufficient. Jesus rejected vain power and deceit in favor of humility and truth.

As Christ's disciples, we share the mission of communicating truth. All of our symbolic action should reflect the truth of God's redemptive history described in the gospel of Jesus Christ. Our yes always should affirm the eternal gospel, not our own petty agendas. We cocreate *with* the Creator, *in* the Creator, and *for* the Creator. Our communication should not merely move people or affect change; it should convey the cosmic point of the matter—the way things really are.

We are called to define reality in a way that is in tune with God's Word. Our lives must be screened through the gospel; they should be a meta-narrative of the kingdom. Our deeply prophetic calling is to communicate the language of the Creator. No wonder the disciples often hung on every word of the Master Communicator. His Word is music to the ears of all creation, showing us the way to justice and peace. We must study both the discipline of communication and the ways to spiritual wisdom. If we gain rhetorical savvy but lack knowledge of the truth and a relationship with God, we are incomplete communicators.

The Sermon on the Mount is a crucial part of the music of truth for fallen humankind. In it, Christ taught that there is an enormous gap between reality and how people view reality. He said, "Not everyone who says to me, 'Lord, Lord,' will enter the kingdom of heaven, but only he who does the will of my Father who is in heaven" (Matt. 7:21). The words seem harsh, exclusive, and pointed. Indeed they are. The sermon challenged common-sense thinking and angered the religious leaders. Jesus taught that Christian communication is gospel-shaped truth telling, not just agreement or impact. Jesus' life on earth is a remarkable testament to the power of the Word to transform people's view of reality and thereby to redeem people's lives and restore cultures.

We might not like it, but we are prophetic communicators of the bad news as well as priestly communicators of the good news. "Beneath our clothes, our reputations, our pretensions, beneath our religion or lack of it, we are all vulnerable both to the storm without and to the storm within, and if ever we are to find true shelter, it is with the recognition of our tragic nakedness and the need for true shelter that we have to start."[5] We are not called to be happy-go-lucky fools who spin symbols without a worry. As *our* words reflect *the* Word, they cut to the core of reality. The light of the gospel has the power to illuminate our ugly hearts and to reveal the principalities and powers of every generation.

Theologian Lesslie Newbigin reveals how, like Jesus in the desert, we are caught between opposing realities. "Our problem is that most of us who are Christians have been brought up bilingual. For most of our early lives, through the accepted systems of public education, we have been trained to use a language which claims to make sense of the world without the hypothesis of God." Meanwhile, we spend only an "hour or two a week" using the language of the Bible. We forget that "the incarnate Word is Lord of all, not just of the Church. There are not two worlds, one sacred and the other secular."[6] As Newbigin suggests, Christian communicators are called to strain all symbols through the sieve of God's reality.

We live in one ultimate reality, but we are caught between two competing cultures. As St. Augustine put it, we live in both the city of God and the city of man. During the Sermon on the Mount, Jesus taught us to pray, "And lead us not into temptation, but deliver us from the evil one" (Matt. 6:13). Can you imagine what the disciples thought when they heard this for the first time? Jesus revealed that evil is palpable, real, and personal, that there are indeed irreconcilable kingdoms in our fallen world. In the large and small decisions of life, we follow either God or the evil one. We act on behalf of the kingdom of light or the kingdom of darkness, heaven or hell, life or death, God or Mammon. Of course we must transform the communication institutions of society, but we must first conform our own hearts and minds to the gospel that we profess. French reformer and social critic Jacques Ellul writes that institutional reforms ought to "spring out of the faith of the Church, and not from the technical competence of a few experts, whether they be Christians or not."[7]

When David Puttnam took over Columbia Pictures, he hoped to change the Hollywood system. But even the success of a major film such as *Chariots of Fire* was no guarantee that Puttnam would have clear sailing. Puttnam wanted to produce stories with socially redeeming value, but the Hollywood system is based largely on the love of riches. Puttnam had to consider very carefully how to work within a fallen system and how to work with others, without giving up his worldview. This is precisely what every professional Christian communicator must do. If we do not have a clear, Christian worldview that is grounded in the truth and fostered by community, the system will likely beat us every time. We study communication to become much wiser and more realistic ambassadors of the gospel in a fallen world.

As we take our seats in the Creator's orchestra, we must know the musical score: the gospel. As we study both communication and God's Word, we are better able to play that score in every one of life's venues. The name of the conductor is Jesus Christ.

Singing Holy Love Songs

After Jesus preached the Sermon on the Mount, his ministry on earth expanded from city to city. Threatened by his growing popularity, religious leaders tried to discredit Jesus by tricking him into giving a false answer about Jewish law. There were over six hundred major and minor laws that governed a complex religious institution, and some leaders taught that all laws were equally binding. One of the teachers of the law asked, "Of all the commandments, which is the most important?" Jesus replied, "The most important one is this: . . . 'Love the Lord your God with all your heart and with all your soul and with all your mind and with all your strength.' The second is this: 'Love your neighbor as yourself.' There is no commandment greater than these" (Mark 12:28–31). Nothing is more important for how we communicate than love for God and neighbor. Without love, shalom is only a dream. Our symbolic action must be a passionate love song for all of creation.

There is an enormous difference between merely spreading truth and communicating in love. The church should be the champion of the message of grace, but it often unvirtuously sows seeds of pride and arrogance. We forget that truth without love can easily turn people away from the gospel. Our love should enable people to identify us as Christian communicators.

Loving our neighbor and loving our work are never enough. We all know gifted, passionate communicators who love what they do but who do not love God. We are called as communicators to love God as well as to love each other. In a world that is fallen from grace, we easily love what we create or the process of creating more than we love the Creator. Instead of letting the Conductor take the first bow, we proudly stand up for others to admire. Christian communicators not only identify with others and enjoy their craft, they also love the Person who created their gifts.

We must ask tough, introspective questions about our motives: Do we truly love God and other people? Do we honestly identify with our neighbor's humanity, not just with our own weaknesses and sin? Can we see the image of God in others? Does our symbolic action reflect the kind of respect and patience that we desire from others? In short, do we treat our neighbors as ourselves in all of our personal and professional communication?

Our communication, like love, cannot be reduced to a set of guidelines. We have to be able to empty ourselves and to take on the burdens of others. We have to practice truthfulness and be virtuous. We must ask for the grace to dig deep into God's Word to see and hear what our Creator intends for us. We have to examine every ethical dilemma we face to learn how we can reflect God's love in a fallen world. Love might require the courage to speak up in one situation and the patience to remain silent in another. Love means letting our decisions be God's call, reflecting God's desire, not our own. Love is not just a feeling or emotion but wisdom and passion garnered ultimately from the Creator. Loving God through our communication takes a great deal of hard work, serious study, wise discernment, and lifelong practice.

The doctor who cared for John Merrick learned to love. He began by protecting the badly deformed man from the circus owner, the newspapers, and public humiliation. But later when Dr. Treeves heard Merrick reciting the Twenty-third Psalm, he also gained love for the man. He realized that the elephant man was not merely a little better than a freak: John Merrick was a full person bearing the image of God. Jesus Christ died for John Merrick, not just for doctors and for attractive people. Dr. Treeves opened his home to Merrick, introducing him to his wife and communing with him as he would with any person. Merrick could barely believe that anyone would be so kind to him. He felt God's grace in the doctor's loving actions. Together Dr. Treeves and John Merrick played a love song composed by a generous God.

Conclusion

Our call to Christian discipleship is rooted in the person of Jesus Christ, not merely in noble theories and effective methods. As C. S. Lewis said, Jesus' rhetoric made it very clear that he was not just a fine orator or a great moral teacher. If Jesus were merely a person, his own words would condemn him as either a lunatic or a demon. "You can shut him up for a fool," Lewis said. You "can spit at him and kill him as a demon; or you can fall at his feet and call him Lord and God. But let us not come with any patronizing nonsense about his being a great human teacher. He has not left that open to us."[8]

I conclude our journey through the world of human communication where we began—with grace. As God's caretakers of creation, we have much to do and some important tools to use. When it comes to symbolic action, no combination of technologies will free us from confusion and regret, so we can be thankful that God started the symphony and invites us to take our seats in the orchestra. Our Creator has equipped us with the gospel and has given us the necessary gifts to play our parts with each other as cocreators of culture. God first loved us, so now we can love Jesus Christ and each other. Shalom is God's symphony, and the orchestra is gathering to rehearse on earth what we will play eternally in heaven.

Sometimes shalom seems like a distant echo, barely a one-note peep. But when we communicate the truth together in love, God works wonders through fallen human beings. It is the Holy Spirit's business and our calling. I invite you to call on the name of the greatest being who ever lived, in heaven and on earth. God says, "I am." We sing, "We are yours." In a nutshell, that is the love ballad of communicating for shalom.

Notes

Introduction

1. Simon Wiesenthal, *The Sunflower: On the Possibilities and Limits of Forgiveness* (New York: Schocken, 1997), 25.

2. Ibid., 54.

3. Ibid.

4. Eugene H. Peterson, *A Long Obedience in the Same Direction: Discipleship in an Instant Society* (Downers Grove, Ill.: InterVarsity Press, 1980), 177.

5. C. S. Lewis, *The Problem of Pain* (New York: Macmillan, 1958), 93.

6. Peterson, *Long Obedience,* 158.

7. For a critique of media theory's secular bias, see Stewart M. Hoover and Shalimi S. Venturelli, "The Category of the Religious: The Blindspot of Contemporary Media Theory," *Critical Studies in Mass Communication* 13 (1996): 251–65.

8. St. Augustine, *De Doctrina Christiana,* ed. and trans. R. P. H. Green (Oxford: Clarendon, 1995), bk. 2.

9. St. Augustine, *Confessions,* trans. Henry Chadwick (Oxford: Oxford University Press, 1991), 94.

Chapter 1

1. Quoted in Tim Stafford, "God's Green Acres," *Christianity Today,* 15 June 1998, 34.

2. Ibid., 35.

3. Ibid., 37.

4. Kenneth R. Chase, "Abundant Life," *Wheaton College Alumni Magazine,* spring 1998, 19.

5. Clifford G. Christians, "The Sacredness of Life," *Media Development* 45, no. 2 (1998): 4.

6. Ibid., 3.

7. Ian Johnson, "The Ann Landers of Beijing Is Adored by the Lonely, Shunned by Colleagues," *The Wall Street Journal Interactive Edition,* 10 December 1998, 1–3, Online: http://interactive.wsj.com/articles/SB913242401254712500.htm.

8. T. S. Eliot, *Notes toward the Definition of Culture* (Reinbek bei Hamburg: Rowohlt, 1961), 29. For a provocative look at cultural theory in the contemporary academy, see Nicholas B. Dirks, ed., *In Near Ruins: Cultural Theory at the End of the Century* (Minneapolis: University of Minnesota Press, 1998).

9. James W. Carey, *Communication as Culture: Essays on Media and Society* (Boston: Unwin Hyman, 1988), 18.

10. Tony Castle, ed., *The New Book of Christian Quotations* (New York: Crossroad, 1982), 259.

11. Beth L. Bailey, *From Front Porch to Back Seat: Courtship in Twentieth-Century America* (Baltimore: Johns Hopkins University Press, 1988).

12. For a very helpful discussion of the distinction between society and culture, see Michael Warren, *Communications and Cultural Analysis: A Religious View* (Westport, Conn.: Bergin and Garvey, 1992), 23–28. Warren traces the history of the concept of culture as outlined in the work of Raymond Williams, an important British intellectual who grew up in a working-

class family and community. Says Warren, "In a relatively short period, culture moved from its specific, local meaning of the cultivation of some particular thing to a word synonymous with the Enlightenment idea of civilization, then to a synonym for nature, and then to signify inner, spiritual development" (28). I tend to use the original meaning of the word: cultivation, namely, cultivating God's creation.

13. Teresa Watanabe, "Heaven and Hell: Rabbis, Pastors and Other Faithful Flow into Environmental Movement," *Grand Rapids Press,* 16 February 1999, A2.

14. Richard J. Foster, *Celebration of Discipline* (San Francisco: HarperCollins, 1998), xii.

15. Nicholas Wolterstorff, *Divine Discourse: Philosophical Reflections on the Claim That God Speaks* (Cambridge: Cambridge University Press, 1995).

16. Martin Luther as quoted in Castle, *New Book of Christian Quotations,* 99.

17. Larry Woiwood, "A Fifty-Year Walk: Reflections on God's Immanence in Creation," *Books and Culture* (November/December 1998): 14.

18. Bill Hybels, *Making Life Work: Putting God's Wisdom into Action* (Downers Grove, Ill.: InterVarsity Press, 1998), 104.

19. Ernst Cassirer, *Language and Myth,* trans. Susanne K. Langer (New York: Dover, 1946), 58.

20. Rolf Bouma, "Grace in Creation," *The Banner,* 13 April 1998, 25.

21. Potter Stewart in *Jacobellis v Ohio,* 378 US 184 (1963).

22. G. K. Chesterton, *G. F. Watts* (London: Duckworth, 1904), 43–44.

23. For a splendid discussion of the connection between theological thought and our capacity for the negative, see Kenneth Burke, *The Rhetoric of Religion: Studies in Logology* (Berkeley: University of California Press, 1970), 17–23.

24. Eugene H. Peterson, "What's Wrong with Spirituality?" *Christianity Today,* 13 July 1998, 55.

25. Larry Tye, *The Father of Spin* (New York: Crown, 1998), 23–50.

26. Haig A. Bosmajian, *The Language of Oppression* (Lantham, Md.: University Press of America, 1983).

27. Frederick Dale Bruner, *Matthew: A Commentary by Frederick Dale Bruner* (Dallas: Word, 1990), 1098–2001.

28. Peter DeVos et al., *Earthkeeping: Christian Stewardship of Natural Resources* (Grand Rapids: Eerdmans, 1980), 210.

29. Kenneth Burke, "(Nonsymbolic) Motion/ (Symbolic) Action," *Critical Inquiry* 4 (1978): 810.

30. Nicholas Wolterstorff, *Art in Action* (Grand Rapids: Eerdmans, 1980), 72–83. Lee Hardy, *The Fabric of This World: Inquiries into Calling, Career Choice, and the Design of Human Work* (Grand Rapids: Eerdmans, 1990), 71.

31. As quoted in Tim Stafford, "God's Missionary to Us," *Christianity Today,* 9 December 1996, 30.

32. Roderick T. Leupp, *Knowing the Name of God: A Trinitarian Tapestry of Grace, Faith and Community* (Grand Rapids: Eerdmans, 1996).

33. Philip Yancey, "What's a Heaven For?" *Christianity Today,* 26 October 1998, 104.

34. Eugene H. Peterson, *A Long Obedience in the Same Direction: Discipleship in an Instant Society* (Downers Grove, Ill.: InterVarsity Press, 1980), 170.

35. Nicholas Wolterstorff, *Until Justice and Peace Embrace* (Grand Rapids: Eerdmans, 1983), 72.

36. Ibid., 70–71.

37. Peterson, *Long Obedience,* 52.

38. Wolterstorff, *Until Justice and Peace Embrace,* 72.

39. Gunter Virt, "The Life of the Spirit in a Mass-Mediated Culture," in *Mass Media and the Moral Imagination,* ed. Philip J. Rossi and Paul A. Soukup (Kansas City, Mo.: Sheed and Ward, 1994), 59.

40. Don Phillips, "Inside a Tower of Power and Pressure: Air Traffic Controllers Strive to Maintain Order in a World of Motion," *The Washington Post,* 22 June 1998, A1.

41. Parker Palmer, *To Know as We Are Known: A Spirituality of Education* (San Francisco: Harper & Row, 1983), 43.

42. Eugene H. Peterson, *Subversive Spirituality* (Grand Rapids: Eerdmans, 1994), 27.

43. Robert E. Webber, *God Still Speaks* (Nashville: Thomas Nelson, 1980), 13.

44. Wolterstorff, *Divine Discourse*.

45. Michael Yaconelli, *Dangerous Wonder: The Adventure of Childlike Faith* (Colorado Springs: NavPress, 1998), 87.

46. See C. S. Lewis, The Chronicles of Narnia series (San Francisco: HarperCollins, 1998).

47. Gregory Boyd, *God at War: The Bible and Spiritual Conflict* (Downers Grove, Ill.: InterVarsity Press, 1997).

48. Richard Hays, *The Moral Vision of the New Testament: Community, Cross, New Creation: A Contemporary Introduction to New Testament Ethics* (San Francisco: HarperCollins, 1996).

49. Burke's work is sometimes difficult to interpret, but it is infused with religious language and Christian metaphors. While I refer to his work frequently in this book, even Burkean scholars disagree on how to interpret some of his ideas. Early in his academic career Burke became interested in "words about words," especially words about God—what he called *logology*. "Theological doctrine," wrote Burke, "is a body of spoken or written *words*. Whatever else it may be, and wholly regardless of whether it be true or false, theology is preeminently *verbal*." Burke, *Rhetoric of Religion*, vi.

50. Kenneth Burke, *Language as Symbolic Action: Essays of Life, Literature, and Method* (Berkeley: University of California Press, 1966), 16.

51. Kenneth Burke, "Poem," in *The Legacy of Kenneth Burke*, ed. Herbert W. Simons and Trevor Melia (Madison: University of Wisconsin Press, 1989), 263.

Chapter 2

1. Bob Stewart, *Revenge Redeemed* (Tarrytown, N.Y.: Revell, 1991), 118.

2. Ibid., 233.

3. Jane Ammeson, "Peace on Turf," *World Traveler*, December 1997, 53.

4. Ibid., 54, 78.

5. Ibid., 78.

6. Dale L. Sullivan, "Kairos and the Rhetoric of Belief," *Quarterly Journal of Speech* 78 (1992): 317–32.

7. Robert Coles, *The Moral Intelligence of Children: How to Raise a Moral Child* (New York: Random House, 1997), 144.

8. Greg Spencer, "Jesus at the Lyceum: Incarnational Principles for Rhetoric" (paper, Westmont College, 1999).

9. J. C. Pollock, *Hudson Taylor and Maria: Pioneers in China* (Grand Rapids: Zondervan, 1974), 156–61.

10. William Bausch, *Storytelling: Imagination and Faith* (Mystic, Conn.: Twenty-Third Publications, 1984), 62.

11. Martin Buber, *Between Man and Man*, trans. Ronald Gregor Smith (New York: Macmillan, 1965), 97.

12. See especially Martin Buber, *I and Thou*, trans. Walter Kaufmann (New York: Charles Scribner's Sons, 1970).

13. Marilyn Daniels, *Benedictine Roots in the Development of Deaf Education: Listening with the Heart* (Westport, Conn.: Bergin and Garvey, 1997), 15.

14. Ibid., 1.

15. Ibid., 15.

16. Ibid., 100–101.

17. Susan Meiselas, "Susan Meiselas," *U.S. News & World Report*, 6 October 1997, 71.

18. Aleksandr I. Solzhenitsyn, quoted in Fred E. Katz, *Ordinary People and Extraordinary Evil: A Report on the Beguilings of Evil* (New York: New York State University Press, 1993), vii.

19. Lewis Smedes, *The Art of Forgiving* (Nashville: Moorings, 1996), 6.

20. Wray Herbert, "Listening to Each Other," *U.S. News & World Report*, 1 September 1997, 65.

21. Sheldon Vanauken, *A Severe Mercy* (New York: Harper & Row, 1977), 42.

22. For further discussion of this phenomenon, see Katherine A. Dettwyler, *Dancing Skeletons: Life and Death in West Africa* (Prospect Heights, Ill.: Waveland Press, 1993), 16–21.

23. Constantin Stanislavski, *Building a Character*, trans. Elizabeth Reynolds Hapgood (New York: Theatre Arts Books, 1981).

24. Quentin J. Schultze et al., *Dancing in the Dark: Youth, Popular Culture, and the Electronic Media* (Grand Rapids: Eerdmans, 1991), 99–103.

25. Colin Soloway, "In Cars, Serbs Skirt a Ban on Marches," *Chicago Tribune*, 6 January 1997, 6.

26. Richard J. Mouw, *Consulting the Faithful: What Christian Intellectuals Can Learn from Popular Religion* (Grand Rapids: Eerdmans, 1994), 11.

27. Gary M. Burge, "Are Evangelicals Missing God at Church? Why So Many Are Rediscovering Worship in Other Traditions," *Christianity Today,* 6 October 1997, 22.

28. Kenneth Burke, "Poem," in *The Legacy of Kenneth Burke,* ed. Herbert W. Simons and Trevor Melia (Madison: University of Wisconsin Press, 1989), 263.

29. Isocrates, *Antidosis,* trans. George Norlin (London: William Heinemann, 1929), 2:329.

30. Max DePree, *Leadership Is an Art* (New York: Dell, 1989), 82.

31. Walter Fisher, "Narration as a Human Communication Paradigm: The Case of Public Moral Argument," *Communication Monographs* 51 (March 1984): 6.

32. Chenjerai Hove, "Oral Traditions Claim a Place in Modern Mass Media," *Media Development* 3 (1997): 13–14.

33. John Dewey, *Intelligence in the Modern World* (New York: Modern Library, 1939), 385.

Chapter 3

1. James W. Carey, *Communication as Culture: Essays on Media and Society* (Boston: Unwin Hyman, 1988), 18.

2. Ibid., 29.

3. Shearon Lowery and Melvin L. DeFleur, *Milestones in Mass Communication Research: Media Effects* (New York: Longman, 1983), 34–35.

4. Ibid., 54.

5. William Albig, *Public Opinion* (New York: McGraw-Hill, 1939), 290–91.

6. See James W. Carey and Albert L. Kreiling, "Popular Culture and Uses and Gratifications: Notes toward an Accommodation," in *The Uses of Mass Communications: Current Perspectives on Gratifications Research,* ed. Jay G. Blumler and Elihu Katz (Beverly Hills, Calif.: Sage, 1974), 234–35.

7. Daniel J. Czitrom, *Media and the American Mind: From Morse to McLuhan* (Chapel Hill: University of North Carolina Press, 1982), 126. For a personal account from one of the founders of the field of social-scientific communications research, see Paul F. Lazarsfeld, "An Episode in the History of Social Research: A Memoir," in *The Intellectual Migration: Europe and America 1930–1960,* ed. Donald Fleming and Bernard Bailyn (Cambridge: Harvard University Press, 1969), 270–337.

8. Leo Lowenthal, "Historical Perspectives of Popular Culture," in *Mass Culture: The Popular Arts in America,* ed. Bernard Rosenberg and David Manning White (Glencoe, Ill.: The Free Press, 1957), 55.

9. Wilbur Schramm, "The Nature of Communication between Humans," in *The Process and Effects of Mass Communication,* ed. Wilbur Schramm and Donald F. Roberts (Urbana, Ill.: University of Illinois Press, 1971), 8–11.

10. For one interpretation of the history of this model of communication, see James Curran, Michael Gurevitch, and Janet Woollacott, "The Study of the Media: Theoretical Approaches," in *Culture, Society and the Media,* ed. Michael Gurevitch et al. (New York: Methuen and Co., 1982), 11–29. For an opposing view of the history of the hypodermic-needle model of communication, see Jeffery L. Bineham, "An Historical Account of the Hypodermic Model in Mass Communication," *Communication Monographs* 55 (September 1988): 230–46.

11. Carey, *Communication as Culture,* 14.

12. Phillip J. Tichenor and Douglas M. McLeod, "The Logic of Social and Behavioral Science," in *Research Methods in Mass Communication,* 2d ed., ed. Guido H. Stempel III and Bruce H. Westley (Englewood Cliffs, N.J.: Prentice-Hall, 1989), 11. Also see Bruce H. Westley, "Scientific Method and Communication Research," in *Introduction to Mass Communications Research,* ed. Ralph O. Nafsiger and David Manning White (Baton Rouge: Louisiana State University Press, 1958), 238–76.

13. Carey, *Communication as Culture,* 16.

14. Leonard Sweet, ed., *Communication and Change in American Religious History* (Grand Rapids: Eerdmans, 1993); David Paul Nord, "The Evangelical Origins of Mass Media in America," *Journalism Monographs* 88 (May 1984).

15. Harry S. Stout, *The Divine Dramatist: George Whitefield and the Rise of Modern Evangelicalism* (Grand Rapids: Eerdmans, 1991).

16. Raymond A. Bauer, "The Obstinate Audience: The Influence Process from the Point of View of Social Communication," in *The Process and Effects of Mass Communication*, 326–46.

17. Harold D. Lasswell, "The Structure and Function of Communication in Society," in *The Process and Effects of Mass Communication*, 84.

18. John Bachman, "Theology and Communication: Towards a Theological Context for the Role of the Church in Dealing with Modern Media of Communication," *World Association of Christian Communications Journal* 23, no. 2 (1976): 14.

19. Clifford Geertz, "Deep Play: Notes on the Balinese Cockfight," in *Myth, Symbol, and Culture*, ed. Clifford Geertz (New York: W. W. Norton, 1971), 8–9.

20. Ibid., 23.

21. Carey, *Communication as Culture*, 18.

22. Two of the best essays about how communication scholars conduct research from a ritual perspective are Clifford G. Christians and James W. Carey, "The Logic and Aims of Qualitative Research," in *Research Methods in Mass Communication*, 354–74; and Robert S. Fortner and Clifford G. Christians, "Separating Wheat from Chaff in Qualitative Studies," in *Research Methods in Mass Communication*, 375–87.

23. I suggest that one's religious faith provides "control" beliefs that shape how one views the world. See Nicholas Wolterstorff, *Faith within the Bounds of Religion* (Grand Rapids: Eerdmans, 1976), 72.

24. Nicholas Wolterstorff, *Divine Discourse: Philosophical Reflections on the Claim That God Speaks* (Cambridge: Cambridge University Press, 1995).

25. Michael Traber, ed., *The Myth of the Information Revolution: Social and Ethical Implications of Communications Technology* (London: Sage, 1986).

26. Isaiah wrote, "So justice is far from us, and righteousness does not reach us. We look for light, but all is darkness; for brightness, but we walk in deep shadows. Like the blind we

grope along the wall, feeling our way like men without eyes" (59:9–10).

27. This may be one of the reasons that even in the scientific study of mass communication there are now few milestones with groundbreaking findings. The transmission view of communication may be giving way to the cultural view even in mass-media research. See Melvin L. DeFluer, "Where Have All the Milestones Gone? The Decline of Significant Research on the Processes and Effects of Mass Communication," *Mass Communication and Society* 1, no. 2 (winter/spring 1998): 85.

28. Max DePree, *Leadership Is an Art* (New York: Dell, 1989), 3.

Chapter 4

1. Martha Manning, "In My Fantasy, I'm Slim, Long Legged, and Drop-dead Gorgeous. In Reality, I'm at War with My Body. Why Can't I Be Happy with an Imperfect Beauty?" *Health*, September 1997, 82–84.

2. Karen Lee-Thorp, "Is Beauty the Beast?" *Christianity Today*, 14 July 1997, 31.

3. Walker Percy, *Lost in the Cosmos: The Last Self-Help Book* (New York: Farrar, Straus & Giroux, 1983), 29.

4. Amy White, "IC Vandalism Sparks Rally," *The Phoenix Online* (November 1998). Online: http://www.sccs.swarthmore.edu/org/phoenix/archives/98/11/02/31.html.

5. John Leo, "Good Hair, Bad Cake," *U.S. News & World Report*, 14 December 1998, 16.

6. Lauran Neergaard, "Drug Name Similarities Can Be Toxic," *Grand Rapids Press*, 29 November 1998, A10.

7. Tina Lassen, "Say What?" *World Traveler*, October 1998, 38–43, 83.

8. For a critique of the Jesus Seminar, see C. Stephen Evans, *The Historical Christ and the Jesus of Faith: The Incarnational Narrative as History* (New York: Clarendon, 1996).

9. J. I. Packer, *The Apostles' Creed* (Berkshire, England: Marchum Books, n.d.).

10. Ralph Graves, "Who Are Those Guys?" *Smithsonian*, January 1999, 110.

11. David Lyon, *Postmodernity* (Minneapolis: University of Minnesota Press, 1994), 2.

12. Ibid., 13.

13. Ibid., 77.

14. St. Augustine, *De Doctrina Christiana,* ed. and trans. R. P. H. Green (Oxford: Clarendon, 1995), bks. 2–3.9, 223.

15. Percy, *Lost in the Cosmos.*

16. Kenneth Burke, *Language as Symbolic Action: Essays of Life, Literature, and Method* (Berkeley: University of California Press, 1966), 16.

17. Simon Winchester, *The Professor and the Madman: A Tale of Murder, Insanity, and the Making of the Oxford English Dictionary* (New York: HarperCollins, 1998).

18. James C. McCroskey, "Why We Communicate the Ways We Do: A Communibiological Perspective" (paper presented at the annual convention of the National Communication Association, Chicago, 20 November 1997), 11.

19. St. Augustine, *De Doctrina Christiana,* bk. 4, sec. 62.

20. Ibid., sec. 21.

21. Elisabeth Elliot, *Love Has a Price Tag* (Ann Arbor, Mich.: Servant, 1979), 113.

22. James Billington, "The Future Face of Russia" (paper presented at the January Series Lecture, Calvin College, Grand Rapids, 15 January 1999).

23. Harold A. Innis, *The Bias of Communication* (Toronto: University of Toronto Press, 1964).

24. Joshua Meyrowitz, *No Sense of Place: The Impact of Electronic Media on Social Behavior* (New York: Oxford University Press, 1985).

25. Barbara Reynolds, *Dorothy Sayers* (New York: St. Martin's Press, 1993), 369.

26. Walter J. Ong, *The Presence of the Word: Some Prolegomena for Cultural and Religious History* (New Haven: Yale University Press, 1967), 17–35.

27. Martin Buber, *I and Thou,* trans. Walter Kaufmann (New York: Charles Scribner's Sons, 1970).

28. Wendell Berry, *Sex, Economy, Freedom, and Community* (New York: Pantheon, 1993), 14.

29. Ibid., 120.

30. Chenjerai Hove, "Oral Traditions Claim a Place in Modern Mass Media," *Media Development* 3 (1997): 13–14.

31. Jaques Ellul, *Propaganda: The Formation of Men's Attitudes* (New York: Alfred A. Knopf, 1971).

32. Robert Fortner, "Excommunication in the Information Age," *Critical Studies in Mass Communication* 12, no. 2 (1995): 133–54.

33. David Shenk, *Data Smog: Surviving the Information Glut* (San Francisco: Harper, 1997).

34. Clifford Stoll, *Silicon Snake Oil: Second Thoughts on the Information Highway* (New York: Anchor, 1995).

35. James W. Carey, *Communication as Culture: Essays on Media and Society* (Boston: Unwin Hyman, 1988), 33.

36. Marshall McLuhan, *The Medium Is the Message* (New York: Bantam, 1967).

Chapter 5

1. Michael Ryan, *Secret Life: An Autobiography* (New York: Random House, 1995), 335.

2. Cornelius Plantinga, *Not the Way It's Supposed to Be: A Breviary of Sin* (Grand Rapids: Eerdmans, 1995), 12.

3. Ryan, *Secret Life,* 8–9.

4. David C. Mortensen and Carter M. Ayres, *Miscommunication* (Thousand Oaks, Calif.: Sage, 1997), xiii.

5. C. S. Lewis, *Mere Christianity* (New York: Touchstone, 1996), 75.

6. Tim Keller, "Brimstone for the Broadminded," *Christianity Today,* 13 July 1998, 65.

7. Mortensen and Ayres, *Miscommunication,* xiii.

8. Dietrich Bonhoeffer, *Creation and Fall: A Theological Interpretation of Genesis 1–3* (New York: Collier, 1959), 77–82.

9. Ibid., 82.

10. Kofi Annan, "The Lord Had the Wonderful Advantage of Being Able to Work Alone," *Time,* 24 February 1997, 15.

11. Plantinga, *Not the Way It's Supposed To Be,* 75.

12. William Stringfellow defines principalities and powers as "ideologies," "institutions," and "images." See William Stringfellow, *Free in Obedience* (New York: Seabury Press, 1964), 52–53.

13. Ibid., 56.

14. Ibid.

15. Angelo B. Henderson, "Some Black Entrepreneurs Prefer a Low Profile in Suburban Areas," *Wall Street Journal,* 26 January 1999. Online: http://interactive.wsj.com/articles/SB917310194885785500.htm.

16. C. S. Lewis, *The Screwtape Letters* (New York: Simon and Schuster, 1996), 8.

17. Abraham Kuyper, *Lectures on Calvinism* (Grand Rapids: Eerdmans, 1931), 27.

18. Lewis, *Screwtape Letters,* 8.

19. Peter F. Drucker, *The Effective Executive* (New York: HarperBusiness, 1967), 27.

20. Jerry Kosinski, "A Nation of Videots," interview by David Sohn, in *Television: The Critical View,* ed. Horace Newcomb (New York: Oxford University Press, 1976), 148–49.

21. Patricia Bizzel and Bruce Herzberg, *The Rhetorical Tradition: Readings from Classical Times to the Present* (Boston: Bedford, 1990), 4.

22. Gene Edward Veith Jr., *The Gift of Art: The Place of the Arts in Scripture* (Downers Grove, Ill.: InterVarsity Press, 1983), 43–61.

23. Richard J. Mouw, *Consulting the Faithful: What Christian Intellectuals Can Learn from Popular Religion* (Grand Rapids: Eerdmans, 1994), 23.

24. Andrew M. Greeley, *God in Popular Culture* (Chicago: Thomas Moore, 1988).

Chapter 6

1. Merrill Goozner, "The Mensch of Malden Mills Inspires," *Chicago Tribune,* 26 December 1996, 1.

2. Richard Mouw, *Uncommon Decency: Christian Civility in an Uncivil World* (Downers Grove, Ill.: InterVarsity Press, 1992), 48.

3. Madeleine L'Engle, *Walking on Water: Reflections on Faith and Art,* commemorative ed. (Wheaton: Harold Shaw, 1998), 51.

4. Alexis de Tocqueville, *Democracy in America,* trans. Henry Reeve (New York: Colonial Press, 1899), 2, 79.

5. Clinton E. Arnold, *Power and Magic: The Concept of Power in Ephesians* (Grand Rapids: Baker, 1998).

6. Robert W. Jenson, *Essays in Theology of Culture* (Grand Rapids: Eerdmans, 1995), 40–49.

7. Ibid., 41.

8. Wray Herbert, "A Georgia Farmer Takes Stock," *U.S. News & World Report,* 9 December 1996, 86.

9. Martin Luther King Jr., "I Have a Dream," in *Martin Luther King, Jr.: A Documentary: Montgomery to Memphis,* ed. Bob Fitch (New York: W. W. Norton, 1976), 218.

10. Martin Luther King Jr., as quoted in "Reflections," *Christianity Today,* 11 January 1999, 80.

11. J. I. Packer, *Knowing God* (Downers Grove, Ill.: InterVarsity Press, 1973), 29.

12. Michael Astor, "Father Pop," *Grand Rapids Press,* 28 December 1998, A2.

13. Quintilian, "Institutes of Oratory," in *Readings in Classical Rhetoric,* ed. Thomas W. Benson and Michael Prosser (Davis, Calif.: Hermagoras Press, 1988), 126.

14. St. Augustine, *De Doctrina Christiana,* ed. and trans. R. P. H. Green (Oxford: Clarendon, 1995), bk. 4, 59–63.

15. Quentin J. Schultze, *Televangelism and American Culture: The Business of Popular Religion* (Grand Rapids: Baker, 1991), 69–95.

16. Ben Witherington, *The Paul Quest* (Downers Grove, Ill.: InterVarsity Press, 1998).

Chapter 7

1. Henri J. Nouwen, *Here and Now* (New York: Crossroad, 1994), 100.

2. Ibid., 98–99.

3. Many of the ideas in this section are from Greg Spencer, "Jesus at the Lyceum: Incarnation Principles for Rhetoric" (paper, Westmont College, 1999).

4. Robert E. Webber, *God Still Speaks* (Nashville: Thomas Nelson, 1980), 97.

5. Gerald Hawthorne, *Philippians, Word Biblical Commentary,* vol. 43 (Waco: Word, 1983), 84.

6. St. Thomas Aquinas, quoted in Hugh T. Kerr, *Readings in Christian Thought* (New York: Abingdon, 1966), 120.

7. Dietrich Bonhoeffer, *Letters and Papers from Prison* (New York: Macmillan, 1967), 189–90.

8. Bonhoeffer, *Letters,* 193.

9. David Mamet, *Some Freaks* (New York: Viking, 1989), 97.

10. J. R. R. Tolkien, *The Return of the King* (New York: Ballantine, 1965), 273–77.

11. Ken Blue, *Healing Spiritual Abuse: How to Break Free from Bad Church Experiences* (Downers Grove, Ill.: InterVarsity Press, 1993), 13.

12. Sheldon Vanauken, *A Severe Mercy* (New York: Harper & Row, 1977), 163.

13. Robert Coles, *The Moral Intelligence of Children: How to Raise a Moral Child* (New York: Random House, 1997), 177–78.

14. Bonhoeffer, *Letters*, xx–xxi.

15. Brendan I. Koerner, "Parental Power," *U.S. News & World Report*, 18 January 1999, 73.

16. Vanauken, *Severe Mercy*.

17. Lawrence L. Langer, "Pre-empting the Holocaust," *Atlantic Monthly*, November 1998, 5, 73.

18. Edward E. Ericson, *Solzhenitsyn: The Moral Vision* (Grand Rapids: Eerdmans, 1980).

19. Kyong-Hwa Seok, "Sex Slavery Museum Keeps Memory Alive," *Grand Rapids Press*, 24 January 1999, A17.

20. Lori Wiechman, "Body Fails; Implant Taps Brain Signals," *Grand Rapids Press*, 21 October 1998, A1, A4.

21. Scott Turow, *One L: An Inside Account of Life in the First Year at Harvard Law School* (New York: Penguin, 1978), 220.

22. Gordon Spykman et al., *Let My People Live: Faith and Struggle in Central America* (Grand Rapids: Eerdmans, 1988), 146–50.

23. Elizabeth Gleick, "Belated Outrage for Girl X," *Time*, 24 February 1997, 31.

24. Chris Meehan, "Actor Rallies for Senior Services," *Grand Rapids Press*, 30 October 1998, C3.

25. Guta Cvetkovic, "The Untold Story in the Information Age," *The Banner*, 19 January 1998, 29.

26. T. K. Thomas, "Towards the Decolonisation of Christian News," *Media Development* 18 (1980): 16.

27. Ibid., 18.

28. LeAlan Jones and Lloyd Newman, *Our America: Life and Death on the South Side of Chicago* (New York: Scribner, 1967), 87.

29. Jacques Ellul, *The Presence of the Kingdom* (Colorado Springs: Helmers and Howard, 1989), 94.

30. Aristotle, "The Function of Rhetoric," in *The Rhetoric of Aristotle*, trans. Lane Cooper (New York: Meredith, 1960), 7.

31. Lewis Carroll, *Through the Looking Glass, and What Alice Found There* (London: Macmillan, 1880), 163.

Chapter 8

1. Andrew Yule, *Fast Fade: David Puttnam, Columbia Pictures, and the Battle for Hollywood* (New York: Delacorte Press, 1989), 89.

2. Ibid., 92.

3. Ibid., 88.

4. Ibid., 97.

5. Walt Mueller, "Marilyn Manson's Revenge," *New Man Magazine* (September/October 1998). Online: http://www.newman-mag.com/issues/nm998/nm9985.htm.

6. Quentin J. Schultze, *Winning Your Kids Back from the Media* (Downers Grove, Ill.: InterVarsity Press, 1994), 119–20.

7. Quentin J. Schultze et al., *Dancing in the Dark: Youth, Popular Culture, and the Electric Media* (Grand Rapids: Eerdmans, 1991), 66–67.

8. Daniel Boorstin, *The Americans: The Democratic Experience* (New York: Random House, 1973), 89–90.

9. Ibid., 422–23.

10. Robert J. Price, "We Are God's Angels: Reach Out and Touch Someone," *The Banner*, 16 February 1998, 25.

11. One of the best essays on the historical connection between consumerism and the Christian faith is Rodney Clapp, "The Theology of Consumption and the Consumption of Theology," in *The Consuming Passion: Christianity and the Consumer Culture*, ed. Rodney Clapp (Downers Grove, Ill.: InterVarsity Press, 1998), 169–204. Clapp writes that "Christians were in a remarkable number of cases architects of twentieth-century consumer culture" (181).

12. James Billington, quoted in Nathan VanderKlippe, "Russia Needs the Support of the West," *Calvin College Chimes*, 2 January 1999, 5.

13. Wendell Berry, *Sex, Economy, Freedom, and Community* (New York: Pantheon, 1993), 23.

14. Quentin J. Schultze and William D. Romanowski, "Praising God in Opryland," *The Reformed Journal* (November 1989): 10–14.

15. Bob Briner, *Roaring Lambs* (Grand Rapids: Zondervan, 1993). For more on Chris-

tians' responsibility to transform the systems in which they work, see Lee Hardy, *The Fabric of This World: Inquiries into Calling, Career Choice, and the Design of Human Work* (Grand Rapids: Eerdmans, 1990), 107–11. Also see Bob Briner, *Lambs among Wolves: How Christians Are Influencing American Culture* (Grand Rapids: Zondervan, 1995).

16. Jacques Ellul, *The Technological Society,* trans. John Wilkinson (New York: Vintage, 1964).

17. Daniel J. Czitrom, *Media and the American Mind: From Morse to McLuhan* (Chapel Hill: University of North Carolina Press, 1982), 10–11.

18. Ben Armstrong, *The Electric Church* (Nashville: Thomas Nelson, 1979), 8–9.

19. James W. Carey, *Communication as Culture: Essays on Media and Society* (Boston: Unwin Hyman, 1988), 16–17.

20. Quentin J. Schultze, *Televangelism and American Culture: The Business of Popular Religion* (Grand Rapids: Baker, 1991), 187–90.

21. Robert Fortner, "High-Tech Worship: The Electronic Church as Technology and Cultural Form," *The Reformed Journal* (January 1984): 19–23.

22. Larry Cuban, *Teachers and Machines: The Classroom Use of Technology Since 1920* (Williston, Vt.: Teachers College Press, 1986).

23. Todd Oppenheimer, "The Complete Delusion," *Atlantic Monthly,* July 1997, 45–48, 50–56, 61–62. Cuban, *Teachers and Machines.*

24. Robert S. Fortner, "Saving the World? American Evangelicals and Transnational Broadcasting," in *American Evangelicals and the Mass Media,* ed. Quentin J. Schultze (Grand Rapids: Zondervan/Academie, 1990), 315.

25. Jacques Ellul, *The Presence of the Kingdom* (Colorado Springs: Helmers and Howard, 1989), 113–32.

26. Tom Brokaw, "In Defense of TV News," *U.S. News & World Report,* 13 January 1986, 79.

27. Malcolm Muggeridge, *Christ and the Media* (Grand Rapids: Eerdmans, 1977).

28. Neil Postman, *Amusing Ourselves to Death: Public Discourse in the Age of Show Business* (New York: Viking, 1985).

Chapter 9

1. Jean Shepherd, *A Fistful of Fig Newtons* (New York: Doubleday, 1981), 162.

2. Noel Gallagher, quoted in "Verbatim," *Time,* 21 July 1997, 25.

3. Aristotle, *Poetics,* trans. Ingram Bywater (New York: Random House, 1954).

4. Madeleine L'Engle, *Walking on Water: Reflections on Faith and Art,* commemorative ed. (Wheaton: Harold Shaw, 1998), 50–51.

5. Neil Reynolds, "When Lies Become News," *Christianity Today,* 9 September 1998, 42–43.

6. Jay Newman, *Religion vs. Television: Competitors in Cultural Context* (Westport, Conn.: Praeger, 1996); Linda Degh, *American Folklore and the Mass Media* (Bloomington: Indiana University Press, 1994); Quentin J. Schultze, *Television: Manna from Hollywood?* (Grand Rapids: Zondervan, 1986).

7. Lesslie Newbigin, quoted in Tim Stafford, "God's Missionary to Us," *Christianity Today,* 9 December 1996, 30.

8. Gregor T. Goethals, *The Television Ritual: Worship at the Video Altar* (Boston: Beacon Press, 1981).

9. Quentin J. Schultze et al., *Dancing in the Dark: Youth, Popular Culture, and the Electronic Media* (Grand Rapids: Eerdmans, 1991), 99–103.

10. Kenneth Burke, *The Philosophy of Literary Form* (Toronto: Vintage, 1957), 253–59.

11. Donald B. Rogers, "Maintaining Faith Identity in a Television Culture: Strategies of Response for a People in Exile," in *Changing Channels: The Church and the Television Revolution,* ed. Tyron Inbody (Dayton: Whaleprints, 1990), 147–55.

12. Ian M. Mitroff and Warren G. Bennis, *The Unreality Industry: The Deliberate Manufacturing of Falsehood and What It Is Doing to Our Lives* (New York: Oxford University Press, 1989), xvi.

13. Phillip Yancey, *The Jesus I Never Knew* (Grand Rapids: Zondervan, 1995), 87.

14. David Marc, *Demographic Vistas: Television in American Culture* (Philadelphia: University of Pennsylvania Press, 1996).

15. Martin Marty, *The Improper Opinion: Mass Media and the Christian Faith* (Philadelphia: Westminster Press, 1961).

16. Richard Campbell, *60 Minutes and the News: A Mythology for Middle America* (Champaign, Ill.: University of Illinois Press, 1991).

17. Jacques Ellul, *Propaganda: The Formation of Men's Attitudes* (New York: Alfred A. Knopf, 1971).

18. John Raulson Saul, *The Unconscious Civilization* (Concord, Ontario: Anansi, 1995), 65–66.

19. James B. Twitchell, *ADCULT USA: The Triumph of Advertising in American Culture* (New York: Columbia University Press, 1996), 30.

20. John Updike, "The Golden Age of the 30-Second Spot," *Harper's,* June 1984, 17.

21. "Advertising fetishizes objects in exactly the same manner that religion does; it 'charms' objects, giving them an aura of added value.... It is no happenstance that the advertising executives, or 'attention engineers,' who helped bring about the rise of consumer culture were steeped in the Christian tradition" (Twitchell, *ADCULT USA,* 32–33).

22. Ali M. Metwalli, "A Muslim's Defense of Faith," *Grand Rapids Press,* 3 January 1999, D4.

23. Christopher B. Kulp, "Demonizing Our Opponents," *Issues in Ethics* (summer/fall 1996): 8.

24. Rosemarie Garland Thomson, *Extraordinary Bodies: Figuring Physical Disability in American Culture and Literature* (New York: Columbia University Press, 1997), 55–80.

25. Jurgen Moltmann, *The Open Church* (London: SCM Press, 1978), 38.

26. Cal Thomas, "Media's Mediocrity, Bias Are Showing," *Grand Rapids Press,* 6 July 1998, A7.

27. Kenneth Burke, *The Rhetoric of Religion: Studies in Logology* (Berkeley: University of California Press, 1970), 236.

28. Martin Marty, "On Martin Luther and Hate Speech—Sightings," *Public Religion Project* (10 November 1998). Online: http://www.publicreligionproj.org/services/sightings/archive/11-10-98.html.

29. Ravi Zacharias, "Television as a Medium: A Christian Perspective," *Ravi Zacharias' International Ministries Ministry Letter* (July 1994): 7.

30. Jacques Ellul, *The Presence of the Kingdom* (Colorado Springs: Helmers and Howard, 1989), 114.

31. Ibid., 98.

32. Ibid., 114.

33. Quentin J. Schultze, *Televangelism and American Culture: The Business of Popular Religion* (Grand Rapids: Baker, 1991), 231–36.

34. Cornel West's many books address everything from race relations to international justice. See, for example, *Prophecy Deliverance: Afro-American Revolutionary Christianity* (Philadelphia: Westminster/John Knox Press, 1982); *Keeping Faith: Philosophy and Race in America* (New York: Routledge, 1993); *The Cornel West Reader* (Cambridge, Mass.: Perseus, 1999).

35. World Association for Christian Communications, *Christian Principles of Communication: Statement on Communication* (London: World Association for Christian Communications, 1990), 11.

36. John Wilson, "Mr. Wallis Goes to Washington: The Transformation of an Evangelical Activist," *Christianity Today,* 14 June 1999, 41–43.

37. One of the more provocative attempts to develop a Christian approach to journalism is Marvin Olasky, *Prodigal Press: The Anti-Christian Bias of the American News Media* (Westchester, Ill.: Crossway, 1988).

38. One of the best collections of essays on Jacques Ellul's work is Jacques Ellul, *Interpretive Essays,* ed. Clifford G. Christians and Jay M. Van Hook (Chicago: University of Illinois Press, 1981). For a brief summary of Ellul's work, see Clifford G. Christians, "Propaganda and the Technological System," in *Public Opinion and the Communication of Consent,* ed. Theodore Glasser and Charles Salmon (New York: Guilford, 1995), 156–74.

39. Ellul, *Presence of the Kingdom,* 87, 102.

40. Michael Warren, *Communications and Cultural Analysis: A Religious View* (Westport, Conn.: Bergin and Garvey, 1992), 13.

41. Václav Havel, *The Art of the Impossible: Politics as Morality in Practice* (New York: Fromm International, 1998), 82.

42. Ibid., 54.

Chapter 10

1. Anthony Lewis, "Press Pays High Price for Truth in Latin America," *Grand Rapids Press,* 7 August 1997, A12.

2. Susan Ferriss, "Reporter's Murder, Linked to Traffickers, Haunts Border," *Grand Rapids Press,* 27 July 1997, A24.

3. Dietrich Bonhoeffer, *The Cost of Discipleship* (New York: Macmillan, 1937), 7.

4. Ibid., xviii.

5. Aleksandr I. Solzhenitsyn, *A World Split Apart* (New York: Harper & Row, 1978), 49.

6. See Dave Schelhaas, "Wendell Berry's Beloved Community," *Pro Rege,* March 1997, 15–22.

7. Clifford G. Christians, John P. Ferré, and P. Mark Fackler, *Good News: Social Ethics & the Press* (New York: Oxford University Press, 1993), 27–30.

8. Sissela Bok, *Lying: Moral Choice in Public and Private Life* (New York: Vintage, 1978), 30–31.

9. John Leo, "Stomping on Journalists," *U.S. News & World Report,* 20 July 1998, 14.

10. David Nyberg, *The Vanished Truth: Truthtelling and Deceiving in Ordinary Life* (Chicago: University of Chicago Press, 1993), 24.

11. Frank J. D'Angelo, "Fiddle-Faddle, Flapdoodle and Balderdash: Some Thoughts about Jargon," in *Beyond Nineteen Eighty Four,* ed. William Lutz (Urbana, Ill.: National Council of Teachers of English, 1989), 126.

12. Susan Montoya, "What's in a Name? A Lot of Congregants, Baptists Say," *Grand Rapids Press,* 16 January 1999, B2.

13. St. Augustine, *De Doctrina Christiana,* ed. and trans. R. P. H. Green (Oxford: Clarendon, 1995).

14. Eugene H. Peterson, "What Bible Heroes Can Teach Us about Scandals," *Christianity Today,* 15 June 1998, 40.

15. Eugene H. Peterson, "The Subversive Shepherd," *Christianity Today,* 14 July 1997, 48.

16. Paulo Freire, *Pedagogy of the Oppressed,* trans. Myra Bergman Ramos (New York: Seabury Press, 1970), 119.

17. Ibid., 46.

18. Ibid.

19. "Accuracy Doesn't Equal Fairness, Editor Says," *Media Issues,* 6 June 1998, 9.

20. Edmund P. Clowney, "Wisdom and the Bell Curve," *Tabletalk,* March 1995, 53.

21. St. Augustine, *City of God,* trans. Demetrius B. Zema and Gerald G. Walsh (Washington, D.C.: Catholic University of America Press, 1962), bk.1, chap. 33.

Chapter 11

1. Raymond Fung, *Evangelistically Yours: Ecumenical Letters on Contemporary Evangelicalism* (Geneva: Wee, 1992), 203–4.

2. Ibid., 204.

3. Ibid.

4. For an account of Oscar Romero's life, see James R. Brockman, S. J., *Romero: A Life* (London: Orbis, 1990).

5. C. S. Lewis, *Mere Christianity* (New York: Touchstone, 1996), 72.

6. Oscar Romero, *The Violence of Love,* trans. James Brockman (Farmington, Pa.: Plough, 1998), 198.

7. Plato, *Gorgias,* trans. W. C. Helmbold (New York: Liberal Arts Press, 1952), 107.

8. Nicholas Wolterstorff, "The Grace That Shaped My Life," in *Finding God at Harvard: Spiritual Journeys of Thinking Christians,* ed. Kelly Monroe (Grand Rapids: Zondervan, 1996), 15.

9. Susan VanZanten Gallagher, "Cry with a Beloved Country: Restoring Human Dignity to the Victims of Apartheid," *Christianity Today,* 9 February 1998, 23.

10. David Halberstam, *Playing for Keeps: Michael Jordan and the World He Made* (New York: Random House, 1999), 177.

11. Ibid., 180.

12. Ibid., 184.

13. Eve Stryker and Catherine A. Warren, eds., *James W. Carey: A Critical Reader* (Minneapolis: University of Minnesota Press, 1997), 128–43; Quentin J. Schultze, "Poets for Hire: The Ethics of Consumer Advertising," *Media Development,* 3 March 1987, 2–4.

14. Plato, *The Phaedrus of Plato* (London: Whittaker, 1868), 279C.

15. Isocrates, *Antidosis,* trans. George Norlin (London: William Heinemann, 1929), 2:239.

16. David Broder, "Cynics Subverting Democratic Process," *Grand Rapids Press,* 8 July 1998, A9.

17. For a good discussion of contemporary political rhetoric, see Kathleen Hall Jamieson, *Eloquence in an Electronic Age: The Transformation of Political Speechmaking* (New York: Oxford University Press, 1988).

18. Gloria Borger, "Pity the Poor Consultant," *U.S. News & World Report,* 20 July 1998, 26.

19. Peter Winch, "Nature and Convention," *Proceedings of the Aristotelian Society* 60 (1959–60): 240.

20. Online: http://www.montypython.net/scripts/argument.htm.

21. Robert D. Kaplan, "Travels into America's Future," *Atlantic Monthly,* August 1998, 37–61.

22. Daniel Taylor, "Deconstructing the Gospel of Tolerance, *Christianity Today,* 11 January 1999, 50.

23. Ibid., 52.

24. Tim Stafford, "When Christians Fight Christians," *Christianity Today,* 6 October 1997, 30.

25. John G. Stackhouse Jr., "Fighting the Good Fight," *Christianity Today,* 6 October 1997, 37.

26. Esther de Waal, *Living with Contradiction: Reflections on the Rule of St. Benedict* (San Francisco: Harper & Row, 1989), 96.

27. Susan Schaller, *A Man without Words* (Berkeley: University of California Press, 1991), 44.

28. Ibid., 170–71.

29. Ibid., 191, 193.

30. Frederick Buechner, *Telling the Truth: The Gospel as Tragedy, Comedy, and Fairy Tale* (San Francisco: Harper & Row, 1977).

Chapter 12

1. Doug Frank, "Free to Groan, Free to Think," *Oregon Extension Journal* 5 (winter 1999): 5.

2. Conductor Leonard Bernstein once described his work as turning chaos into the cosmos of music. See Madeleine L'Engle, *Walking on Water: Reflections on Faith and Art,* commemorative ed. (Wheaton: Harold Shaw, 1998), 16.

3. Abraham Kuyper, "Sphere Sovereignty," in *Abraham Kuyper: A Centennial Reader,* ed. James D. Bratt (Grand Rapids: Eerdmans, 1998), 488.

4. Jean Francois Lyotard, *Signed, Malraux,* trans. Robert Marvey (Mineapolis: University of Minnesota Press, 1999).

5. Frederick Buechner, *Telling the Truth: The Gospel as Tragedy, Comedy, and Fairy Tale* (San Francisco: Harper & Row, 1977), 33.

6. Lesslie Newbigin, *Truth to Tell: The Gospel as Public Truth* (Grand Rapids: Eerdmans, 1991), 49.

7. Jacques Ellul, *The Presence of the Kingdom* (Colorado Springs: Helmers and Howard, 1989), 69.

8. C. S. Lewis, *Mere Christianity* (New York: Touchstone, 1996), 56.

Index